Jungle Dragoon

JUNGLE DRAGOON

The Memoir of an Armored Cav Platoon Leader in Vietnam

Paul D. Walker

PRESIDIO

In telling this story, I have either left out or changed the names of some participants to insure that no further pain or suffering is caused to relatives or loved ones. They have endured enough from this war.

Published by Presidio Press
505 B San Marin Drive, Suite 300
Novato, CA 94945-1340

Library of Congress Cataloging-in-Publication Data

Walker, Paul D.
    Jungle dragoon : the memoir of an armored cav platoon leader in Vietnam / Paul D. Walker
        p.   cm.
    ISBN 0-89141-689-7
    1. Vietnamese Conflict, 1961–1975 Personal narratives, American. 2. Vietnamese Conflict, 1961–1975—Regimental histories—United States. 3. United States. Army. Cavalry, 4th. Squadron, 1st—History. 4. Walker, Paul D. I. Title.
    DS559.5 .W345 1999
    959.704'342'092—dc21
                                    99-32631
                                    CIP

Unless otherwise noted, photos courtesy Col. Robert McCormick of the Research Center of the 1st Division Museum at Cantigny.

Printed in the United States of America

Contents

Preface

The most precious commodity with which the army deals is the individual soldier who is the heart and soul of our combat forces.

—Gen. J. Lawton Collins

Hundreds of books have been written about the role the infantry played in the Vietnam War but few have been written about the role of armor. This book is an effort to complete the picture.

Prior to America's entry into the Vietnam War, there was much discussion about how effective tank units would be in that tropical environment. Some doubted that heavy units would be able to operate in the mud of the monsoon season or that their equipment would hold up in the heat and humidity of the tropics.

The French experience was of little help in answering these questions. They had restricted their armored vehicles to the roads, and, as a result, suffered severe losses, the most notable being the destruction of Groupement Mobile 100 west of Nha Trang.

After Congress passed the Gulf of Tonkin Resolution in 1964 giving President Lyndon Johnson virtually unlimited power to deal with American security interests in Vietnam, the marines almost immediately began sending ground combat forces to protect airfields and other American facilities. The first army combat units were shipped to Vietnam in the spring of 1965.

The 1st Infantry Division, one of the army's proudest combat divisions, with a heritage of valor extending back to World War I, was the first army division to deploy to Vietnam, arriving in July 1965. The division took with it a heavily armored cavalry squadron as an experiment to determine if there was a role for armor in Vietnam. It quickly became evident that armor would play a significant role in the war.

The army learned long ago that in order to be effective, infantry, artillery, and cavalry had to work together. Vietnam was no exception. No unit moved anywhere unless it was covered by indirect artillery fire, and convoys did not move on unsecured roads unless they were escorted by armored vehicles.

To avoid the killing effects of American artillery, the enemy sought to get in close to the unit being attacked. When they succeeded in doing this, the nearest armor or cavalry unit was detailed to spearhead a counterattack. The divisions came to rely heavily on their armored cavalry squadrons because of their effectiveness. However, that effectiveness came with a price: cavalry units tended to have a high casualty rate in both men and vehicles.

In addition to their traditional reconnaissance mission, armored cavalry squadrons provided convoy protection, infantry support, and, with attachments, had the ability to operate independently, much like a separate brigade.

There was little standardization among armored units early in the war. Some cavalry squadrons were equipped with tanks and armored personnel carriers. Others traded in their armored vehicles for jeeps outfitted with recoilless rifles and pedestal-mounted machine guns. Some were equipped with M551 Sheridan armored reconnaissance/airborne assault vehicles instead of tanks. Still others were equipped only with armored personnel carriers. However, experience showed that there was a need for heavy tanks on most combat operations.

A debate was still going on in the summer of 1966 regarding the basic load of ammunition to be carried by each tank and armored personnel carrier. Within weeks after my arrival, squadron headquarters directed that each personnel carrier was to be loaded with 5,000 rounds of 7.62mm ammunition for its M60 machine guns and 2,000 rounds of ammunition for its M2 .50-caliber machine gun. Tanks were to carry 5,000 rounds of 7.62mm ammunition for their coaxial machine guns and 500 rounds of ammunition for their .50-caliber machine guns. In addition, each tank was to carry 45 rounds of canister, 12 rounds of high-explosive, seven rounds of white phosphorus, and three rounds of the new "Beehive" ammunition.

None of my vehicles ever carried exactly those amounts. For example, my tank crews usually carried one or more antitank rounds because they were not convinced that the enemy had no tanks. Oftentimes, the desired amounts simply were not available. However, they did serve as a good guide when requesting resupply.

My overall purpose in writing this book, in addition to recounting my own experiences, is to provide the reader with a clear picture of how armored cavalry units operated in Vietnam, and of the many contributions they made to the army's efforts in that war.

Prologue

Out of college less than a year and stationed in Germany, I was a twenty-three-year-old army second lieutenant in the spring of 1966 when I received orders for Vietnam. Like most of my contemporaries, I grew up during the 1950s and had a conservative, traditional view of the world. I managed to avoid the campus unrest that a few short years later would completely change the political face of America, especially how we looked at the war and the kind of people we sent to fight it.

In the mid-1960s, with popular support for the war running at its highest level, America's young men, when called upon to serve, stepped forward with pride and patriotism to do what had to be done to protect freedom and democracy around the world.

Young men entering military service in the early part of 1966 were not reluctant to serve in Vietnam. Most thought they were answering the challenge that President John F. Kennedy made in his inaugural address: "Let every nation know, whether it wishes us well or ill, that we shall pay any price, bear any burden, meet any hardship, support any friend, oppose any foe, in order to insure the survival and success of liberty."

Growing up in the America of the 1950s, we eagerly listened to the stories of adventure and excitement told by our fathers, uncles, and older brothers who served in World War II and Korea. There was much talk of one's duty, of paying your dues for the good life American citizens enjoyed.

When Vietnam came along I just happened to be graduating from college with a commission in the U.S. Army. It was an easy decision: I certainly didn't want to miss the opportunity of participating in what many considered the major event of our generation.

Looking back, I have nothing but positive memories of my tour of duty. I feel no guilt. I experience no thoughts I can't deal with and, except for a dream that crops up occasionally, I feel nothing but pride for myself and the men who served with me during those trying times.

This book is dedicated to those brave young men who served in the 1st Infantry Division's 1st Squadron, 4th Cavalry.

Acknowledgment

It is with warm and grateful thanks that I acknowledge the help so generously given by the Executive Editor at Presidio Press, E. J. McCarthy. I'm particularly grateful for his suggestion to improve the book by increasing its heft and his numerous letters of encouragement.

In Country

Those who do not do battle for their country do not know with what ease they accept their citizenship in America.
— Dean Brelis

The infantry battalion's B Company commander paced nervously off in the distance, a radio handset at each ear. Curious, I tuned one of my radios to his frequency and heard the last frantic calls from one of his platoons, which was outnumbered, surrounded, and in danger of being wiped out. It was the same platoon that we had taken out to start its patrol just a few hours before. The platoon's call sign was Slingshot, and Slingshot Six (the platoon leader) was screaming out the grid coordinates where he wanted artillery fired. Gunfire and explosions boomed in the background as the lieutenant spoke. Then there was silence.

Soon a small, pleading voice came over the radio: "This is Slingshot Kilo [the radio operator], the lieutenant has been hit in both arms and the back of the head. Please get us out of here."

That was the last contact with the ill-fated platoon. I stared at the company commander, who was standing there alone. He looked very old. Feeling sorry for him, I jumped down from my vehicle and ran over to offer my assistance. He still had a handset glued to each ear but he looked at me and nodded, acknowledging my presence. Just then the men on my vehicle yelled that the infantry battalion commander wanted to talk to me on the radio. I ran back to my command track and called him.

In very slow, clipped speech, he instructed me to "assemble your platoon on the main road as quickly as you can. An infantry platoon

1

will be attached to you, we're going to attempt to rescue that platoon."

I contacted my platoon, which was pulling outpost duty on the Tay Ninh road, and, in an equally grim tone, told the vehicle commanders to return to base at top speed. I advised them that we were going after the platoon we had taken out that morning, which was in heavy contact and in danger of being overrun.

As I waited for my platoon to arrive, the battalion operations officer briefed me on the current enemy situation. He explained that the platoon was in contact with an estimated two hundred–plus NVA regulars and that they were literally fighting for their lives. We were the only unit available that had any hope of reaching them in time. Finally, in a burst of emotion, he emphasized that "those men are surrounded and being cut to pieces and if we're going to save any of them, we've got to get moving."

With about thirty infantrymen scattered throughout the platoon on top of our vehicles, we took off at full speed but were held up at the first bridge we encountered. The engineers had removed the center span and it was impassable. I jumped down and spoke with the engineers' senior sergeant, who said that if they did everything they could as quickly as possible it would take at least an hour to make the bridge passable. We didn't have that much time, so I sent out my two scout sections, one upriver and one downstream, to search for a fording site. Within minutes the Bravo Team leader reported they had a vehicle across the river. I immediately ordered the rest of the platoon to move there at once and attempt the crossing.

As soon as we reached the crossing site the remainder of the platoon began lining up to ford the stream. I maneuvered my M113 armored cavalry assault vehicle to the front of the column and, with great difficulty, crossed over in the tracks of the first two scout vehicles.

The fording site was sandy, about fifty feet across with a depth of four to five feet. A tank following me became hopelessly stuck, tilting dangerously to one side. Only five to ten minutes had elapsed since we'd picked up the infantry when the battalion commander called, swearing and cursing and demanding to know my location.

I told him about the dismantled bridge and our efforts at the fording site. Then the commander demanded to know which side of the river I was on. I replied that I was on the far side with three of my scout tracks. He let out another string of curses and then ordered me to have the infantry wade across and load up on my three ACAVs. He wanted me moving in less than five minutes. Did I understand? I understood. I radioed my platoon to dismount the infantry and get them moving across the river. As the grunts waded over I noticed the noise from our supporting artillery battery—six 105mm howitzers firing as fast as they could in support of the platoon in contact. The infantry platoon leader and I waded into the river to help the soldiers with their footing and to speed up the crossing.

I felt great apprehension as the overloaded vehicles finally began to move. I had originally thought the entire platoon was a little light for this mission, but now, with only three of my ten vehicles and no tanks, I didn't feel at all good about the situation. I feared we were charging up the road into certain death.

Reflecting upon how I'd come to be in this situation, I found it difficult to believe that just a couple of months before I had completed the Jungle Warfare School in Panama and returned by chartered plane to Charleston, South Carolina, to continue my journey to Vietnam. An airline strike had closed the major airports, forcing travelers to go by train, bus, or rental car. I chose the train to Washington, D.C., and then took a bus to McGuire Air Force Base, New Jersey, where I boarded the flight that brought me to this bloody, faraway land that few of us then knew anything about.

The night train ride to Washington was like something out of the 1940s—dirty old railroad cars crowded with young soldiers in uniform. An elderly black porter came down the aisle with a huge pot of coffee. It looked like something you'd find over a campfire on a cattle drive. That coffee was the only refreshment I had on the eight-hour train ride.

I was seated next to an older gentleman who was determined to tell me about his experiences in World War I. One incident he recalled with delight occurred on the first day of basic training. His drill sergeant separated out the wooden heads in the platoon and put a piece of straw through the laces of one boot and a piece of hay through the laces of the other so that these halfwit soldiers could tell their right foot from their left. After that, the sergeant called cadence by saying, "Hay foot, straw foot, hay foot, straw foot," instead of "left, right, left."

The war ended before they finished training. Shortly after the armistice was announced, the man said, their camp closed earlier than scheduled and they were all discharged because of the fear of influenza, which had caused numerous deaths in nearby camps.

Directly across the aisle sat two young privates who had removed their shirts because of the heat. I asked them where they were headed and then told them they were in a public place and to put their shirts back on. They did.

When we arrived in the towering, cathedral-like Union Station, I learned that the next bus to McGuire Air Force Base would not be leaving until 10:30 A.M. the following day. Armed with that knowledge, I checked into a nearby hotel and explored our nation's capital.

Everything was within easy walking distance, so I walked the three blocks to the capitol building. Inside the huge marble building I explored the rotunda and the old senate and house chambers. It was a Saturday and the unnatural stillness of the streets was refreshing. I felt as if I had the entire city to myself. Leaving the capitol, I next visited the Smithsonian museums. The Air and Space Museum was my favorite. Finally, I returned to my hotel in time to see *Doctor Zhivago* at the theater next door.

The bus ride to McGuire was uneventful. Upon arrival I was quartered in a World War II–era BOQ a short distance from the officers' club. I walked over to the deserted officers' club and called the post transportation office and asked for a vehicle and driver to pick me up the next morning and take me to the airfield to catch my flight. I explained very firmly to the sergeant that my orders said I was to be at the terminal no later than 7:30 A.M. He assured me that a vehicle would pick me up by 6:30 A.M. and not to worry.

During World War II most existing army posts were expanded using a standard blueprint for light, wood-frame buildings. The designers intended that these temporary structures be torn down or replaced by permanent buildings after the war. Peace brought a rapid demobilization, and most of the temporary buildings, rather than being dismantled, were simply locked up. When the Korean War came along they were reopened for basic trainees. When that war ended, they were used by Reserve and National Guard troops.

By the end of 1965, the active army had reclaimed most of the temporary World War II buildings for use by those being trained for duty in Vietnam. Little had been done to upgrade or even maintain them. Most were still heated by coal-fired boilers and contained the original wire-spring bunks with roll-up cotton mattresses. The men were housed in forty-eight man bays with a communal latrine.

Officers had it a little better than the enlisted men. Our small BOQ rooms were usually equipped with a refrigerator, a writing desk, and a shared, semiprivate bathroom.

It was a very simple life, with just the bare essentials to see us through our training and off to the war.

The next morning, promptly at six-thirty, I was surprised to see an army green eighteen-wheeler with a modified trailer pull up in front of the BOQ. It was a standard trailer with windows cut in the sides, bus seats placed in neat rows, and recessed stairs extending down from one side, with a compressed air-operated door. There was obviously a bus shortage in the area. It was the most depressing vehicle I'd ever seen, and I hesitated to get in. Finally, the driver came around and asked if I had called transportation the night before. When I said that I had, he said, "Then please get in, Sir, we're late."

At first, I was the only passenger, but we soon stopped at a barracks area and some sixty very young, fuzzy-cheeked privates boarded with their drill sergeant. The sergeant saluted and apologized for my having to ride in the cattle truck. He explained that his unit had just finished advanced infantry training and the men were all headed to Vietnam. Then the sergeant moved his soldiers in single file onto the bus. The GIs filled every vacant seat, and the remaining fifteen sat on the floor. I didn't realize it then, but for the next three days I would share the same plane and experiences with this group of fine young men as we traveled to Vietnam.

Most of them were draftees, recent high school graduates who wanted to take care of their military obligation and get on with their lives. President Lyndon Johnson and Secretary of Defense Robert McNamara early on decided to rely entirely upon the active army to fight the war and not to call up the Reserves or National Guard. They wanted the war to cause as little disruption to everyday life as possible so that efforts to build the "Great Society," the president's first priority, could continue unimpeded.

The army relied on the draft for the required manpower. As the war dragged on and became more unpopular, more and more young men sought Selective Service deferments or refused to answer the call to serve. But that was in the future. In 1966, the home front was supportive, and the young soldiers traveling with me were filled with enthusiasm and feelings of great expectations for a war they thought would be a cakewalk.

Three officers and 149 enlisted men were jammed six abreast in one of the new Boeing 707 jets as we flew from New Jersey to Fairbanks, Alaska, then to Japan and finally to Saigon. The flight took about twenty-four hours. My most enduring memory is of eating seven delicious airline meals while scrunched in a tiny seat. As a diversion I read two books—one entitled *The Battle of Dien Bien Phu.*

The stewardesses on the last leg of the flight were older women in their forties. They were good sports who tried to be pleasant and helpful to the young soldiers, talking to them and handing out reading materials. The soldiers were, for the most part, polite, quiet, and well behaved.

As we approached our destination I got into an awkward discussion with the soldiers seated closest to me about the progress of the war. Most of them had great confidence in the ability of the United States, the richest nation on earth, to crush this "peasant uprising," using its superior military might.

Newspaper articles I'd read prior to my departure had indicated the tremendous optimism of the American people for a quick victory. There was even a story about a reporter aboard the aircraft carrier *Ranger* who thought if we could just show this mammoth ship to the Vietcong, it would be enough to make them give up.

All of us had been given a standard army briefing on Vietnam that portrayed the country as being backward and its military primitive, armed with weapons dating back to World War I.

The general feeling was that the world's most powerful nation, with a military that was "second to none," would quickly destroy the Vietcong, restore democracy, and soon build a modern nation in South Vietnam that would be the envy of the Communist North.

At about 2 A.M. the pilot announced that we would be landing in fifteen minutes. Instantly, everyone was awake and trying to see out the windows, hoping to catch a glimpse of the strange land below. Unfortunately, the only thing visible was a darkened sky.

Once we were on the ground a hush fell over the plane. No one spoke as we taxied up to the terminal and stopped. Then a stewardess opened the door and in rushed thick, hot, humid air. It was raining as we made our way down the slick gangway, picked up our baggage from the tarmac, and, soaking wet, boarded one of the six covered two-and-a-half ton trucks that had arrived to take us to the in-processing site.

The trucks ferried us to the other side of the airfield and dropped us off in front of two olive-drab tents with the sides rolled up. Tall, roughly built tables were set up in a horseshoe with places for seventy-five men to stand. Clerks passed out pencils and a pile of blank forms. The intensity of the rain increased and, with water running off the tent in torrents, the sergeant in charge barked orders through a bullhorn. He explained each block of each form as we filled out the various insurance and next-of-kin forms, using the army's tried-and-true "by the numbers" method. This process took about an hour. Then, wet and tired, we were loaded back on the trucks and taken to nearby barracks for the remainder of the night. As we got off, the drivers checked our orders and told us when representatives from various units would arrive the next morning to pick us up.

Most of my traveling companions were going to the replacement battalion located just outside Saigon. From there they would be assigned to different units. I was going to the 1st Infantry Division and was told I would learn my specific assignment when I arrived there.

It was after 4 A.M. when I finally turned out the lights. Outside, I noticed it was just starting to get light. My first day in Vietnam was already beginning.

I awoke to a loud honking noise followed by the revving of a large engine and a husky voice calling, "Anyone going to the Big Red One?" I got up and went to the door and saw an old 1940s flat-nosed bus idling in front of the building. It was painted army green and had chicken wire over the windows. I told the private driving it to wait a minute, that I'd be right out. On boarding the bus I discovered that eight of the twelve soldiers inside had flown over with me the day before and that no one had eaten breakfast, so I asked the driver if we could find a mess hall before leaving the area. After breakfast we headed out of the Tan Son Nhut Air Base compound and into the mass confusion of Saigon traffic. Bicycles, pedicabs, motorcycles, small cars, and trucks flowed in an endless stream of noise and exhaust. Traffic circles had been constructed at major intersections, much as you would find in Paris or London, and traffic was even more congested at those points.

There was a sort of pecking order to the traffic. Larger vehicles crowded ahead and were given a clear right-of-way by smaller and slower vehicles. Two-and-a-half-ton trucks driven by South Vietnamese soldiers were the most aggressive, and cars and bicycles scrambled to get out of their way.

The sidewalks teemed with masses of people—shoppers, school children, women in flowing traditional Vietnamese dresses, and even a few Boy Scouts in uniform.

My first impression of the city was a good one. I had imagined that it would be virtually deserted, with bombed-out buildings and the few people remaining dressed in rags.

Before we left the mess hall, the driver told us the rules of the bus. It was probably his finest hour. In his slow, Georgia drawl, the chubby, pink-faced driver explained why the windows were covered with chicken wire: "Before, little zipperheads on motorcycles would drive up next to buses and throw grenades through the windows. Now, the gooks put a hook on the grenades and just pull the pin and hang them on the chicken wire." He paused and looked around, gauging the effect of his revelation before continuing.

"The worst ones are bad guys on motorcycles who ride up alongside, pull out a pistol, and shoot someone on the bus and then just ride off." After finishing his spiel, the driver assigned us each a window to look out and told us to yell "Bomb!" if we saw someone hook something on one of the screens, or "Sniper!" if anyone pointed a gun at the bus. In either of those situations we were all supposed to dive to the floor. Interestingly, no one on the bus had a weapon.

It took about twenty minutes to pass through the city and into the countryside, during which time we were peering tensely out through the chicken wire, bracing for the impact that we just knew would happen any minute.

We finally emerged from the city unscathed and crossed over the Saigon River into the rice-growing area northwest of the city. Soon, off in the distance, we could see a large, flat military compound built out by itself. Three separate layers of concertina wire ringed the compound, each separated by about ten yards of ground that had been cleared of all vegetation. Inside we could see oiled dirt streets lined with one-story frame buildings that had sandbags halfway up each outer wall. Just inside the compound was a large billboard that read, "WELCOME TO THE BIG RED ONE. THOSE WHO LIKE LONG HOURS AND HARD WORK WILL FIND A HAPPY HOME HERE."

After wishing us all good luck and telling us to keep our heads down, the driver dropped us off at the division personnel office. The enlisted men were led off to fill out more paperwork and I was told to wait for the G1, who would meet with me shortly.

The personnel officer was an older, gray-haired lieutenant colonel who took about thirty minutes to visit with me, find out about my background, and determine what it was that I wanted to do. He also told me that they had not received any lieutenant replacements for several weeks. He told me about what he considered to be the division's premier fighting unit, the 1st Squadron, 4th Cavalry. Wherever there was trouble the cavalry squadron was normally sent in to take care of it. After watching my reaction, he said that unless I had any strong objections the "Quarter Horse" would be my unit of assignment. I said that would be fine with me. It sounded like a real hard-charging unit, which was just what I was looking for.

As I shook his hand and started to leave, he added, "One more thing, Lieutenant, you can't report to your unit until you've attended the division commander's briefing, and the general won't be available until the day after tomorrow."

Faced with the prospect of spending two days on my own at the division's main base camp, I asked a clerk to drive me over to the transient officer's quarters, a low, sandbagged building next to the officers' club.

The General's Briefing

A nation cannot remain great if it betrays its allies and lets down its friends.

—Richard M. Nixon

While patiently waiting for the general to return, I explored every inch of the compound, walking through the miniature city like a tourist.

In September of 1966 most of the division's rear-area support units were located there at Dian: the division headquarters and primary staff sections, the band, finance, personnel, a heavy maintenance company, and a company of engineers, to name a few. In talking to people during my strolls I learned that nearly every week a squad of local Vietcong came within a mile or so of the compound after dark, set up a mortar tube, fired six to ten high-explosive rounds, and then disappeared. Damage from this action was normally slight, more psychological than real. Occasionally, however, they would score a direct hit on a building or piece of equipment and casualties would result. That explained the sandbagged buildings.

One evening at the officers' club, an older AG captain explained in great detail how his unit was doing its part in fighting the war. He related how every two weeks his clerks and typists manned the entire perimeter for a twenty-four hour period and sent a ten-man patrol out to check a nearby section of jungle. Additionally, they set up three-man listening posts a hundred or so yards outside the wire, situated near trail intersections where the enemy was most likely to approach. The captain was obviously very proud of how his men per-

11

formed as clerks and as soldiers. As a green second lieutenant just arriving, it all sounded very impressive to me.

One other observation I made while wandering around was the role local Vietnamese women played in the base's daily routine. At seven-thirty each morning at least a hundred women arrived. Each wore a black silk pantsuit under a skirt slit up both sides to the waist, and a white, conical straw hat. They were all skinny, had old faces and gold teeth, and none was over five feet tall. They performed all sorts of necessary duties around the compound. They did the laundry, cleaned up the BOQs, worked as KPs in the mess halls, sewed patches on uniforms, and helped the garbage-truck crews empty fifty-five gallon drums of trash. It was amazing to see the amount of work done by these sturdy little women. Then, at five each afternoon, they went back out the main gate and into the nearby villages and hamlets.

On one of my strolls I rounded the corner of a sandbagged building and stopped dead in my tracks. About twenty yards in front of me I saw one of the women squatted down cooking her lunch. She apparently had the job of cleaning out the outhouse latrines. These little wooden buildings, normally four-holers, had half of a fifty-five-gallon drum under each seat to catch the waste. Each day the drums were removed through a trapdoor in the rear of each such structure and the contents burned, using a small amount of kerosene. The lucky person assigned this task normally carried a long stick to stir the contents and thus make sure the fire consumed everything.

On this particular day the little Vietnamese woman had strung a short piece of wire above the burning mess and hung her lunch, half of a chicken, from it. She would occasionally raise it up and baste it with a thick red sauce.

After watching for a few minutes, I eventually moved on. Later I wondered if such behavior was caused by a radically different culture or because of extreme hunger and poverty. Perhaps, I figured, our being there would help to educate people like her about proper health and sanitation measures.

The day of the general's briefing, about thirty of us newly assigned officers and senior sergeants were herded into a cramped,

sweltering briefing room in division headquarters. Lieutenant Col.
Alexander Haig (who later served as President Ronald Reagan's
White House chief of staff, commander of NATO, and secretary of
state), the G3, briefed us on the division's current operations. After
imparting forty-five minutes of mind-numbing information, Lieutenant Colonel Haig concluded his remarks by wishing us good luck
and ordering us to stand by for the division commander, Maj. Gen.
William Depuy.

Most of those present had flown over on one of the new jet air-
liners and were still suffering from jet lag. Added to this was the 110-
degree heat and high humidity. Having had a few days to acclima-
tize myself to the time change and extreme heat, I was adjusting
pretty well. However, the men who had arrived the day before were
still suffering.

The army in 1966 tolerated alcohol consumption as long as it
didn't interfere with a soldier's duty performance. Several of those
present had consumed copious quantities the night before and, as
we sat there, hot and uncomfortable, waiting for the general to arrive, the faint odor of alcohol floated through the back of the
crowded room.

Within minutes the outside door burst open and a full colonel
stepped inside and bellowed, "Gentlemen, the division commander." At this, we all scrambled to our feet, and stood at rigid attention. A short man with a deeply lined face and a heavy scowl entered
the room. He was wearing a crisp, freshly starched set of fatigues.
When he reached the front of the room he faced the group and
barked, "Take your seats." Shortly after he began speaking, he
stopped in midsentence, pointed at a sergeant in the back of the
room, and shouted, "Wake that man up!" Hands reached out from
three different directions and shook the sleeping sergeant. When
the man opened his eyes, General Depuy glared at him and said in
a low, growling voice, "I want you out of the division by the close of
business today. Now get the hell out of here."

As the hapless, bleary-eyed sergeant tripped and stumbled from
his seat to the door, the full colonel took him by the arm. At that
point the general hissed to the colonel, the division chief of staff,
"Ed, I want you to find an appropriate home for this one."

"Yes, Sir!" replied the colonel as they both disappeared out the door. The general continued glaring out at the group. It was so quiet you could have heard a pin drop. After what seemed an eternity, the general snapped, "I don't want worthless men like that in the division."

General Depuy talked for thirty minutes about leadership and what he expected of us in combat. One comment has stuck with me over the years: "As combat leaders, I expect you to show your soldiers through your own example how to fight like men and, if necessary, how to die like men." He followed those stirring words with a warning: "If, through your own incompetence or dereliction of duty, you wind up with American blood on your hands, I want to personally assure you that I will do everything in my power to see that you go to Leavenworth for a very long time." After letting that thought sink in, he concluded with, "The division needs you, your country needs you, so don't let us down."

With that, a voice from the rear of the room roared, "Attenhut!" We jumped to attention, the general left the room, and the briefing was over.

It wasn't quite the welcome I'd expected. I had anticipated something a little more positive, something more in the John Wayne tradition, a "let's-get-in-there-and-win-this-war-together" kind of speech.

I later learned that General Depuy relieved more unit commanders than any other division commander in Vietnam.

Not many months later, my platoon was pulling outpost duty along a deserted jungle road. While switching channels on my powerful radios I heard General Depuy grilling an artillery battalion commander about the positioning of his firing batteries. As soon as the battalion commander answered one question, the general asked another. Not satisfied with the answers he was getting, the general finally said, "Diehard Six, you just lost your job. Meet me at the following coordinates, I'm taking you back to base."

He was a tough and demanding commander intolerant of mistakes. Fortunately, I had little contact with him during my tour of duty.

Less than an hour after our briefing I was on a C-123 cargo plane flying up to Lai Khe to join my unit, the ominous "welcome" from my new division commander still ringing in my head.

The trip from Dian to Lai Khe lasted about forty-five minutes, taking us over some spectacular terrain—rice paddies, thick jungle, wild rivers, and rubber plantations. With me were twelve other men going to 1st Infantry Division units at Lai Khe. The plane also carried three heavy pallets of perishable food items for local mess halls. Raw egg yolks oozed out of the crushed corner of one container.

The camouflage-painted plane was powered by two large, noisy piston engines and had two small jet engines to assist them on short takeoffs. Seated along the sides of the cargo bay, it was possible to get a good view of the ground as we passed overhead. After what seemed like forever, the small, gray-haired crew chief pointed at the ground and announced we would be landing soon.

The pilot, using a straight-in approach, quickly dropped the plane in from a height of several thousand feet and within seconds we set down on the PSP runway for a surprisingly smooth landing.

We got off while the engines continued to run, and a forklift rushed out to unload the pallets. In a matter of minutes the plane was gone, leaving us standing there beside the runway with our luggage. It was obvious that we had landed in the middle of a large rubber plantation.

Lai Khe had been a small plantation town; now, however, most of the buildings were deserted and in a terrible state of repair. Rubber trees with eight- to ten-inch trunks and approximately thirty feet tall were planted in neat rows, fifteen to twenty feet apart, reaching to within a few feet of the main road, Highway 13. This was a dangerous highway that I would spend much of my time and energy trying to keep the enemy from closing during most of the next twelve months.

We hadn't been there long when an army jeep driven by a powerful-looking black first lieutenant pulled up. After briefly looking us over he looked at me and said, "You must be Walker." When I nodded he leaped out, came around the jeep, and firmly shook my hand. "I'm Ron Copes," he said with a smile. "Welcome to Lai Khe."

We loaded my duffel bag and small suitcase in the back of the jeep and headed across the road into the rubber trees. It seemed twenty degrees cooler there.

Lieutenant Copes worked at squadron headquarters, which was colocated with C Troop. During the short drive he told me three war stories about the blood and gore of recent battles and the heavy casualties incurred. As he finished the last one we ground to a stop in front of a single-story, army-engineer constructed building. A tanned and grinning captain strode out. "Captain Lettenoff, this is your new lieutenant, Lieutenant Walker," Copes announced.

We shook hands and visited for a few minutes. Then Captain Lettenoff took me on a tour of the area. Our first stop was at my tent, where we dropped my bags. From there we went to the mess hall, then the maintenance area, and, finally, to the motor pool, a cleared dirt area close to our tents and next to Highway 13. The rich, sweet smell of motor oil mixed with diesel fuel filled the air. It was the monsoon season, and the motor pool was one big mud hole. Everything—people, supplies, and vehicles—was covered with thick, red mud. The troop commander pointed out my ten vehicles, but with the mud it was almost impossible to distinguish them from the others. It took me several days to sort them out.

In welcoming me to the troop, Captain Lettenoff explained what he expected of his platoon leaders. Whenever he called my platoon on the radio he wanted to hear my voice right away. If I needed to be off my track for any reason I was to take the PRC-10 portable radio with me. Furthermore, whenever my platoon made contact with the enemy, my place was in the middle of the action—there were to be no secondhand reports. Finally, Captain Lettenoff said the unit had taken a number of casualties during the past few months and many of my men were recent arrivals. "Take advantage of every opportunity to teach the men what you expect of them when the going gets tough," he advised. He ended with an admonition: "I want you to be a calm, steady hand in this platoon. Just use plain common sense and you'll do fine."

When he had finished talking, the CO caught the attention of a sergeant and motioned for him to come over. His name was Staff Sergeant Cowhig, and he had been the acting platoon leader. The

CO instructed Sergeant Cowhig—a tall, slim, quiet man—to introduce me to the men, show me my vehicles, and answer any questions I might have. Then he turned to me and said he would see me later at supper.

After the CO left, Sergeant Cowhig explained that my regular platoon sergeant had been slightly wounded by a booby trap and would not return for about ninety days. Until then, because of seniority, he would serve as my platoon sergeant. Continuing in a concerned tone, he explained that eight of the sixty-three men in our platoon were brought into the army under a special program called Project 100,000. This program was for men who scored low on the army's mental ability test. Under normal circumstances these individuals would not have been admitted into the army, but through this special test program a hundred thousand men who scored in the lowest mental category were allowed in to determine if they could function in nontechnical fields such as the infantry. The eight men we had in our platoon appeared to have normal intelligence but the ones from Puerto Rico had difficulty understanding English. Because of the language problem, these soldiers often misunderstood directions and caused needless casualties. This social experiment was an additional burden throughout my tour.

After meeting the vehicle commanders and saying hello to the men, Sergeant Cowhig and I discussed how the platoon had been operating.

Although junior in rank, Sergeant Cowhig served as platoon sergeant for most of my tour. He was the strong, silent type, who thought carefully before saying anything. All the men had great respect for him. He reminded me of Gary Cooper.

Later, for one brief, six-week period, I had a gung-ho sergeant first class platoon sergeant named Graff, who was a great help in running the platoon. Unfortunately, Sergeant First Class Graff's tour as platoon sergeant ended abruptly when he was riding in the lead tank of a convoy coming out of a rubber plantation west of Phuoc Vinh. Another unit had cleared the narrow, muddy dirt road. All was proceeding smoothly when Sergeant Graff's tank hit a huge mine that blew him right up in the air. From my position about fifty yards farther back in the column I could see his arms blown straight up, like a referee signaling a touchdown, as he was propelled out of the commander's hatch. It seemed impossible that anyone could survive such an explosion, yet Sergeant Graff was almost instantly back on the radio reporting a Russian T-34 tank to his immediate front.

This panicked the platoon, and I quickly ordered the other two tanks to remove the canister rounds from their main guns and reload antitank rounds. Then, with my medic at my side, I cautiously approached Sergeant Graff's disabled tank on foot. We found no Russian tanks, and by the time we reached Graff, he was unconscious. Within minutes a medevac helicopter arrived and we loaded Sergeant Graff and two of his crewmen aboard. That was the last time we saw him, although I did hear later that he recovered fully from his wounds. For several months afterward, whenever there was a lull in a conversation, someone would enliven things by mentioning Sergeant Graff's frantic radio call. We never were able to figure out why he reported sighting a Russian tank. It was probably the shock of the explosion.

Sergeant Cowhig and I were a good match and I considered myself lucky to have a man of such strong character as my platoon sergeant.

Each vehicle in my platoon exhibited a tremendous amount of combat damage. It was clear to me this tour was not going to be a picnic. One tank had twelve jagged bullet holes in its searchlight cover. Three of the ACAVs had been hit by RPGs that went in one side and out the other. The RPG was a dreaded antitank weapon consisting of a shaped explosive charge on the end of a rocket motor. The rockets were normally very accurate when fired from the shoulder. Only the front slopes of our tanks, with their thick armor plating, were safe from these "dragon killers."

My armored cavalry platoon was organized as follows:

- Two scout sections for reconnaissance, each with two M113 armored personnel carriers mounting an M2 .50-caliber machine gun and two smaller M60 7.62mm machine guns.
- One M109 mortar carrier mounting an 81mm mortar for close-in fire support and illumination. This vehicle was very similar in appearance to the M113.

• One tank section. This was the real muscle of the platoon. It consisted of three fifty-two-ton M48A3 tanks that were used for heavy direct fire and shock effect. The main ammunition was 90mm canister rounds filled with small pellets that proved very effective in breaking up ambushes. Each tank also mounted a .50-caliber machine gun at the tank commander's position, and a hull mounted 7.62mm machine gun.

• My command vehicle, an M113 with three powerful radios for long-range communications. The three antennas marked it as a prime target.

• One ten-man infantry squad in an M113 equipped with the same armament as the scouts.

Because of the nature of the war in Vietnam I was forced to make modifications to the platoon's organization, particularly in the infantry squad. I often dispersed these soldiers evenly among the rest of the vehicles in the platoon when our strength fell below authorized levels. The TO&E called for each of the tanks to have a four-man crew and each of the scout vehicles five, except for my command vehicle, which had six. This was very helpful for the normal routine of all-night guard duty.

As we strolled through the motor pool, Sergeant Cowhig pointed out some of the maintenance problems on various vehicles—worn track, broken torsion bars, and leaking oil seals—all of which were primarily due to a lack of spare parts. Each vehicle had caterpillar-type tracks and required large amounts of maintenance for the few miles covered each day.

Finally, we climbed on my vehicle and, with Sergeant Cowhig providing a running commentary, drove north out of the rubber trees, past old men in rice paddies planting rice stems and shoots in the rich black earth, to a makeshift firing range. There I test-fired all the weapons on the vehicle, including my .45-caliber pistol, until we were both satisfied that I could pull my own weight as a member of the crew.

I spent the remainder of the afternoon wandering around asking questions and talking with soldiers who seemed extremely tired and listless. The one exception was my medical specialist. He was a big, blond-headed young man named Trosper, and he always had a cheerful smile and boundless energy. He was my constant companion for the next six months, saving countless lives with his expert first aid and sound advice.

Whenever we made contact with the enemy, I raced to the scene of the action, either on foot or in my command vehicle, and my medic was always right at my side. During my eleven months as a platoon leader, I had three different medics, and I recommended each of them for either the Silver Star or Bronze Star for heroism. Numerous times, with total disregard for their own safety, they went out in the face of enemy fire to help recover members of the platoon and treat their wounds.

The medics also showed tremendous concern for the health and welfare of our soldiers. One incident, in particular, illustrates this caring. A stray dog bit a soldier when the platoon stopped briefly in one of the villages we often passed through. The man in question was a good friend of the medic and told him he was afraid of taking the series of rabies shots. My medic didn't want to cause the soldier more pain or discomfort, but he also wanted to ensure he was treated properly. He shared his dilemma with me. I explained the seriousness of the situation to the soldier and urged him not to let the rest of the platoon down by becoming a casualty. I then ordered him to take the shots and explained that our medic would administer them. That solved the problem; it also increased my appreciation of the tough job the medics performed. I always had the highest respect for them and the medical advice they provided.

When we finished my day's orientation I had an accurate picture of the situation in order to fight the platoon or to call for fire support and then report to headquarters. I thanked Sergeant Cowhig for his assistance and headed off to the mess hall—a long, low, structure similar in design to a stateside mess hall. It had a kitchen and serving line at one end, then the main dining area. At the other end of the building was a separate dining area for officers. All of the kitchen equipment—tables, chairs, curtains, serving trays, and utensils—were the same as those in a regular mess hall. It was comforting to find such familiar surroundings here at our little outpost in Vietnam.

At supper that evening I joined the rest of the troop's officers at a double table. Two mess personnel served us food brought on metal trays. The menu included roast beef and gravy, mashed potatoes, peas and carrots, hot rolls, iced tea, and ice cream for dessert. Captain Lettenoff directed the conversation during the meal, which was very relaxed. When we finished eating the CO put six cigars on a plate and passed them around the table. We all lit up and pushed back our chairs for more light conversation. Right outside our window two large dogs—one brown, one gray, both with short hair like bulldogs—got into a gnawing, growling, yelping fight. All of us officers jumped up and ran outside to watch the determined struggle. The dogs put on a good show for about ten minutes—until the first sergeant came out with a pan of ice water and threw it on the combatants, sending them running off in opposite directions.

About the time the dogfight ended, a young soldier came by and announced that the movie *Thunderball* with Sean Connery would be starting in five minutes. Captain Lettenoff and the executive officer had work to do, so they said goodnight. We platoon leaders and the artillery forward observer walked over to where the troop clerk had hung a brown-looking sheet between two rubber trees and set up the unit's 16mm movie projector for the evening show. The four of us, still with our cigars, took seats on empty ammo boxes and waited for the movie to begin. The unit had received this film about ten days before and this was the third showing. In spite of that, about a hundred soldiers attended.

After the movie I made my way back to my tent in the dark, unpacked my gear, set up my cot, blew up my air mattress, hung up my mosquito netting, and settled down for a good night's sleep. I awoke about midnight when a nearby 155mm artillery battery began shooting a fire mission. The concussion from the big guns' blasts made my air mattress quiver and shake; so I reached down, pulled out the mattress plug, and was soon sound asleep again on my hard cot.

A Platoon Lost

The most terrible job in warfare is to be a second lieutenant leading a platoon when you are on the battlefield.
—Dwight D. Eisenhower

Soon after joining C Troop I was the only officer platoon leader remaining; the others were either recovering from wounds or away on R and R. It was during this period that the 1st Infantry Division busily prepared for a major campaign northwest of Tay Ninh. The objective was to disrupt one of the enemy's main infiltration routes into Saigon.

Late one evening I was walking back to my tent after the nightly movie when the troop clerk handed me a note from the CO. My platoon was to depart early the next morning to take part in a division-level operation and I would be gone for about two weeks.

In preparing for this elaborate campaign in the vicinity of Soui Da, the division determined that before major units could move into the area an airstrip needed to be constructed for resupply and a local bridge rebuilt. Consequently, in the first week of December a task force consisting of the following elements was assembled for the mission: an infantry battalion, a 105mm artillery battery, a signal platoon for communications, a medical detachment, a support company, an engineer company, and my armored cavalry platoon.

Simply stated, the engineer company was going up to do the work and everyone else was going along to watch, provide security, or for logistical support.

We needed little preparation. Our vehicles were always topped off and ready to go. Early the next morning, with one extra set of fatigues and our army-issue shaving kits, we climbed on our vehicles and were off to join the task force, which was at the compound at Phu Loi some forty-five miles south on Highway 13.

Highway 13 was an old, French-built, two-lane asphalt road running some sixty miles between Saigon and the Cambodian border. Its original purpose had been to link the various plantations of French Indochina with the seaport in Saigon. Cargoes such as rubber, hardwoods, rice, and charcoal were transported over it.

The Vietcong used Highway 13 for another purpose: to show local villagers the weakness of the Saigon government and its inability to keep the road open. These determined soldiers, with orders and equipment from the North, buried antitank mines in the roadway at the same place, month after month. Whenever a unit was successfully ambushed along the highway, chances were good the enemy would repeat the effort using exactly the same tactics. This situation was a direct result of MACV's policy of controlling the countryside during the daytime and then withdrawing to our bases at night, allowing the Vietcong to move back in and regain control. However, knowledge of these enemy habits did allow us to be particularly alert as we passed through areas of previous contact.

My orders were to report to Lieutenant Colonel Martin, the infantry battalion and task force commander. Upon arrival at Phu Loi I learned that I had missed an important task force meeting held earlier in the day. Not wanting to get off to a bad start, I immediately reported to Lieutenant Colonel Martin, an unsmiling officer with a stutter, who reprimanded me for missing his meeting and refused to listen to my explanation why. He glared at me for a moment and then barked, "This will not be a picnic, Lieutenant, people will probably be killed on this operation." With that he turned me over to his operations officer for the details and left the room.

The operations officer, Major Edwards, a slim man with thin, hard lips, explained that there would be eighty-four wheeled vehicles in the task force column and my ten armored vehicles were to provide security for the convoy. Furthermore, the infantry would be flown into the objective by helicopter and my vehicles would be the convoy's only protection from Saigon north. He asked how I would deploy my platoon for this assignment, and I said I would place four vehicles in front, three in the middle, and three at the rear of the column, with one tank in each group. The major nodded his agreement. He then explained that we would depart at midnight and arrive in Saigon no later than 4 A.M. so as to avoid the heavy traffic in the city. Finally, he instructed me to have my men eat in the local mess hall, get a couple of hours' sleep after chow, and then have my platoon lined up on the perimeter road ready to roll no later than 11:30 P.M.

We were lined up along the perimeter road when, at midnight, the first infantry trucks began to arrive. Lieutenant Colonel Martin gave the order to move out and I started out the gate in the lead with my four armored vehicles. I got an eerie feeling when I looked over my shoulder and saw the faint glow from what appeared to be a thousand headlights snaking along behind like tiny fireflies. The small hamlets and villages along our route were like ghost towns, their streets empty, seemingly devoid of life.

We eventually came to the Saigon River. As soon as we crossed the bridge, Lieutenant Colonel Martin radioed me to stop the column and announced that he would lead the way through Saigon. That was fine with me. Road signs were often stolen or destroyed and you had to guess where you were. I'd rather have him do the guessing.

With the war on, I was surprised to see so many streetlights and storefronts lit up. However, since there was no threat of enemy air attack, there was no need for a blackout. In any event, it made finding our way much easier. Even at that early hour there were masses of people along every street, apparently getting an early start on the day.

The trip north from Saigon was uneventful except for two trucks breaking down and a sniping incident that occurred in the middle of the column. The two trucks were hooked to a large wrecker and towed the rest of the way. A sniper fired on the column during the recovery operation, so I ordered my middle security element to drop out and fire high in the direction of the distant sniper to avoid hitting the nearby village. This ended the sniping incident and my crews rejoined the rear of the convoy.

One evening back in Lai Khe, our artillery forward observer tried to explain the struggle to win the "hearts and minds of the people" to me. He stated that the Vietcong were constantly trying to portray the government as heartless, uncaring, and unable to protect the people or their property. According to him, part of this effort involved having snipers fire on U.S. or South Vietnamese government convoys as they passed through villages along major highways. The convoys' normal reaction to being fired upon was to return fire with all weapons. This usually resulted in much property damage and killed many villagers. As you can imagine, this practice didn't win us very many friends. U.S. forces were better about holding their fire, but South Vietnamese forces normally returned fire with reckless abandon. Consequently, one good sniper could win many converts to the Vietcong cause. That thought was in my mind when I ordered my men to fire high.

Due to the poor condition of the roads and our close interval, we were soon covered with thick dust and exhaust grime. We finally reached our destination after more than ten grueling hours on the road. All of us were filthy and completely exhausted.

Upon pulling into the large, brush-covered assembly area, I was assigned to defend a small sector near the road. The area was covered with a low, sagebrush-like plant and there was a single tall hardwood tree. I instructed my men that the tree and vegetation would have to be removed to clear fields of fire for the machine guns. While they were clearing this brush a runner arrived from the infantry battalion to notify me of a commanders' meeting scheduled for 1 P.M.

All commanders were present as Lieutenant Colonel Martin briefed us on the enemy situation, defensive positions, and his expectations regarding the appearance of our men. He explained that large enemy elements had been sighted in the area. He said he wanted everybody alert and that he expected shirts and helmets on at all times and everyone carrying a personal weapon. He then assigned specific missions. My platoon was to take three ten-man ambush patrols out at dark and pick them up at first light in the morning. We were also to secure the road to Tay Ninh each day.

By the time I returned to the platoon area the men had rigged three blocks of C-4 explosive around the base of the lone mahogany tree and were waiting for my permission to blow it up. I radioed the task force CP and informed them of our plans. After getting clearance, I ordered my men to light the fuse and then we all ran to get under or behind something. A tremendous explosion echoed across the area. When the smoke cleared the tree was still standing. A few leaves and a small patch of bark appeared to be the only things disturbed. That stout tree defied two more attempts to bring it down so we finally gave up.

That evening we loaded up the thirty infantrymen for the ambush patrols and dropped them off in their assigned areas. The patrol members looked like killers of the night. With their uniforms and equipment taped to reduce noise, and with black and green camouflage paint on their faces, they were a bunch of frighteningly ugly men. That night the patrols were scattered around the base, one a mile to the north, another to the south, and the largest off to the west. Their mission was to give early warning of enemy forces moving in to attack the task force. The remainder of the night was uneventful and my men were able to get some much-needed sleep between their two-hour guard shifts.

We picked up the ambush patrols at first light and returned to base. None of them had made contact with the enemy. Later, as we prepared to move out and begin opening the road to Tay Ninh, I received a call from the CP instructing me to pick up an infantry platoon and drop it off northwest of our area so they could begin a special reconnaissance sweep.

The Ho Chi Minh Trail ended about fifteen miles north of our area and just inside the Cambodian border. This trail brought a constant flow of enemy personnel, supplies, and equipment into our area. Lieutenant Colonel Martin decided to put one of his platoons in the general area to ensure that no large enemy force was assembling for an attack.

On this particular day, the battalion's other two rifle companies were conducting reconnaissance-in-force sweeps near Nui Ba Den, a very prominent mountain to our southwest. The mountain jutted several hundred feet right out of the level rice fields and dominated the surrounding countryside.

A Special Forces outpost was located on top of the mountain, and Vietcong occupying the lower slopes could observe our movements from their positions. The previous night we spotted their fires burning in several places on the mountain below the Special Forces camp. We were certainly aware of the enemy's nearby presence.

The infantry platoon leader and his artillery forward observer rode on my track. Both were friendly and energetic young men who took their jobs seriously. I distributed the remainder of their thirty-one men evenly among the other vehicles. We moved out of the compound and crossed the bridge north of camp, which was scheduled for repair later that day. After traveling about five miles up an old forest road through thick groves of hardwood trees and underbrush, I stopped the column at a slight bend in the road and the infantry platoon dismounted. I tossed the infantry lieutenant a C-ration cookie and told him to call me if he needed a ride back. Then we watched as they waved and disappeared into the thick brush.

Leaving the infantry, we moved back down the road and across the bridge. The engineers had already begun dismantling it. After clearing the bridge I positioned my ten vehicles about fifty feet off the road but within sight of each other, although sometimes as much as five hundred yards apart. I then went all the way to Tay Ninh and satisfied myself that the road was clear before calling the CP to report the road was open. That done, I moved back to the task force area, determined to find a company mess where I could get my platoon at least one good, hot meal a day. My search led me to the engineer company area. After telling me that feeding an additional fifty people would not be a problem, Capt. Bob Lucas, the company commander, took me over to see his kitchen setup. It was a very elaborate affair consisting of a pair of two-and-a-half-ton trucks backed up together with two mess stoves in the back of one and two field ovens in the back of the other. One side of the trucks was for cooking and baking, the other side was for serving. Men walked up a ramp with their trays, got their food, and then went down the other side of the ramp. It was a very efficient setup that could operate day or night and, with some canvas overhead, in rain or shine. The mess sergeant was very proud of his mobile kitchen and gave me a fresh-baked apple pie for my crew. I thanked the captain and told him we would see him at supper.

I walked back to my command vehicle with the warm apple pie, where Sp4 Carl Weaver wasted little time cutting it into six pieces. It was while we were savoring that delicious cinnamon-apple pie that I noticed the B Company commander off in the distance in an agitated state with a radio handset at each ear. I switched to his frequency and learned that the platoon we had dropped off earlier was in danger of being overrun and I was ordered to take another infantry platoon and go rescue it as described earlier.

After the infantry platoon leader and I got his men across the river at the fording site, I had them mount up on our three ACAVs. Because of the heavy weight of thirty-six infantrymen and sixteen cavalrymen, we could manage only fifteen to twenty miles per hour. We must have been a real sight, what with men and equipment covering every square inch of our vehicles. The forest road was totally deserted and full of potholes. Eighty- to one-hundred-foot tall teak and mahogany trees lined the edge of the road and thick underbrush carpeted the ground.

After ten long minutes we turned off the main road and began smashing through the thick, tangled brush. I ordered the infantry to dismount and move out ahead of us. The artillery fire stopped at that point and I was told to proceed cautiously to the location we'd been given.

A few yards ahead the brush thinned out and I left my vehicle and walked behind the infantry with PFC Jorge Borgos, my RTO, covering me with his M14. We soon smelled the powder and could see where our artillery had been exploding. To our front was a grove of trees with a clearing in the center. Around the near side of the clearing we found most of the bodies of the men in the platoon we had carried out earlier. The mutilated bodies of the two lieutenants were next to a small bush and, because of their condition, were identifiable only by their nametags and rank insignia. We posted local security and searched the battlefield. We were able to locate twenty-seven bodies and three badly wounded soldiers, leaving one soldier unaccounted for. The infantry platoon leader and I had our men bring the dead to the center of the clearing and wrapped the bodies in their ponchos while my medic worked on the three wounded. The smell of gunpowder and death hung heavy in the air.

Two helicopters landed. One was a supply helicopter and the other carried Brig. Gen. Bernard Rogers, the assistant division commander. I reported to the general and then we questioned the wounded in an effort to find out what had happened. The three men had been wounded in the stomach or chest and were covered with blood. They said they pretended to be dead as enemy soldiers moved around the battlefield and shot anyone showing signs of life.

One of the men said that as the platoon entered the grove of trees, two enemy soldiers ran out the far side and about ten GIs ran after them. When the grunts reached the center of the clearing, all were cut down by heavy enemy fire. The enemy seemed to be all around them, firing rifles and machine guns and throwing hand grenades; the platoon didn't have a chance.

Brigadier General Rogers ordered me to load the wounded on his helicopter and put as many bodies as we could on the other bird, then put the remaining bodies on my vehicles and return to base. He indicated he would try to intercept the fleeing enemy with artillery and tactical air strikes.

The helicopters departed, leaving us with seventeen dead soldiers to load into our three vehicles. The enemy had picked up their dead and wounded and most of the U.S. weapons, radios, packs, ammunition, and rations—anything they could carry off.

With the infantry fanned out in front of my vehicles, we headed back to the forest road without incident. I halted the column when we reached the road and loaded up the infantry. Standing there with the infantry lieutenant, we verified that all thirty-six of his men were on board. As we prepared to mount up, I noticed that my driver was motioning for me to come forward. About two hundred yards farther down the road was a fresh pile of dirt. I yelled for the infantry lieutenant to come forward and we scanned the entire area with binoculars but could see nothing else unusual. Next I radioed our base to request assistance but received no response. Unable to reach Sergeant Cowhig, I tried another radio, again without success. I'd run into situations where I could not send or receive on the radio before. The solution was to move a short distance to get out of the dead spot. Apparently we were in one of those communications black holes.

I unfolded my map and, with the infantry lieutenant looking over my shoulder, tried to find another route back to base. We could hear artillery exploding in the area of the recent battle, so that was not a possibility. If we went north it would take us into

Cambodia and farther away from base. That, too, was out of the question. Cambodia was off limits and, in the event of enemy contact, we would be entirely on our own. I imagined the platoon, out of radio contact, being surrounded by numerically superior forces, overrun and butchered to the last man, and no one ever knowing what had happened to us or ever finding our bodies. It was a chilling thought.

The sergeant on my middle vehicle frantically waved for me to come forward. When I reached his track he pointed into the brush about fifty yards away and said he'd just seen two men out there and they appeared to be enemy soldiers. That discovery ended our discussion about what route to take. I quickly ordered everyone to mount up and prepare to move out. We needed to get out of there fast if we were going to survive, and continuing on our present course seemed to me the only viable option.

With the road ahead apparently blocked, danger felt very near. I started to breathe a little faster. My plan was to make a run for it and have everyone open up with all weapons when we reached a large tree about fifty yards farther down the road. Each vehicle had three machine guns and the infantry platoon had three more, giving us a total of twelve. With those plus forty or so M14s we could put out a heavy volume of fire and keep the enemy down in their holes. I got on the platoon radio frequency so all could hear and explained my plan and the need to keep up a steady stream of fire. I also directed that if a vehicle was disabled the other two were to stay with it and make a stand until reinforcements arrived. I had no intention of leaving anyone behind.

I leaned forward over the driver's hatch and told my driver to watch the road for mines or signs of freshly dug ground and to drive on the far left side of the road, away from the mound of fresh dirt in front of us. I put my snub-nosed .38-caliber revolver in his hand and said, "You might need this." I tried one last time to call base, again without success except for a very broken transmission that was unintelligible because of heavy static. Then I raised my hand and, much like the old wagon masters on the frontier, radioed the other vehicles and signaled for everyone to move out. We hadn't gone more than ten yards when an RPG slammed against the side of my vehicle, exploding just in front of the gas tanks. The blast wounded six men, one very seriously. We continued to roll, however, and everyone who was able began to fire. The noise was deafening. Three more RPGs were fired at the column, one of which hit the last vehicle and caused slight casualties to those on board. As we moved, picked up speed, and approached the pile of dirt in the road, the enemy fire increased. More RPGs *whooshed* and exploded in our midst and machine-gun and AK-47 fire peppered our vehicles. Two more men on my track were hit. By this time we were only a few yards from the pile of dirt, which we could now see was a trench about ten feet long, two feet wide, and placed in a narrow part of the road so that we couldn't avoid it. I yelled at the driver, "Don't slow down. Hang on!" We hit the pile with a great impact, jarring everyone considerably. Although knocked around, no one fell off. Fortunately, the most seriously wounded had been put in the troop compartment just before impact. Looking back I saw my two trail vehicles hit the dirt pile hard, slow down, and then continue moving with guns blazing.

I again tried to radio our base camp. On the third try a loud, clear signal came through: "This is Seven-Seven. Send your message." It was Major General Depuy! In as calm a voice as I could muster, I told him our location and situation and that we had taken about twelve casualties. With all the loud firing and explosions in the background, I'm sure it was convincing. The general informed me he was directly overhead, that artillery fire would be immediate, and that I should prepare to adjust the artillery fires.

"Negative!" I shouted. "It's too hot down here!"

A hundred yards beyond the pile of dirt we stopped receiving enemy fire. About a mile later I ordered everyone to cease firing and asked for a status report from each vehicle. We had eight wounded on my track, two wounded on the middle vehicle, and six wounded and one killed on the trail vehicle, which was also having engine trouble.

After passing slowly over the now-reconstructed bridge I again contacted base. This time someone in the CP answered. I reported our status and requested they notify the aid station that we were bringing in sixteen wounded, three very seriously.

The TC on the rear vehicle called me and reported his engine was smoking badly and that they were going to have to stop.

"Negative!" I replied, "No matter what, don't stop until you reach the aid station!"

We pulled up so close to the aid station that we almost ran over the tent pegs. After checking our three most seriously wounded, the doctor called for a medevac helicopter to take them to Saigon. The other thirteen men were put on stretchers and cots for examination and treatment.

The last vehicle would not start, so we unloaded the bodies and placed them in my vehicle for the trip over to graves registration. We then said good-bye to the infantry platoon that had been attached to us for the rescue mission. Sergeant Cowhig pulled up in his tank and informed me that he had heard everything loud and clear on the radio, and that he hadn't expected to ever see me again after we hit the ambush. While we were talking, a jeep from the command post arrived with a message that Lieutenant Colonel Martin and the division commander wanted to see me.

I instructed Sergeant Cowhig to take over and hopped into the jeep. It occurred to me as I was riding to the CP that I might be in a lot of trouble for saying "no" to Major General Dupuy when he ordered me to hold up and adjust artillery fire. When we reached the command post Major Edwards pulled me aside and said, "Don't go in there." He then proceeded to warn me that they had heard all of my radio calls. He said I shouldn't complain to the general about not getting support from the battalion since it was my own radios that were inoperative. He then asked for my status of killed and wounded and we also discussed the status of the Slingshot Platoon's casualties. When the major told me the final count was thirty and that all the men were accounted for, I said, "Sir, thirty-one men went out with me this morning, so one is still missing."

The major glared at me for a moment. "You're wrong, Lieutenant," he said sharply. Then he turned and walked away.

I was correct, though. One man apparently was taken prisoner. The major's concern stemmed from the fact that few things in the army reflect more adversely on a unit or its commander than to come in from a field training exercise and not be able to account for all of your men and equipment, especially weapons and ammunition. In combat it's even worse. It was not uncommon for units, when it was determined that a man or piece of sensitive equipment was lost, to spend days or even weeks searching for the lost person or equipment. Commanders thus were slow to admit that they couldn't account for someone.

This was the only incident during my twelve-month tour of duty where I was closely involved in a situation where a soldier couldn't be accounted for and was presumed to be missing in action.

As I stood outside the command post tent in the hot sun, Major General Depuy strode out, followed closely by Lieutenant Colonel Martin.

"Where's Lieutenant Walker?" the general asked.

"Here, Sir," I replied, holding up my hand.

"Walker, you did all right out there today," he barked. "By the way, what were they doing with that hole in the road?"

"Probably getting ready to bury a five-hundred-pound bomb, Sir."

He shook his head as he walked away and muttered, "You're real lucky." With that he marched over to his waiting helicopter, climbed in, and soon disappeared over the trees. I waited for thirty minutes to see if Lieutenant Colonel Martin wanted to speak to me. When he failed to call for me, I got a supply truck to take me back to my platoon area. Some time later I learned that Major General Depuy had taken the task force commander apart verbally and almost relieved him on the spot for sending the Slingshot Platoon out without proper support.

Later that afternoon I held a meeting with my vehicle commanders. Sergeant Cowhig did most of the talking. He reported that the engineers had helped recover the stuck tank from the river, that our two wounded soldiers would be returned to duty the next day, that a new motor and radiator had been ordered for the One-Three vehicle,* and that he had found a small tent for our supplies and for

---

* The first number indicates the platoon. Since we were the 1st Platoon, all of our vehicles were One-Something. Scout Section A had vehicles One-One and One-Two, and Scout Section B had vehicles One-Three and One-Zero. The mortar track was vehicle One-Nine. My command vehicle was One-Six (commander's always get the number six). The infantry carrier was vehicle One-Eight. The three tanks were vehicles One-Four, One-Five, and One-Seven.

me to sleep in. He also informed me that he had sent the two vehicles that had carried the dead soldiers down to the river to be washed out. "One more thing," he added, "the local signal platoon has agreed to let us use their showers tonight."

When he was finished I quickly summarized the rescue operation and told the sergeants how much I had missed not having them along, especially the tanks. I also mentioned that if our vehicles hadn't been able to jump the trench there would have been a massacre. In closing, I told them about my meeting earlier in the day with the engineer company commander regarding our eating at his mobile kitchen. After that I dismissed them with the comment that we had just enough time for a shower before supper.

It had been a very intense and tragic day. We had been very fortunate, and it felt especially good to have all of my men and vehicles back together and to be surrounded by the warm glow and security of the platoon.

Ike Pappas

Vietnam was the first war ever fought without any censorship. Without censorship, things can get terribly confused in the public mind.

—Gen. William C. Westmoreland

In the fall of 1966 we almost always found the enemy dug in and waiting for us when we went out on large-scale division operations. Heavy American casualties generally resulted and much effort was expended to discover who was leaking our plans to the Vietcong.

In early September our G2 section gleaned some critical information from prisoner interrogations. Apparently there was a network of spies and agents stationed in local villages. They were able to figure out where and when our operations would be conducted by observing our helicopters. This was primarily because of our extravagant practice of repeatedly sending helicopters into specific areas at low level to gather information prior to sending in ground forces.

The division staff soon put together a scheme to use this knowledge to our own advantage. By using heavily scripted helicopter reconnaissance flights we were able to lure the enemy to deploy forces in selected areas such as along abandoned roads or in jungle areas with good access to roads. Then, by careful design, a small unit such as a platoon or troop would be sent in as bait in the hopes the American unit would be small enough to tempt the enemy into attacking it. At the same time, the division would have two or more infantry battalions deployed nearby with helicopters ready to transport them to the battle zone.

The only problem with this plan was that during the ten to fifteen minutes the bait unit was left holding off the enemy force it was in danger of being badly mauled or overrun. Although no small unit wanted to be the bait, the tactic proved to be successful in killing large numbers of enemy soldiers. The official rationale for these entrapment operations was that by sacrificing a small number of U.S. troops we were destroying a much larger number of enemy soldiers and in the process wearing down the enemy's ability to make war.

In November of 1966 the division was again preparing to use this successful gambit to make contact with the enemy. It was on this particular operation that C Troop, 1st Squadron, 4th Cavalry, was chosen to be the bait. By then our troop was operating in the vicinity of An Loc near the Cambodian border, and we were conducting daily search-and-destroy operations to the northeast in heavily wooded terrain.

At about 2 P.M. one day all platoons were ordered to return to the troop assembly area and the platoon leaders were to be prepared to conduct an aerial reconnaissance with the troop commander at 3 P.M.

Upon returning to the assembly area, I turned the platoon over to Sergeant Cowhig with instructions to begin preparing our night defensive positions. Then, with map and notebook in hand, I walked over to where a squadron helicopter was waiting. When all of us were together, the troop commander explained the purpose of our reconnaissance.

"First," he said, "we are to add to the activity along a particular road to make the enemy believe an American unit will soon move through the area. Second, we will look for signs of enemy activity, trails, holes being dug, people moving around, and things like that. Finally, we will look at the condition of the road and try to locate good turnaround points for the column."

The four of us boarded the helicopter, an older model Huey without places for door gunners. After lifting off the pilot circled our assembly area several times, gaining altitude to approximately three thousand feet. Then we followed Highway 13 north to Loc Ninh. From there we followed an old logging road heading east. This pockmarked old asphalt road had not been used for several years and brush and small trees grew right up to its edges. We flew over the road for about fifteen minutes then dropped down to about five hundred feet and followed it back to Loc Ninh. My most vivid memory of this area was of a totally abandoned, utterly desolate road with no signs of life other than the heavy, lush vegetation.

At one point the CO thought he saw something suspicious and asked the pilots to make a second pass. Using his binoculars, he announced that it appeared to be the remains of three scout cars left over from when the French were fighting the Vietminh.

Having read *The Battle of Dien Bien Phu,* I was reminded of the many battles Gen. Christian de Castries and his armored forces had fought with the Vietminh in this particular area. Those Frenchmen, poorly supported and little appreciated by their countrymen, displayed tremendous courage in trying to keep the local road networks open against the ever-mounting strength of their enemy.

Knowing a little about the enemy's tactics, my guess was that whatever their reasons for choosing to attack the French column along this bend in the road so many years before may have been, they would probably still be valid today. I mentioned this to the CO and he nodded his head in agreement as he placed an X on his map marking the location of the French vehicles.

Looking at the CO's map, we compared notes as he pointed out reference points on the ground. The helicopter began to vibrate noticeably as we neared our assembly area. From our position in the rear we could see the pilots anxiously checking their instruments. As we set down inside our perimeter the shaking became almost violent. The pilots quickly shut down the engine and we wasted no time getting out. The engine smelled extremely hot, and smoke billowed out from around the transmission access plates. Aviation mechanics quickly repaired the craft's transmission and by dark it was operational again.

After our air reconnaissance, the CO gathered us together and informed us that as soon as it was dark we would load our vehicles and move twenty miles north, stopping just short of Loc Ninh and remain there overnight, hidden in the rubber trees. The next morning we would move down the road we had just reconnoitered, serving as the bait for a division-sized operation being set up nearby.

The night move was designed to further confuse the enemy into thinking our unit was only a platoon of ten vehicles rather than a troop of approximately forty.

The last time the troop had drawn this type of mission heavy casualties resulted. No one was eager to be the lead platoon. I made a mental note to write home before we pulled out—just in case.

As darkness approached, we loaded our barbed wire and equipment and moved onto Highway 13. Then, at the CO's direction, we moved north in column without lights. A clear sky with plenty of stars and an almost-full moon provided surprisingly good visibility. With first platoon in the lead and Sergeant Cowhig in the lead tank, I had no difficulty locating the rubber plantation road where we would spend the night. The road ran parallel to Highway 13 and about twenty-five yards inside the rubber trees.

When we were well clear of Highway 13 I stopped my platoon and had my vehicles make a hard left turn, move off the road, and stop just inside the trees. Second Platoon moved up and stopped on the road just behind us. Those vehicles executed a right turn and moved into the trees on the other side of the road. Third Platoon and troop headquarters executed the same maneuver a short distance down the road behind 2d Platoon. After stretching barbed wire across the road at either end of the troop and positioning a trip flare in front of each vehicle we were set for the night.

Around nine-thirty, when I was half-asleep, I received a radio call saying that the CO wanted to meet with platoon leaders at his location. He had received some last-minute information and wanted to pass it along to the platoons, to better prepare us for the next day's operation.

The sky was cloudy now and, with the cover of the rubber trees, it was almost impossible to see anything. By following the sound of my feet on the hard road and asking directions as I passed various vehicles I managed to locate the CO's command track.

The four of us climbed through the combat hatch in the back of the CO's ACAV and huddled together under the red glow of the vehicle's interior lights. To get our attention, the CO began by warning us that he didn't want anyone to be alarmed. Earlier in the evening he had received a message from squadron headquarters that an infrared aerial reconnaissance photograph indicated the presence of up to three thousand enemy soldiers along the road that we would be traveling on in the morning. Because of this, our plan was now changed. Upon contact with the enemy we would throw CS tear-gas grenades from each vehicle, close all our hatches, and call for airburst artillery fire on our positions. We would then remain buttoned up until reinforcements arrived.

We sat there quietly in the dark for a long moment as our tired minds absorbed what he'd just said. Then the 2d Platoon leader spoke up, asking if anyone had ever called airburst artillery in on top of armored vehicles before and what the effect might be on the men inside. No one knew. Then we talked about the accuracy of our artillery and the size of the guns that would be firing on us—would they be 155mm or 105mm, or both?

I asked the CO to reconsider this plan since most of our weapons would be inoperable if we were buttoned up. If we didn't keep the enemy pinned down by immediately returning fire, they might slaughter us with RPGs while we sat there waiting for reinforcements. After more discussion the CO agreed to rethink the latest plan. Dismissing us, he told us to return to our vehicles, locate our gas masks, and ensure they were in working order.

Airburst artillery for our protection was a harebrained idea; perhaps the CO wasn't getting enough sleep. We left the meeting in disbelief, shaking our heads as we disappeared into the night.

Apparently unknown to the CO, we had only a few serviceable protective masks on each vehicle and those were used only for checking out tunnels. Normally, when we discovered a tunnel, the practice was to throw in a CS grenade and allow time for the gas to settle in all the low areas of the tunnel complex. This usually forced whoever was inside to come out, generally coughing and with their hands up.

The hard part came when I had to choose a courageous volunteer to search the tunnel. I would put a mask on him and watch as the unlucky soldier disappeared into the tunnel with ear plugs in place and a flashlight in one hand and a .45-caliber pistol in the other.

Inside, the tear gas left the air clouded and the mask further reduced visibility, leaving the soldier at a great disadvantage in his search for booby traps or enemy soldiers who may have remained inside despite the noxious gas.

I always felt that I was condemning a young man to certain death when I sent him into one of those tunnels.

Rather than wake up my track commanders and having them stumble around in pitch darkness trying to locate my vehicle, I decided to assemble them early the next morning. Since the vehicles were so close together, I only required a guard for every two vehicles, pairing up crews to work out a guard schedule requiring only a one-hour shift for each man.

The night was uneventful, and the next morning at stand-to we were informed that a helicopter would be arriving at about six with hot chow for everyone. Morale soared. The late road march coupled with the helicopter breakdown had resulted in no meal deliveries the previous evening. The old saying that an army travels on its stomach is absolutely correct; a good meal always does wonders for morale.

I decided not to inform the track commanders about the gas-mask contingency plan since so few men had them. I was confident the CO would reconsider. I also withheld the news that three thousand enemy soldiers might be waiting for us alongside the road. It would only cause needless worry. Besides, there was nothing we could do about it except do our jobs the very best we could and hope the shock action of the tanks would save the day.

There was something very psychologically demoralizing about a fifty-two-ton tank bearing down on you belching fire and hot steel. The effect was very noticeable, especially when compared to our lightly armored ACAVs, which weighed about twelve tons and mounted just the three machine guns. In the middle of an ambush, with the enemy dug in next to the road and bullets flying in all directions, the enemy would usually stand their ground if faced only with armored personnel carriers. It was a different story when the tanks pulled into the line and started raking the bunkers with

90mm canister rounds. Few of the enemy's weapons could harm a tank and, after a few rounds of 90mm fire, the enemy would usually start to disappear. In many cases the psychological effect was so overwhelming that enemy troops would jump up from their positions without weapons and stampede wildly into the jungle. Some armor units enhanced this effect by painting eyes on their tank turrets or drawing a dragon-like mouth on the front slope of their vehicles' hulls.

The resupply helicopter landed down the road. One of the headquarters tracks went out to meet it and bring in the supplies. Then, with its rear ramp lowered to where it was parallel with the ground, the vehicle moved slowly down the line serving breakfast. As it passed, 3d Platoon and headquarters personnel moved out to the road and filled their paper plates. Two men stood on the ramp ladling out hot coffee from insulated food containers and handing out large, grapefruit-sized cinnamon rolls, two per man. That was it, nothing but coffee and rolls. We had been served a similar light breakfast just before a large battle the previous month, so the men started calling it our "battle breakfast."

I wandered out with the men to get my coffee and rolls when the breakfast wagon rolled up behind my platoon. While I was standing there next to the vehicle stirring my coffee, one of the men handing out rolls motioned me over and said, "Lieutenant Walker, here's an extra roll for you." Then, with a large roll in his hand, the man jumped off the ramp and came over to where I was standing. He looked about thirty-five and wore no rank or name tag on his fatigues. At first I took him for a new track commander reporting for duty.

"I'm Ike Pappas with *CBS News,*" he said as he handed me the roll and then stuck out his right hand. "Your CO told me I could tag along with you today. I hope that's all right."

I shook his big fleshy hand and said, "Sure. We can use another good man today."

He explained that he had been briefed about our mission the day before in Saigon at MACV headquarters. The word was that our troop was certain to make contact with the enemy today and he was hoping to put together a good story for the *CBS Evening News* about the pending battle.

As he talked, I remembered seeing him occasionally on television and recalled that he had a reputation for honest reporting. Also, he was one of only a handful of reporters who ventured out from the "Pentagon East" in Saigon to report on the combat side of the war.

Most reporters—and there were plenty in Vietnam—preferred to get their information from the daily Saigon PIO briefing jokingly referred to as the "Five O'clock Follies." Their idea of a good story was to visit the rear-echelon soldiers and write about GI drug addicts, the black market in U.S. goods, or about how unlucky some poor soldier was to be spending a year of his life in this godforsaken place.

When I first arrived in country, the following story was making the rounds about one of the Saigon-based reporters:

> An infantry major returning from R and R spent the night in downtown Saigon while awaiting transportation back to his unit. That evening, coming back from dinner, the major walked past what looked to him to be a disheveled GI. The man was wearing unbloused jungle-fatigue trousers, no name tag or other identifying insignia on his shirt, was hatless, and had hair far exceeding the regulation length.
>
> Oblivious to the teeming masses flowing by on the sidewalk, the major yelled, "Get over here, soldier!" As the man came forward, he ordered him to halt and shouted, "Stand at attention when I speak to you!" Not getting the desired response, the major lit into the man. "Look at you!" he roared. "You're a disgrace to the army and a disgrace to your country! What unit are you with?"
>
> "*NBC News,*" the man had replied.

Ike Pappas was friendly with everyone, shot lots of film, and tape-recorded all of his interviews. I took him to each vehicle and he tried to interview at least one person in each crew, starting with, "Are you ready for today?" and "What do you think is going to happen?"

It was a further morale boost to the platoon to know that a famous TV reporter was going into battle with us and would be sending a full report of the expected battle back to hometown viewers all across America.

The CO called the platoon leaders together for a short meeting before we moved out and informed us that we would go with the original plan. There would be no airburst artillery and no gas masks. After that we mounted up and prepared to move out.

The final battle plan called for 2d Platoon to move out alone down the abandoned road. I was to follow about two minutes later with 1st Platoon. Immediately behind us would be the troop headquarters' six vehicles, and 3d Platoon would bring up the rear. Following the bait script, the plan was to convince the enemy that this was a lone platoon, just ten armored vehicles and approximately fifty men moving down an abandoned road, and thus provoke them to attack with their sixty-to-one advantage.

Lined up on the road with engines running, we checked and loaded weapons while waiting for the CO to coordinate our departure with division. I took this opportunity to instruct the track commanders to have extra belts of ammo ready for the machine guns and to ensure that each man had at least two grenades hung on his flak jacket. While they were complying, Ike Pappas wandered around taking pictures of men draping belts of ammo over the gun shields and around their necks.

After what seemed an eternity the CO came up on the troop radio net and ordered us to move out. The long-awaited words made our hearts pound. Second Platoon rumbled off in a cloud of diesel exhaust and headed east down the deserted road to meet its destiny. I ordered 1st Platoon to move up to the road and wait for my command to follow 2d Platoon.

As our column crept slowly up to the jump-off point at the edge of the trees, Ike Pappas, who was sitting next to me and filming while holding a microphone in front of the radio speaker, leaned over and said, "These things actually shake the ground when they move." I nodded my head and continued to watch the second hand of my watch. A minute and forty-five seconds after the last 2d Platoon vehicle disappeared from view I alerted the platoon and fifteen seconds later gave the order to move out. As we rolled out onto the road I looked back to make sure the headquarters and 3d Platoon vehicles were following us. It was comforting to see so many tanks and machine guns following me and to feel the earth shake beneath us.

All attention was now focused on 2d Platoon as we listened to their lieutenant describe over the radio the terrain up ahead and announce the passage of various checkpoints. Battles of the type we expected to engage in usually began with the lead tank hitting a mine and being disabled. If that happened, the engaged platoon was supposed to herringbone—that is, pull half of its vehicles off to one side of the road and the other half on the opposite side at about a forty-five degree angle and return fire with all weapons.

At the first sign of an attack, I was to rush forward at top speed, move through 2d Platoon, and position my vehicles alongside their tracks. Headquarters would deploy to our rear, and 3d Platoon was to move through the formation and deploy in front of us. We would remain in that position and attempt to hold off the enemy while the infantry battalions were airlifted in.

We crept along at about fifteen miles per hour with our ears straining to catch every word as the 2d Platoon leader reported their progress. After about forty-five minutes of moving along in this manner the CO came on the radio and said, "It looks like Charlie isn't going to take the bait. Second Platoon, turn around and rejoin the troop."

As we turned around and began heading back, the CO halted the column at what he considered the most likely spot for an ambush and had all vehicles face the same direction and fire all available weapons at a nearby tree line. Two air force jets that had been on station circling out of sight and waiting for the battle to begin swooped in and dropped napalm on the tree line rather than take it back to base.

About fifty thousand rounds of ammunition later, the CO ordered us to cease firing. Then, with my platoon leading, we headed back through Loc Ninh and down to the vicinity of An Loc, where we had been patrolling the previous day.

The column halted briefly as we passed through Loc Ninh, our previous night's stop, while Major General Depuy landed his helicopter for a meeting with our CO. A few minutes later the CO returned to his vehicle and radioed me that Ike Pappas would accompany the CG for the remainder of the day. When I informed Ike of this, he seemed disappointed. Earlier he had told me he was looking forward to spending a few days with us. Orders were orders, though, and Ike grabbed his camera and tape recorder and, with a handshake and big smile, jumped to the ground and walked over to the CG's helicopter.

Standing at the edge of the road, the general gave each vehicle a thumbs-up as our column rumbled by in a cloud of dust and exhaust smoke.

No one ever mentioned hearing from their families in subsequent letters from home that they had seen Ike Pappas reporting about a cavalry unit on a bait mission, so I guess we didn't make the cut.

As our armored column moved south to perform another search-and-destroy mission, I felt just a tiny bit of disappointment—but not much.

About three months later, a sergeant from division PIO flew out on a resupply helicopter to spend a few days with our platoon. He was a very cocky young man who insisted he was going to make us all famous with the story he planned to write about our activities.

He was with us less than three hours when the vehicle he was riding in hit a large command-detonated mine. The blast flipped the track upside down, killing two men and wounding four. The would-be reporter was one of the wounded, suffering a broken leg and severe burns.

While snipers peppered the area, I assisted with the evacuation of the injured crewmen. As we loaded the reporter aboard the medevac chopper, I patted him on the shoulder and said, "As soon as you're well, you'll have to come back and try it again."

"Sir," he replied through gritted teeth, " I'm never goin' back out with the Cav again!"

The Bob Hope Show

We played remote bases, the kind of bases where guys went to bed with their rifles by their sides, not for security, but for companionship.

—Bob Hope

Toward the end of December 1966 C Troop completed a civic-action mission in support of the division's 3d Brigade. The area involved was about thirty miles north of Saigon and was known as the Iron Triangle. The region was an infamous enemy staging area. Covered with thick woodlands and heavy underbrush, it was a perfect hiding place for large Vietcong units.

Our 3d Brigade was involved in a large-scale search-and-destroy operation against suspected enemy bases code-named Cedar Falls. In all, some thirty thousand U.S. troops were sent into this Vietcong stronghold.

After B-52s saturated the area, helicopters airlifted thousands of specially trained combat forces into the villages. Then, after removing the villagers to refugee camps, giant Rome plows leveled the area, leaving the guerrillas no place to hide. The region was then burned and bombed again to destroy the miles of underground tunnels the enemy had constructed.

Afterward we learned that although more than seven hundred Vietcong were killed in this operation, the enemy's main force was able to escape.

Our mission was to assist the 3d Brigade with the relocation of four Vietnamese villages on the edge of the Iron Triangle. The villagers had either willingly or unwillingly been supplying Vietcong units for many years.

The villagers—along with their possessions, harvested crops, and farm animals—were loaded onto trucks and hauled to a refugee camp in the vicinity of Saigon. There, huts had been constructed, wells dug, and land set aside for farming so they would be content and not want to or try to return to their old villages.

Our job was to provide security for the villages during the loading and road security for the move to the new location. The enemy did not attempt to interfere with this operation and it was completed without incident. I was surprised when I learned that all of the villagers had been permitted to see the refugee camp prior to the move and accepted it. Many even seemed happy about it.

One particularly strange incident occurred while we were loading the villagers and their livestock. We had just escorted several truckloads of grain and livestock to the new village and were preparing to spend the night near the old village. Later that evening, after setting up our defensive perimeter, I toured the almost-deserted village with four of my men. As we were walking through the area we came upon some villagers gathered around a huge pig. They were feeding and petting it and having what appeared to be a lively discussion about the animal, which must have weighed in at about five hundred pounds.

Moving on around the village, we could see that it had been stripped of everything usable. Roofing tin, bamboo poles, clay stoves, and even fruit trees had been removed and taken to the new village. After assuring myself that everything was secure, we returned to our vehicles and spent an uneventful night.

At first light the next morning, while out checking vehicles and crews, I spotted the five-hundred-pound pig lying dead in the middle of the road outside our perimeter. Seeing no one around, I went over to investigate. There was no sign of a wound or injury and no one came forward to claim the carcass throughout the rest of the day. My guess was that the pig was some sort of sacrifice left to watch over the old village. It seemed strange to us that, as much as the people valued their animals, no one claimed this one—for its food value if nothing else. I considered burying the pig but decided against it for fear I might interfere with religious ceremonial rites or the ancestral worship we'd heard so much about.

After completing that mission, we returned to Lai Khe with the realization that during the coming three-day Christmas truce all U.S. units would remain in their base camps. We, however, no longer had a base camp. This was because of the division commander's recent decision that our region needed more secured areas in order to provide greater security to the local countryside. The general considered it a great waste of assets to allow our heavy firepower to remain overnight inside a secure compound. His logic was that platoon-sized and larger cavalry units should set up night defensive positions outside the regular bases. That doubled the number of secure areas and further restricted enemy movement.

It sounded great, except that it forced us to be out every night, pulling guard duty and sending out ambush patrols and listening posts. At the same time we were forced to give up our comparatively comfortable quarters at Lai Khe. However, looking back on the different techniques used to provide security for the surrounding area, this was one of the few that appeared to work.

When we set up at night I generally positioned the platoon on high ground with good observation all around. This certainly didn't stop the Vietcong, but it at least caused them to move into areas that were not as well guarded. It also provided a psychological boost for local South Vietnamese forces in the area and demonstrated to the local villagers that we weren't abandoning them to the dangers of the night. On two different occasions Vietcong patrols unaware of our presence walked into our trip flares. We fired on both of the surprised patrols and, in one case, inflicted heavy casualties on the enemy.

When we reached Lai Khe we pulled into the rubber trees close to our old area, which had been occupied by a new unit. Arrangements had been made for us to use their showers and eat in shifts at the mess hall, and our men would sleep on their own vehicles. For soldiers to constantly complain about all the little inconveniences of life is normal. This situation, however, moved complaining to a new level. There were even fistfights over trivial matters with those who now occupied our former quarters.

It was important to keep the men busy, so on Christmas Eve and Christmas Day we replaced worn track and changed engine oil and oil filters. Around noon on Christmas Day we stopped work and went to the mess hall for what, to us, could only be described as a feast.

Our six cooks had been working since midnight baking pies and cooking turkeys. The men were on their best behavior as we filed through the serving line in our old mess hall. The menu included shrimp cocktail, mixed nuts, fresh fruit, and, of course, turkey with all the trimmings. Apple, pecan, and mincemeat pies, ice cream, cranberry sauce, rolls, coffee, tea, milk, and soft drinks were also available in abundance. It was a wonderful meal and a fine reminder that the richest nation on earth had not forgotten its fighting men.

Our mess sergeant was a perpetually smiling, slightly overweight, cigar-smoking character named Riley. His mess team stayed in the rear and sent hot chow out to the platoons in insulated containers. My question to him was always, "When are you going to start sending us some real food?" We were always getting on him about the amount of chili and rice he sent to the field. I learned later that when the system broke down, which was often, he always had plenty of rice and canned chili on hand as a substitute. The Christmas, Thanksgiving, and Easter meals were his times to shine. He rose to the occasion, posing for pictures with the turkeys or hams, and was forever shaking hands with the men.

The plan was for us to eat in the mess hall, but some of the more hard-core crews carried their food back into the rubber trees and ate on their dusty tracks.

After dinner, I challenged the 2d Platoon to a game of softball and we had a very spirited two-hour game in our old motor pool. There were many spectators and lots of cheering advice. The winner was supposed to get a case of iced beer, but it somehow disappeared during the game.

Just before dark the troop commander ordered all five of us lieutenants into his jeep with his old Vietnamese dog, and drove us around the compound perimeter checking security. The jeep's top was off and the windshield was down so it was a very cool and relaxing ride. The CO explained that our noble enemy might use the truce as an opportunity to attack, knowing that we Americans would be preoccupied celebrating Christmas. Although the perimeter was well-manned, the CO outlined a plan for our three platoons to move forward and reinforce the line if the base was attacked during the night.

The day after Christmas we were offered the choice of working on our vehicles or road marching down to Phu Loi to see Bob Hope's USO show. My men were all eager to go but some of the men in the other two platoons voted to stay behind and do maintenance work.

Around nine o'clock the next morning, quite late for normal operations, those of us going to the Bob Hope show loaded up and moved out in fighting formation. The trip to Phu Loi was slowed by the requirement to sweep the road with hand-held minesweepers. In spite of this, we arrived a little after noon and the MPs directed us to an area near the airstrip where the show was to be performed. After we parked and locked up our vehicles, I released the men with instructions to be back on their tracks and ready to roll within thirty minutes after the show.

One end of the small airstrip had been roped off for the show and ten flatbed trucks arranged as a theater. Six trailers placed in a semicircle served as the stage. A curtain had been set up on top, forming a backdrop. Four trailers parked about fifty yards in front of the stage formed the theater's rear boundary. Within this area, three to four thousand enthusiastic soldiers eagerly waited for the show to begin. Helicopter gunships circled overhead providing security for the event while MPs on the ground did a fine job of controlling the crowd and directing traffic.

I moved in and sat on one of the flatbed trailers in the middle of a group of soldiers from my platoon. After a few minutes, it was obvious that we had arrived early and the show would not start for some time. I spent the next thirty minutes visiting with other members of the division with whom I had worked on various operations. Most didn't know my name but instead referred to me by my radio call sign, "Dragoon Charlie One-Six," or simply "Charlie One-Six."

Soon the advance team arrived and began hooking up the sound system and setting up the stage lights. Then jeeps began pulling up to the rear of the stage area and dropped off the actors and actresses. While this was going on, Bob Hope walked out on the stage in old, sweaty clothes and checked the placement of various items of equipment. When the crowd saw him people began to applaud. He waved and then turned his back on the audience as he continued to direct the placement of things on stage. Finally, while checking out the sound system, Hope announced that the show was going to be filmed for the folks back home and asked us to please bear with them while they finished setting up.

Hope was clearly in charge, pointing and telling technicians where he wanted various lights and cameras, even bringing actors out to show them their places on stage. Les Brown's band was there and rehearsed a couple of numbers before the show.

It was interesting, after having observed the set-up process, to see how smoothly everything flowed when the cameras began to roll. Bob Hope, the hard-working director, instantly became Bob Hope the polished actor, stepping out from behind the curtain with an ear-to-ear smile, clean clothes, an army hat, and swinging a golf club. He was now energized, looked much younger, and told several jokes. Funny or not, we all laughed.

The cast consisted mostly of beautiful young girls—with the exception of Phyllis Diller—and they performed many songs, dances, and skits. The most memorable performance was a song and dance by Joey Heatherton (a well-built young lady wearing a *very* short skirt). All too soon they launched into the final number, *Silent Night,* sung by Bob Hope and his wife, Dolores. Everyone was invited to join in and we enthusiastically obliged, knowing full well that we were being recorded on film. After the show, the cast came out and graciously shook hands and signed autographs.

Bob Hope was not just an actor but an enduring symbol of America's appreciation for its servicemen. That tradition extended from World War II to Korea and now to Vietnam. His coming to Vietnam with a famous cast and film crew sent a strong message that we were not forgotten at home. His sincere message of appreciation came across loud and clear during the show's serious moments.

We all knew that with his money and fame he could have been anyplace in the world he wanted to be, but he had chosen to come here, to the middle of an increasingly unpopular war, to help brighten our Christmas. We all admired and appreciated him and the rest of the cast very much.

As instructed, my men reassembled on their vehicles after the show and, after a brief stop at the Phu Loi PX, we headed back to Lai Khe. All went well as our column moved north in military formation. Then, while passing through a small, unnamed village, I saw an RPG explode against the tank ahead. Most ambushes began with a hail of RPGs, but this time only one rocket was fired. I immediately sent out the scout sections to try and locate the ambushers. I radioed the damaged tank and was told that there was only slight damage to the vehicle but that the TC was badly injured. I moved up and dropped off the medic, then followed the scout sections into the nearby village, where we were unable to find any signs of the enemy.

Soon I received a call from the medic. The tank commander was seriously wounded and we needed an immediate medevac helicopter to get him to a hospital or he would die. I called for the chopper and then returned to the damaged tank to assist.

Sergeant Richard Keith had been riding behind the .50-caliber machine gun located on top of the turret with his arms draped over the armor shield surrounding it. The enemy rocket either hit his arm or exploded very close by. As I climbed down into the turret, I could see that his right arm had been blown off at the shoulder. Blood was everywhere and the floor of the turret was slippery with it.

Sergeant Keith was unconscious when I arrived and the medic, a very capable young man, was in the process of taking his pulse after having put a tourniquet on the stump of his arm. The medic said his pulse was very weak and I suggested giving him plasma or a blood expander right there on the tank floor. The medic inserted an IV into his good arm there on the cramped floor, and we tried to elevate his legs and cover him with a blanket until the helicopter arrived.

Removing a wounded crewman from inside a tank is a difficult task. The height from floor to hatch is about six feet at the loader's position and seven to eight feet at the TC's position. The hatches themselves are very narrow. Then, once you get out, you're normally on a hard, sloping surface ten feet above the ground.

About ten minutes later I heard the helicopter approaching and we began moving Sergeant Keith up and out of the tank. The normal method is to loop a rope or cord under the arms and lift the man out, or to pull him up by the back of the collar. In Sergeant Keith's case neither of those options was possible due to the location of his wound, so I wrapped my arms around his chest and began to slowly climb up through the open hatch. The medic and two other men pulled him through from the top. We placed him on a stretcher with the IV still attached and carried him to the waiting Huey, which Sergeant Cowhig had directed in.

As the helicopter disappeared, we looked ourselves over. It was readily apparent just how much blood Sergeant Keith had lost: My hair, boots, pants, and shirt were soaked with blood, and the medic was in the same condition. Later that evening I was notified that Sergeant Keith died while en route to the hospital.

After speaking briefly with the tank crew to ensure that they would be all right, we resumed our march to Lai Khe. It was after 6 P.M. when we arrived. I had the men top off all the vehicles and we washed out Sergeant Keith's tank. When we finished I took a long shower, put on a clean uniform, and ran to the mess hall for a late supper that had been held for me. After eating I watched the last part of a Peter Sellers' movie and then went to bed early.

I woke up at about ten with horrible pains in my stomach and a general feeling of nausea. My first reaction was to find our medic and see if he could figure out what was wrong with me, but I decided there was no need to wake him and the rest of the platoon just because I had a stomachache.

Remembering that the brigade aid station was located near the center of Lai Khe, I found an old Vietcong motorbike that we had captured a few weeks before and, armed with an M14 slung across my chest, started down the road with just the moonlight to guide me. I pulled up in front of the aid station and leaned the motorbike against a tree. The building appeared to be one of the original brick plantation buildings. Inside, I told the duty sergeant that I thought I had appendicitis. The doctor was across the room and overheard my comment. He put a thermometer in my mouth and said, "Let's see if you have a fever."

Within seconds, my stomach started rumbling like a volcano and I rushed to the door just in time to throw up like a wide-open fire hose. After I finished heaving there in the doorway, the doctor said, "Lieutenant, I think we can rule out appendicitis." He then asked what I'd eaten for dinner and said my symptoms sounded more like food poisoning. He gave me a white, chalky liquid to calm my stomach and told me to come back if that didn't solve the problem.

I was already feeling better by the time I arrived back in the troop area. All the lights were out except for a dim light in the CQ's room, so I went back to my track and tried to get some sleep. I knew that in the morning, with the end of the Christmas cease-fire, our unit would be heading north to participate in another campaign along the Cambodian border and I would need all the rest I could get.

Wounded

I could have ended the war in a month. I could have made North Vietnam look like a mud puddle.

—Barry Goldwater

After four months of continuous operations as platoon leader of the 1st Platoon I was better acquainted with this fine group of young men. Most were very bright, had big plans for the future, and were only there, like me, to fulfill their military obligation.

After I joined the platoon we were often sent out alone to patrol or to conduct an extended reconnaissance. My greatest fear during these initial operations was of being cut off or surrounded by the enemy and wiped out before help could arrive. However, it didn't take me long to develop an appreciation for the vast firepower the platoon could bring to bear on our overrated enemy. I soon realized that as long as our little group of vehicles kept close together we could hold out against anything the enemy threw at us.

One morning after stand-to, Private Borgos jumped down inside the cargo hatch of my ACAV. A few seconds later he breathlessly scrambled back up and shouted, "Sir, there's a live grenade down there!" I quickly ordered the driver out and we took cover for a few minutes. Nothing happened; there was no explosion. We waited a little longer and then I slowly and cautiously climbed back up on the vehicle and peered into the cargo hatch. Sure enough, there was a live grenade on the floor of the track. However, the handle, pin, and the top of the blasting cap had been pinched off. In a situation like that, the slightest bump or jar is often all it takes to set it

off. We couldn't just leave it there, nor could we blow it in place—
that would destroy the vehicle.

Getting no volunteers, I cautiously climbed inside the track, got
out a quarter-pound block of C-4, rigged up a blasting cap with
about three minutes worth of timed fuse, slipped them in my
pocket and then carefully picked up the live grenade and inched
my way out. Once on the ground, I moved about thirty yards in
front of the vehicle and set the grenade down on the far side of a
large tree. I placed the block of C-4 next to it, lit the fuse, and ran
back to my vehicle with just enough time to get everyone down before the sharp sound of the explosion sent hundreds of tiny pieces
of metal raining down all around us.

Afterward, in an effort to determine what had happened, I had
the driver lower the infantry ramp. There, in the lower crack of the
doorframe, were the missing pieces of the grenade. They had been
crimped off the last time the door was raised.

It wasn't hard to figure out how that occurred. On extremely
dark nights the men would sleep with grenades beside them. In case
of an enemy attack they could throw the grenades as they jumped
inside the vehicle for cover. Apparently, someone had left one on
the ramp and it was crushed when we raised the ramp at stand-to
that morning. I don't know why it didn't explode—I guess it was just
our lucky day.

We were participating in another bait mission and would be departing later than usual to allow us to load extra ammo and prepare
our equipment. It was also malaria pill day. As the drug began its
predictable work, I grabbed a roll of toilet paper, our metal folding
chair with a hole cut in it, a shovel, and the latest copy of the *Pacific
Stars and Stripes,* and headed for the center of the perimeter.

Artillery units were located near us, so there were helicopters
and jeeps arriving and leaving all the time. As I sat there on my folding chair reading the paper, a jeep pulled up and stopped about ten
feet away. The driver grinned at me and said, "Lieutenant, could
you tell me where Alpha Battery is located?"

Barely looking up, I said, "See that large antenna over there?
That's it."

"Thanks," said the driver.

I looked up as he drove off and saw that he had two beautiful Red Cross girls in the jeep with him. Both were grinning and one of them gave me a tiny little wave, which I acknowledged. I then looked in the direction of the platoon and saw at least a dozen of my soldiers breaking up with laughter. They had sent the jeep over for directions. These guys were not above a good practical joke.

The Red Cross girls (sometimes called Donut Dollies) were paid volunteers who worked in the hospitals and at Red Cross centers at the larger base camps. They would occasionally visit the field on a supply helicopter to help serve food or hand out the mail. These brief visits were a tremendous morale booster. I'm not sure why, but they never visited any of our cavalry units during my twelve-month tour.

For the past several days, division helicopters had been making runs over a particular stretch of abandoned jungle road in preparation for our bait mission. A battalion of infantry we normally worked with was standing by on an airstrip about twenty minutes away. All the necessary preparation and coordination had been made for the operation to begin at ten that morning.

The plan was the same one I described earlier except that this time 3d Platoon would lead the way. If they were engaged, the remainder of the troop, with my platoon leading the way, would charge forward to reinforce them. We then would hold out until the infantry battalion was brought in to destroy the enemy. It was a simple plan, yet the enemy fell for it time after time.

The monsoon season was upon us, and we sat there in the warm rain, uniforms plastered to our skin, watching 3d Platoon line up at the edge of the clearing. At exactly 10 A.M. the column groaned and creaked slowly out of the perimeter. We had been briefed to stay on the road because the marshy ground on either side would not support armored vehicles.

As 3d Platoon disappeared down the steam-covered jungle road, I formed up 1st Platoon and prepared to follow. Troop headquarters and 2d Platoon would follow closely behind us.

After giving 3d Platoon a five-minute lead, we slowly moved out with two tanks in front followed by my command vehicle. Monitoring the radio, I could hear the 3d Platoon leader, a tall, skinny lieutenant from Oklahoma, calling out various checkpoints in a high-pitched, singsong voice. Suddenly, he screamed, "The lead tank's just been blown up and we're getting a wall of fire from all sides! Get up here quick!"

That was our cue. I notified my platoon that 3d Platoon was in heavy contact and told the lead tanks to "put the pedal to the metal." Soon we were moving at full speed—bobbing, weaving, and swaying on top of our vehicles, desperately holding on to anything solid. As the column came up a slight incline and started around a sharp, narrow bend in the road, heavy fire erupted directly in front of the lead tank, which was hit by RPGs. Its right track was blown off and the main gun disabled.

This was a new wrinkle: We had been ambushed about three miles short of where 3d Platoon was being torn to pieces. I radioed for artillery fire as the second tank and my vehicle came under heavy fire from the ambush site. The gunners responded with an accurate barrage within seconds. I ordered my driver and the TC of the other tank to draw back about thirty yards so as to avoid being hit. The radio was hot with calls from the CO, who wanted me to "get moving now, regardless of the costs, we have to reach Third Platoon fast!"

The 3d Platoon leader's calls became increasingly hysterical as he described his losses and asked repeatedly where we were.

With those messages still ringing in my ears, I pulled my track out from behind the second tank to check the effectiveness of our artillery fire. We advanced with all our guns blazing and, as we pulled up even with tank number two, an RPG slammed into the front of my vehicle, killing the driver instantly, seriously wounding the gunner in the TC's position, and wounding me and Private Borgos in the legs.

Smoke began to fill the track as I attempted to remove the driver. When I realized he was dead I turned my attention to the gunner and, with Private Borgos's help, pulled the large man out through the combat hatch. By then the medic had arrived and he took charge of the wounded gunner. I crawled back inside my burning vehicle and had Private Borgos unhook the PRC-10 portable radio.

I stuck my head up through the cargo hatch for one last look around. Bullets were flying everywhere and the tank was blazing away over us with its .50-caliber and main guns. I glanced quickly around and detected movement in the brush not more than ten yards away. Borrowing Borgos's M14, I fired two magazines into the nearby brush and received a hand grenade in return. I ducked back inside and the grenade exploded harmlessly on top of the vehicle.

We climbed out through the cargo hatch and, with Borgos close on my heels carrying the radio, I moved on foot to the right rear of tank number two. There, from behind a giant anthill, I called the platoon and had three vehicles move over to the left side of the road in staggered formation and begin firing their weapons up and down the area where I'd seen the enemy movement. Next, I switched the radio to the troop's frequency and gave the CO a SITREP. I advised him that the artillery had been ineffective, that the enemy still had at least three rocket launchers in operation, and that two of our vehicles were destroyed and blocking the road. Finally, I let him know we had as many as five dead and at least three wounded.

The CO, who was only about a hundred yards away from the action, listened to my report and replied, "Third Platoon is being wiped out. I don't care what the costs are, but do something and do it right now."

I acknowledged and switched back to the platoon frequency.

Private Borgos and I remained huddled behind the anthill as I took stock of our situation. The noise was deafening and bullets were flying in all directions. Borgos was losing blood from a deep wound on his right leg, which I wrapped with my battle dressing. I should have sent him to the rear, but I had no replacement for him and the radio was strapped to his back. He was a small man but very courageous—and extremely loyal and dedicated to me. I simply couldn't spare him. The road ahead was still blocked by the lead tank and we had no contact with the crew. Either they were all dead or their radio was inoperative. The enemy controlled the road with their anti-tank weapons, and the surrounding area was marshy and wouldn't support an armored vehicle. It was a perfect place for an ambush.

Only four or five minutes had elapsed since the lead tank was hit, but it seemed much longer. Furthermore, time was running out for

3d Platoon. The CO was right: We had to get moving regardless of the circumstances.

With Borgos close behind, I moved up beside the still-firing tank to check the drainage ditch that ran alongside the road. It was covered with small trees, vines, and heavy brush, but it was just high enough that it might support a tank. It appeared to be our only hope of getting around the disabled tank and through the trees and brush, then back up on the road, partially bypassing the ambush and maybe catching the enemy off guard.

Borgos and I climbed up on the back deck of the tank and onto the turret. There was an explosion nearby and shell fragments hit me in the chest and collar, knocking the breath out of me. As soon as we were safely inside I explained my plan to the tank commander and then called the platoon and told everyone we were going cross-country and to close it up and follow the number two tank. No matter what happened to the vehicle in front, I stressed, they were to go around and not stop until they reached 3d Platoon.

"This isn't going to work!" the TC exclaimed.

"Let's make it work," I replied as I loosened several 90mm canister rounds. I told the TC that Private Borgos would load for him. Then I pointed out the general line we would follow through the brush and said, "Move out."

The tank leaped forward like a thoroughbred, jumped the drainage ditch, and then slowed as its fifty-two tons ground through the brush and its tracks sank into the soft ground. Although the tank slowed it didn't stop. We fired the main gun as fast as we were able, spraying the jungle with deadly canister pellets. The ACAVs appeared small as they snaked through the jungle behind us, their .50-caliber and 7.62mm machine guns blazing.

I stood on the floor of the turret with my head sticking out through the loader's hatch. Ahead of us I could see standing water and motioned frantically for the TC to head back to the road. We cut back just in front of the disabled tank and, with the engine straining, hit the drainage ditch hard. We came out on line with the enemy positions as the tank turned sharply on the road's hard surface. We had fired two canister rounds directly into the enemy positions while crossing the drainage ditch and enemy fire seemed to have slackened somewhat. Just as we finished our turn and the driver began to accelerate, an RPG smashed into the side of the tank commander's gun shield, killing him instantly. His body slid down through the open hatch and hit the floor hard. There was no need to check for a pulse, the blast had literally cut him in two. We continued to move as the rest of the platoon ran the gauntlet, coming out of the brush and back up on the road.

Firing as they came, the column continued to move, but at a heavy price—the infantry track exploded and was left burning beside the road. Three men lay dead inside and six more were wounded. Shortly after the third tank entered the bypass it became mired in the marshy ground, almost even with the lead tank. The enemy gunners wasted no time focusing their attention on it.

The current situation was that 2d Platoon and the troop headquarters were isolated, blocked by my disabled tank on the road. My third tank was stuck in the bypass, preventing them from maneuvering around the heavy enemy small-arms and antitank fire to their front. That meant I had only one tank and five ACAVs left with which to save what was left of 3d Platoon. Radio calls from their platoon leader were not encouraging. He had kept up a running commentary on the battle, stating in his latest transmission that the enemy was up on the road and moving in among his destroyed vehicles.

We charged up the road with a large cloud of dust and diesel smoke billowing out behind us. I didn't feel we were bringing much to the battle as I stood there in the turret over the dead tank commander and looked at my loader, Private Borgos.

I called my platoon on the radio and ordered everyone to fire to the left side of the road in the direction of the ambush. Then I began firing the main gun and the TC's .50-caliber machine gun. We were riding to the rescue with guns blazing in the finest tradition of the old cavalry, for whatever that was worth.

As we got closer to 3d Platoon's position it was apparent that the ambush had been sprung where the heavy brush came closest to the road. I counted a half-dozen helicopter gunships overhead firing their rockets and miniguns at targets within fifty feet of the armored vehicles.

The 3d Platoon crews waved and cheered as we joined their column. Mounds of empty shell casings covered the tops of their vehicles. I counted one tank and two armored personnel carriers destroyed and still burning. The latter had been destroyed where the brush came closest to the road. I stopped my tank there and fired six main-gun canister rounds point-blank into the dense vegetation to my front. The other vehicles moved in alongside 3d Platoon's tracks and continued to fire everything they had.

When I radioed the 3d Platoon leader, he whined, "Is this all that's coming?"

"This is all you're going to need," I replied. He said two of his vehicles were almost out of ammunition and that his medic needed help. I said we'd try to help out.

We kept up a steady volume of fire into the enemy positions and I moved my tank down to the end of the line, pulled forward maybe twenty yards, and told the gunner to start firing high explosive rounds rather than canister. Small-arms fire peppered the tank, sounding like hail. After firing about ten rounds of high explosive into the main part of the ambush site, we backed out of our exposed position and returned to the road. There, Private Borgos and I threw boxes of .50-caliber and 7.62mm ammo to the 3d Platoon vehicles as we passed down the line.

Approaching the burning tank at the end of the column, we could see enemy soldiers on the road behind it firing down our line of vehicles. Moving to the side of the road for better aim, I was preparing to fire more canister rounds when an RPG slammed into the tank's searchlight with a deafening roar. Pausing only briefly after this distraction, we fired four canister rounds behind the burning tank, effectively clearing the enemy from that part of the road.

Along with small arms and antitank weapons, the enemy was also firing mortars and throwing grenades. The latter were beginning to take their toll on the men in my platoon. I told each vehicle commander to get his people down inside and slow up their rate of fire or we'd soon be out of ammunition.

There was only one radio on my tank, which I kept tuned to the platoon frequency so I could command the platoon. Periodically the CO came on my frequency and asked for situation reports, particularly the casualty count. So far we had five men dead and twelve wounded. On one of those calls I asked how things were going where he was. He said that 2d Platoon was organizing a dismounted patrol to move around and attack the enemy position from the flank.

The battle in our location continued for another ten minutes as gunships, artillery fire, and air force fighter-bombers pounded the nearby jungle. Off in the distance we could see dozens of helicopters dropping off elements of the infantry battalion. Their job was to sweep around behind and destroy the enemy.

Within a few minutes the enemy fire slackened and we could see movement to our front. At this point I had my platoon fire farther out from the road in hopes of hitting more of the enemy as they withdrew.

With the infantry closing the trap, the battle shifted away from us and we began to take stock of our situation. Up and down the road were burning vehicles. The road was littered with empty 90mm shell casings, and .50-caliber and 7.62mm brass was scattered everywhere. A brass merchant would have had a field day.

The 3d Platoon leader and four of his men joined up with Private Borgos and me, and together we began extinguishing the fires on the burning vehicles. At the same time we checked up on our men and helped to remove the wounded. Medevac helicopters soon began landing on the road to evacuate our dead and wounded to the nearest hospital or graves registration unit. I personally put Private Borgos, who had begun limping badly and needed to get his wounds properly treated, on one of the helicopters. He waved to me as the chopper disappeared over the trees.

The CO informed me that the enemy at his location had vanished and that the crew of my lead tank managed to get out through the escape hatch located under the driver's seat. The men then joined up with the crew of the third tank. Only two of them were lightly wounded.

Buoyed by that good news we were able to put together an approximate casualty report for the two platoons that had been in contact: My platoon had suffered 4 dead, 19 wounded, and 4 vehicles destroyed; 3d Platoon's losses were 5 dead, 16 wounded, and 3 vehicles destroyed.

As we continued to evacuate the wounded and consolidate our positions, forward elements of the infantry battalion arrived and started searching the area to our front. The infantrymen brought wounded enemy soldiers out to the road for evacuation. The enemy casualties were placed in front of one of my vehicles so we could keep a machine gun trained on them while our medics treated their wounds.

Curious about the enemy's ambush site, I collected three soldiers and, armed with M14s, we began to tour the enemy positions. The VC had done a beautiful job of camouflaging their positions. It was almost impossible to see them from the road. The ambush site consisted of three rows of connected trenches with logs and dirt for overhead cover. The complex extended at least one hundred yards along the road.

Enemy bodies were scattered throughout the area. We found twelve dead VC clustered together in the thick brush where I had initially pulled up my tank and fired six rounds of canister. Their bodies had been shredded by the thousands of sharp canister pellets.

Not wanting to get into the tunnels for fear of booby traps, we carefully walked around the edges of the trenches to get a better idea of their size. The nearest trench was about thirty feet away, the middle one seventy-five, and the third a little over a hundred feet back from the road. The entire complex was big enough to accommodate a battalion-sized unit or larger. Much work had gone into preparing the positions, but it was obvious they offered little protection from our helicopter rockets and artillery fire. In all we found eighty-four enemy bodies, treated six wounded, and recovered thirteen weapons. The VC and NVA normally carried off their dead and wounded and rarely left any weapons on the battlefield, so the actual casualty figures were probably much higher.

As our little patrol returned to the road, the troop commander and 2d Platoon were just arriving, towing my three disabled vehicles at the rear of their column. I checked on my two tank crews after reporting to the CO. The crew of tank One-Four told me that they had been forced to escape out the bottom of their disabled tank after a second RPG jammed their turret mechanism. After talking things over, I instructed the men from tank One-Four to help clean and man tank One-Five, the vehicle I'd just been crewing.

Major General Depuy and our squadron commander, Lieutenant Colonel Lewayne, arrived on the scene and began inspecting the battlefield. The 3d Platoon leader was called over to provide the briefing, so I took this opportunity to sort out my platoon before we returned to base.

The CO ordered me to escort the troop maintenance section, which was towing our damaged vehicles, back to the squadron rear and get my new command track rigged up with the proper radio configuration. He also instructed me to take out an ambush patrol from the nearby artillery position there at dusk. While we were in the rear he also wanted us to clean up and get a hot meal since we looked "pretty rough."

I selected the track with the most inexperienced commander for my new command vehicle. Although I rode in the infantry compartment so I could better manage the radios, I still commanded the vehicle. It thus provided me the opportunity to put a less experienced man in the TC's position and train him so he could take over another track when its commander went home or became a casualty.

After some awkward jockeying on the road, the platoon, now little more than a ragtag column, headed back to the rear minus many fine young men. I stopped the column when we reached the first ambush site and dismounted with three men. We found the enemy bunkers set deeply into the ground and so well hidden that I almost completely overlooked one on the far side. That position must have been the one that killed my tank commander. We found the mangled bodies of two enemy soldiers inside, the obvious victims of our 90mm canister rounds.

Since 2d Platoon had been given the mission of destroying the tunnels and bunkers, I radioed the platoon leader and described what I'd found. I recommended that he get a detail over there to destroy the position as soon as possible so it couldn't be reused.

Our move back to the squadron base camp was uneventful. After making sure new radios were installed in my new track and that the men got showers and chow, several of us visited our casualties in the 24th Evacuation Hospital. It seemed like half my men were there. They were in good spirits and it appeared that all but three would quickly return to duty.

The most seriously wounded men were usually kept at the 24th Evacuation Hospital just long enough to be stabilized and then evacuated to Saigon. Those cases usually didn't return to duty. Ninety-five percent of those who remained at the evacuation hospital normally returned to duty within three to five days. I had eleven men there who fell into that category.

The most common wound received by men in the cavalry was concussion. Large antitank mines exploding under a vehicle often caused internal injuries that were difficult to detect at the evacuation hospitals. Soldiers suffering from concussion were transported down to the more specialized hospital in Saigon. Injuries of that type could keep soldiers out of the line for thirty days or more.

Men suffering serious gunshot or shrapnel wounds were usually evacuated to Japan, and amputees and other seriously wounded men were shipped back to the States as soon as their condition permitted.

Many of those returning to us could have resumed light duty sooner, but there was nothing light about duty in the cavalry platoons, so they remained in the rear until they were completely healed. Soldiers returning after a hospital stay of three or four weeks never seemed the same. They were extremely cautious and acted as though their luck had been used up.

Freshened up and feeling much better, we said good-bye to our comrades in the hospital and mounted up for the approximately ten-mile road march north to pick up our ambush patrol. On the return trip I increased the interval between vehicles so we wouldn't eat quite so much dust. As we turned off the paved road and headed down an old, dirt logging road, my driver swung wide to miss a large mud hole and, *KABLOOM!* I had the painful sensation of being blown into the air and not coming back down. I regained consciousness on the floor of my vehicle, my head, left hand, and arm bleeding heavily. I groggily pulled myself up and, looking out the cargo hatch, I could see that a mine had blown a large hole in the road and that we were sitting in it at about a forty-five-degree angle with the engine racing out of control.

I crawled across the top of the track to the driver's hatch, stuck my head in, and reached down to turn off the master switch. The driver, who had apparently suffered a concussion, and the other crewmen had managed to get clear of the vehicle or were blown off. Only the vehicle commander remained on board. He was still sitting behind his .50-caliber machine gun, obviously in great pain. I motioned for others to help, and we lifted the sergeant to the ground. Once he was clear of the vehicle I jumped down and ran to the closest track and got on the radio. I ordered the scout teams out, called for a medevac, and then notified the CO of our latest misfortune. The medevac helicopter arrived while I was explaining our situation, so I broke off our conversation and helped load the wounded. When I returned to the radio I found the medic talking with the CO, who said he wanted to speak with me. The CO ordered me to turn the platoon over to the senior vehicle commander and get on the medevac. He said he wanted the people back at the hospital to look at my wounds. I informed him that it was too late, the helicopter had already departed. He told me that was no problem, and then called the medevac pilot, who returned within minutes and took me and the other casualties on board to the hospital I had just visited that afternoon. Nurses and medics ran out to the helipad when we landed and insisted we be carried in on stretchers.

The hospital consisted of six large, olive-drab tents with bright red crosses painted in white circles on the roofs. Inside the operating tent I stripped to my waist. When they saw the blood on my trousers from the leg wounds I suffered earlier in the day they had me take my pants off, too. I wore no underwear during the monsoon season because the cotton never dried and the elastic waistband chafed your skin and frequently caused rashes to develop, so this was extremely embarrassing. As soon as I sat down I set my helmet on my lap and let them go to work. After cleaning and bandaging my wounds and putting my left arm in a sling they moved me to an army cot and placed ice cubes all around me on the bare canvas. I really wasn't seriously injured. My wounds were all superficial and only a few tiny metal fragments remained inside my skin.

After lying there for about an hour with nothing but a sheet draped over me, I heard the sound of armored vehicles outside. In a few minutes members of my platoon were standing around my cot asking if I was going to be all right. Overwhelmed by their concern, I asked the senior vehicle commander what they were doing at the hospital goofing off when there was a mission to perform. He said the CO had radioed him and said that with the platoon down to just three ACAVs and two tanks he didn't think they could handle the mission so he was giving it to 3d Platoon. He added that the CO then told him to "take what remains of your platoon to the evac hospital, remain there until your platoon leader is released, and then rejoin the troop as soon as possible."

I decided it was time to get back to the platoon. My medic could provide any needed treatment. Besides, with six men standing around with rifles and flak vests, and other wounded platoon members coming over to inquire about me, the ward was becoming a circus. I looked under my cot and found my boots, rifle, helmet, and flak vest, but there was no pants or shirt. I sat there with the sheet draped across my lap, a sling on my arm, and fourteen little bandages scattered over my body and asked my men if they could find my uniform. A few minutes later, one of the NCOs returned with it tightly wadded up. He said they had found it in a trash can behind the operating room.

I got dressed and informed the ward nurse that I was checking out.

"First let me get the doctor's okay," she said, motioning for me to sit down. Then she left the tent to go look for him.

Instead of waiting, I headed for our vehicles. On the way out I visited each of my men still being treated to see how they were doing. I patted them on the arm or leg and told them I hoped to see them back soon. Private Borgos asked if he could go with me but since he was on crutches I told him he would have to remain.

Outside, I mounted up on the closest tank and, as we passed by the ward tent headed for squadron maintenance, I saw the nurse standing in the doorway with her hands on her hips glowering at me. I waved, but she just glared back.

Squadron maintenance, which consisted of three two-and-a-half-ton trucks, two armored vehicles, and two fuel trucks, fitted one of my ACAVs with a new set of command radios for the second time that day. We were back in business.

It was too dark to rejoin the troop, so we spent the night there at squadron maintenance. The CO had arranged for us to pick up two vehicles to replace our recent combat losses, and I spent part of the evening figuring out who would man them. One possibility was to break out a couple of our healthier soldiers from the hospital.

Later, sitting there in the bright moonlight unable to sleep, I reflected that, all things considered, it had been a lucky day for most of us. But the day was not yet over. I was still awake at about 11 P.M. when a runner from the headquarters of the infantry battalion that was guarding our perimeter came over and said that his commander wanted to speak with me. With my arm still in a sling and iodine swabbed over half of my face, I hobbled along in the dark behind the soldier.

I entered the small command-post tent and saw a lieutenant colonel and three other officers poring over a large map. The colonel looked up and exclaimed, "What the hell happened to you, Lieutenant?"

"We ran into a small ambush this morning, Sir," I replied. "But it's a long story. What can I do for you?"

He explained that one of his long-range reconnaissance patrols had run into a superior enemy force, gotten surrounded, and that he wanted my platoon to go out and rescue it. The plan was for us to move about two kilometers out on an old logging road with our headlights on and firing high to drive the enemy away. He put his finger on the map and said, "You'll wait here in the dark for the patrol to come out to your location, then load them up and return to base. It's just that simple."

Not impressed with his plan, I told the colonel he would need to contact my CO for authorization and I gave him the radio frequency to call. I listened as the colonel explained his plan to my CO. He made a strong argument, but the CO apparently didn't think any more of it than I did. However, rather than refuse our support outright, he cited my physical condition, the platoon's reduced strength, and the very real possibility of a night ambush as his rea-

sons for declining. The conversation ended abruptly when the
colonel cut my CO off and said he was going to call his brigade commander.

Thinking the issue had been settled, I hobbled back to my vehicle and lay down on my stretcher to try to get some sleep. About
five minutes later the radio crackled with a call from my CO. He
curtly informed me that my platoon was being attached to the infantry battalion effective immediately and that I should switch to
their radio frequency for further instructions. He told me to keep
my vehicles in a tight column, wished me luck, and abruptly signed
off.

I switched to the infantry battalion frequency and the S3 informed me that ground guides with red-filtered flashlights would
arrive any minute to guide my vehicles across the base camp to the
logging road we were to follow. Then, almost as an afterthought, he
asked, "Are you ready to move out?"

"Give us three minutes to load up and we'll be set," I replied.

I contacted the rest of the platoon and informed them we were
going to conduct a night rescue and to get their people loaded up
and be ready to move out in two minutes. While the crews reacted
to my announcement I gathered the still half-asleep TCs together,
told them what I knew of the mission, and sent them back to their
tracks.

Finally, with all five vehicles lined up on the road just inside the
barbed wire, the S3 called me over for a final briefing. He said he
would be going along and that we would have one infantry squad attached. When he finished, he asked me where I wanted him and the
rifle squad to ride.

"I'll ride in the lead tank, Sir," I replied. "You ride in the second
tank, and spread the squad out on the three armored personnel
carriers."

"Fine," he answered. "Now let's get moving."

He and the infantrymen quickly loaded up and I slowly hobbled
forward to the lead tank. As I struggled to climb up over the rear
sprocket, the tank commander came back to help me aboard. After
painfully lowering myself into the turret through the loader's hatch
with the TC's help, I raised my good hand and motioned what was

left of the 1st Platoon, C Troop, 1st Squadron, 4th Cavalry, forward. We roared out the gate and into the night with headlights on.

After about ten minutes I located the logging road and we turned off the main road and slowly inched our way down what appeared to be a heavily traveled footpath. Finally, after topping a low crest, the major ordered me to stop the platoon and have my tank crew begin firing their .50-caliber and coaxial machine guns high and to the northwest.

Bright tracer rounds arced into the night sky, and after about a minute the major told me to fire two high-explosive main-gun rounds in the same direction. We promptly complied. Every Vietcong within a ten-mile radius now knew our location. He next directed us to turn off our engines and lights and sit quietly while his infantry squad dismounted and moved forward about fifty yards in front of my tank.

We sat there in total darkness with brush pressing against the sides of our vehicles and limbs and vines hanging over our heads. I imagined that every Vietcong in the area was moving in our direction. I didn't have a very good feeling about the situation, and my rear vehicle commander apparently didn't either. He called me and asked for permission to put a two-man listening post to the rear. I approved the request, but cautioned him to not let them go out more than twenty-five yards.

The major was in contact with the patrol and every few minutes he ordered me to elevate our .50-caliber machine gun and fire a few rounds.

After a long fifteen minutes, the seven-man recon patrol finally linked up with our infantry squad and we loaded everyone aboard. The patrol had one casualty and I instructed my medic to take care of him.

As we cranked up our vehicles, I verified with the major that all of his people were on board, then I checked with the last vehicle to ensure that the listening post had been called in. Satisfied that everyone was aboard, I gave the order to move out with the rear vehicle leading. Trees and brush were so thick around the trail that we were forced to back the vehicles almost all the way out to the main road before we were able to turn around.

As soon as we were back on the main road we turned on our headlights and returned to base, stopping at the perimeter to allow the GIs manning the gate to pull back the barbed wire for our entry.

While riding along in the dark I considered the great risk involved with this type of operation. We would really be pushing our luck if we did something like this again very soon. Sooner or later the enemy would be waiting out in the dark to ambush us as we dashed out to rescue a patrol. Few things are more terrifying or deadly than a night ambush.

We dropped off the major and his men in the infantry battalion's area and that was the last I saw of him. I never did receive a full accounting of the patrol's enemy contact.

It was after midnight when we pulled back into our previous positions. I had been standing in the loader's hatch for more than an hour and the pain in my legs and left shoulder was very noticeable. Getting off the tank was particularly difficult, so both the TC and medic helped steady me as I climbed to the ground.

Just before I got out of the tank I heard the infantry battalion call for an emergency medevac for the wounded man from the patrol we had picked up and who we had dropped off with the rest of the infantrymen at their compound. It was a rare occurrence for a medevac chopper to go out at night, so we knew his wounds must have been serious.

Once I was back on my own vehicle, the medic insisted on rebandaging two of my most serious wounds. When he finished I lay down on my stretcher for the third time that night and, totally exhausted, was instantly asleep.

A Classmate Visits

Our presence in South Vietnam has but one purpose, and that is to help keep the peace, and to keep ambitious aggressors from helping themselves to the easy prey of certain newly formed independent nations.

—Harry S. Truman

Early one morning a few days later we were lined up waiting for the order to move out and the platoon seemed particularly slow in responding to radio calls. This was due, I was sure, to the men being awake most of the night enduring another enemy mortar attack.

A normal mortar attack would last just a few minutes as the enemy dropped in six to ten 82mm rounds and then disappeared. The previous night was different. The entire troop was gathered into a night defensive position with perhaps twenty trucks parked near the center. About midnight the first mortar rounds began to land among our armored vehicles—first three, then a pause of about five minutes, then three more, and then about twelve landed, one right after the other. This odd pattern continued for more than three hours.

I ordered everyone off the ground and into the vehicles with all hatches closed except for one. To ensure that the enemy was not using the cover of the mortar attack to sneak up on us, I directed each vehicle to post one person at the TC's position at eyeball-level behind the .50-caliber machine gun, observing to the front. Of course it didn't take long on a hot, humid night with five or six men cooped up inside for things to grow uncomfortable fast. Adding to our discomfort was the fact that there was no moon and a slight overcast, which made visibility almost nil. Being under the trees also hampered our vision.

The troop commander called me during this extended mortar attack and said that most of the rounds were falling into my sector of the perimeter. Since we weren't able to determine their direction, we were unable to provide much guidance to our supporting artillery. Then he finally got to the purpose of the call: "We've got to find out where these rounds are coming from, so I want your platoon to find one of the shell craters and get me a shell report."

I had an ambush patrol about a hundred yards out in front of the platoon. Although they hadn't made contact with the enemy, they thought they could hear the sounds of mortars being loaded and fired to their front. I passed this information along to the troop commander and he called artillery in on the suspected locations, but the enemy fire continued.

Knowing that I wouldn't be able to find anyone who knew what a shell report was in my young and inexperienced platoon, I told Private Borgos to put on the PRC-10 portable radio and get ready to accompany me outside. While we waited for a pause in the shelling I asked the other vehicle commanders if they'd observed any mortar rounds landing within our sector. The three vehicles on my left flank reported hearing and feeling mortar rounds land close by their positions.

When the next lull came I announced to the platoon that Private Borgos and I would be on the ground looking for a shell crater so I could send in a shell report. I explained that I would have a flashlight with a red filter on it so no one would think we were the enemy.

Unable to find a crater in the dark, we huddled behind a nearby tree while I radioed Sgt. Richard Cramer, the track commander who had seemed the most confident that we would be able to find craters near his vehicle. I told him I wanted him outside to help me. He acknowledged, and I shined the red light in the direction of his vehicle so he could find us. He joined us about a minute later.

Sergeant Cramer took the lead as he moved straight out in front of our line of vehicles. When he reached our defensive barbed wire he knelt down and motioned for me to join him. Borgos and I moved up and, with all three of us flat on our chests, I shined the filtered light into a crater that was almost directly under the wire. I was looking for the high and low sides of the crater so I could determine the direction from which the round had been fired. The high side of a shell hole supposedly faced in the direction from which the round came. Lying there in the dark I found it almost impossible to determine anything. However, by running my hand around the edge of the crater, I could definitely feel a disturbed and undisturbed side. By laying my compass on the ground next to the hole and shining the red light on the dial I was able to determine a pretty accurate direction of attack.

With Sergeant Cramer and Private Borgos hard on my heels, we raced to the closest vehicle and piled in. About thirty seconds later another wave of mortar rounds began to fall. By then I was on the radio with the troop commander giving him the approximate line to the enemy tubes.

We sat there in the cramped confines of the armored vehicle and listened to our own artillery landing in the designated area. Our artillery fire continued for about five minutes, then there was a thirty-minute lull. The enemy apparently still had some fight left in him, though, because three more rounds landed close by. I again called for a fire mission and this time it brought an end to the enemy shelling for the night.

I had started to return to my own vehicle a number of times but finally decided we had pushed our luck far enough. Borgos and I remained where we were until stand-to.

I inspected the area at first light and found little damage from the enemy fire but located at least fifty craters in front of or behind my platoon's sector.

The attack was probably the work of two or three determined Vietcong with a mortar tube and lots of ammunition. I figured they probably fired three rounds, jumped into a deep bunker until our artillery stopped, and then got back out and fired three more, keeping it up almost all night.

Later that day, after escorting a resupply convoy to Loc Ninh and back, we entered a division resupply point that had been set up a short distance off Highway 13. After picking up food, fuel, and ammunition, we were directed over to our troop supply truck. As each vehicle pulled alongside, the supply personnel exchanged our old M14 rifles for the new M16s, a one-for-one trade. My M14 did not get exchanged because I was off my vehicle attending a meeting when the turn-in occurred. Due to the limited number of rifles available, individual soldiers had to personally exchange their weapons.

We had heard a great deal about the outstanding qualities of the M16, both from those who had already been issued the weapon and through articles in magazines and the *Pacific Stars and Stripes* newspaper.

The new rifles came in regular cardboard boxes, five to a box, with a large exploded diagram showing how to disassemble the weapon. Compared to our old M14s, the M16 was a major technological advance. Originally developed for the Special Forces for close-in jungle fighting, they were lightweight, had a high rate of fire, and used the same sights as the M14. The real novelty was the small buffer in the stock and the much smaller 5.56mm round that the weapon fired. These features reduced the recoil considerably, allowing the firer to hold it steady for up to twenty rounds of extremely accurate and rapid fire.

That same day, as we headed north to begin a new campaign in the Michelin rubber plantation, we found an old, deserted section of road, stopped the platoon briefly, and allowed each soldier to fire his new weapon. The men had each been issued five hundred rounds of the new, smaller, faster ammunition, and I directed that only two twenty-round magazines be fired—one on semiautomatic and one on full automatic.

They fired their new weapons with great enthusiasm. I noticed that on full automatic the M16 sounded like a horse snorting. I borrowed Private Borgos's rifle and ripped off an entire twenty-round magazine in a couple of seconds. It was a very smooth weapon to fire and we all were amazed by its firepower.

Later in the evening, when we entered our night defensive position and began to put out barbed wire and clean our weapons I had everyone break down the M16s and clean them just as we had done with our old M14s. We had been provided no instructions or supplies for the care and cleaning of the new rifles, so we used our homemade solvent consisting of 50 percent motor oil and 50 percent gasoline. This mixture, with the help of an old toothbrush, was effective for cleaning dirt and grime from our machine guns and had worked well on the M14. We figured it would be equally effective on our new M16s. The men soaked the parts in the cleaning solution, scrubbed them with toothbrushes, wiped off the excess, and then reassembled the weapons using the large exploded diagrams that came with each box as a guide.

The night was uneventful other than a few enemy mortar rounds being fired into the perimeter at about 2 A.M.

At first light the platoon mounted up and moved out to clear and pull outpost duty along a section of the old plantation road that had not been used for several years. Minesweepers cleared a five-mile section of road, then I positioned my vehicles within sight of each other to allow for a clear view of the road.

About three hours after taking up our positions I received a call from troop headquarters instructing me to provide two armored vehicles to escort four artillery supply trucks. The trucks were leaving from a large, cleared artillery position located about a mile off the main road in a heavily forested area and my tracks were to accompany them into the town of An Loc, about fifteen miles away, and then return.

This was a simple mission of the type we were often given, so I picked my most inexperienced scout team, with Sergeant Reeves in charge, to provide some training for them.

The two vehicles headed south and were soon out of sight. I adjusted my position to cover the area of road left open by the departing scout team. About a half an hour later I received a frantic radio call from Sergeant Reeves saying that their little convoy had been ambushed a half mile from the artillery position and that they had taken casualties. I could hear the sounds of heavy firing and explosions in the background and knew his situation was serious.

I immediately called the rest of the platoon and ordered them to move to tank One-Four's position at top speed and organize into a fighting formation with tanks leading.

We headed south as soon as we were formed up and I called the beleaguered scout-team leader to determine their status. After several calls, an out-of-breath Sergeant Reeves excitedly told me that they were still receiving heavy enemy fire and that they were located at the narrowest point in the road, where the Rome plows had stopped work. He said his other track and two of the trucks were on fire and that they appeared to have three dead and six wounded. "I don't know how much longer we can hold out," he added, "our rifles are jamming up on us."

"The new M16s?" I replied.

"Affirmative," he responded. "All of ours have stopped working."

Approaching a small bend in the dirt road, I could see smoke rising above the trees and knew the enemy was still attacking. I ordered my three tanks to start firing their main guns high and wide and then we charged into the deadly enemy fire. The tanks, with about fifty feet between them, stopped beside the burning vehicles, pivoted to the right, and continued to fire all their weapons point-blank into the enemy positions.

I led the ACAVs down the other side and we came up on the road between the convoy's vehicles and poured a steady stream of fire into the jungle. I radioed the artillery unit and requested an immediate fire mission two hundred yards off the road and behind the enemy positions.

As I was repositioning my vehicles around the battlefield I heard one of my sergeants shout over the radio, "None of these damn '16s will work."

On my own vehicle I could see that Private Borgos and two other crewmen were having difficulty ejecting spent rounds from their rifles. Borgos at one point used the auxiliary antenna to ram down the barrel and dislodge a stuck casing.

As the enemy fire began to die down, I dismounted with two men and my medic, arming one with my M14, and moved around the ambush site putting out the fires and helping the wounded. The final count was four dead and seven wounded (one of the dead and two of the wounded were my men).

An infantry company soon arrived from the artillery position and began to sweep the area.

While a medevac chopper loaded up the dead and wounded, Sergeant Reeves explained that when he first passed by the ambush position everything had looked normal. However, after picking up the four trucks and starting back through the area he noticed fresh footprints on the dirt road and signs of digging. Just as he yelled for his driver to slam on the brakes, a command-detonated mine blew a crater in the road no more than ten feet in front of them. That triggered the ambush and the track at the rear of the convoy suffered the brunt of the attack.

When the rear vehicle was set on fire, the crew took shelter behind a five-ton truck and attempted to return fire with their rifles but the weapons jammed. That truck was soon destroyed and my men, joined by several wounded men from the truck, moved behind the second truck in line. That was where we found them when we arrived: huddled behind the truck's wheels or lying in the muddy drainage ditch next to the road. Their vehicle was destroyed by three RPGs, which exploded the track's ammunition and caused the fuel tank to explode. All that remained of it was a melted, burned-out aluminum hulk.

We hooked tow cables on the trucks and pulled the aluminum hulk off the road, then we dragged what was left of the trucks back inside the artillery perimeter.

The artillery battalion commander met us at the edge of the perimeter and I reported all the details of the ambush, including the problem with our malfunctioning M16s. I also radioed our headquarters and reported the enemy contact and the loss of three men and one vehicle. The CO called me back in about fifteen minutes and we had a lengthy discussion about my malfunctioning rifles. According to him, we were the only unit in the squadron to report problems with our M16s. Everyone else was very happy with them. I told him my men considered the M16s to be defective and that they wanted their M14s back. He said he would look into the matter and get back to me shortly.

Before leaving the artillery position, I met with all my vehicle commanders to discuss the performance of their M16s. All reported problems with the weapons, mostly a failure to extract spent casings properly. At this meeting I discovered we had three other M14s still in the platoon, all of which had been pressed into service during the ambush. Of the forty-eight M16s issued to the scouts, mortarmen, and infantrymen in my platoon (tank crewmen weren't issued rifles), forty-three jammed completely, and the remaining five would fire only on semiautomatic.

This was serious. However, we still had three machine guns on each ACAV, and the tanks were not affected, so our overall firepower was not too greatly reduced. The real concern was how to arm the dismounted ambush and reconnaissance patrols we had to send out until the problem could be solved. It looked like our four M14s would be doing yeoman service for the time being.

My initial rifle marksmanship training was with the old M1 Garand, the standard World War II infantry rifle. It's still a great weapon and accurate to about four hundred yards. The sights are easy to use and it will operate under almost any conditions. You can pull the bolt back and pour a handful of dirt into the chamber and it will still fire. The M14 is almost the same in design. The big difference is that it uses a twenty-round magazine instead of an eight-round clip, and it has a selector switch that allows for automatic or semiautomatic fire. It also uses the same 7.62mm ammunition as the M60 machine gun.

Comparing the M14 to the M16, I found very few things to like about the new rifle. To me it was not as accurate, it was too short, and it didn't seem to have the same stopping power as the M14. I now understand why so many soldiers in the early days carried their M16s around in the original plastic packing—almost as if they were undecided as to whether they wanted to keep them or not.

The artillery battalion S3, Major Lyons, radioed and explained that the two artillery batteries at his location still needed their resupply. He wanted to know if I had the resources to escort four supply trucks up to the resupply point in An Loc and shepherd them back before nightfall.

"Yes, Sir," I replied.

I again detailed Sergeant Reeves to lead the mission but this time assigned two tanks to accompany him and then led the rest of the platoon back out to the main road, where we resumed our outpost duty.

The second escort mission was accomplished without incident. While Sergeant Reeves and his vehicles were returning, the troop commander called and advised me an expert from the division ordnance unit would be coming out on the evening resupply helicopter to look at our M16s and come up with a solution to the problem.

The resupply bird arrived shortly after we set up our night defensive position. I ran out to greet our visitor and was surprised to see 1st Lt. Jim Wise, a classmate from my college days. As we shook hands, Jim explained that he had been tasked with coordinating and supervising the issue of the new rifles to division units.

After unloading our supplies, which included a hot meal, the helicopter departed and I took Jim back to my vehicle, where I told him about our sad experience with the highly touted rifle earlier that day. He was shocked when he learned how the rifles were issued to us. A required orientation class was supposed to be given to all soldiers prior to receiving the new weapon. Part of the orientation included a section on care and cleaning, and each rifle was supposed to be issued with a small plastic bottle of silicone lubricant specially designed for the rifle's precise tolerances.

After examining several weapons and hearing about their failure in the ambush, Jim asked to see all of my soldiers armed with M16s. I told him that would be no problem but that he would have to conduct two sessions since I couldn't take everyone off the line at the same time.

Jim began his briefings by showing the men how to clean off all of the oil and dirt from the rifle with just plain gasoline and a clean toothbrush. Next, he showed them how to apply a tiny amount of the special silicone cream to the rifle's working parts. He also explained the importance of keeping the weapon clean, pointing out that even a small amount of dirt or sand could cause the weapon to jam.

The men asked several good questions concerning how to get the best results when firing the weapon. He said there was no problem with firing long bursts on automatic, but he recommended short bursts for better accuracy and to preserve ammunition. Some of the men wanted to know why the army would issue a weapon that required such careful handling to men who operated in constant dirt, dust, water, and mud. Jim didn't have an answer for that, but he agreed that proper field testing should have revealed the weapon's flaws.

After the briefings I instructed the men to return to their vehicles and thoroughly clean each rifle as they had been shown, adding that Lieutenant Wise would personally come around and inspect their weapons.

Since Jim was assigned to the division support command, I figured he might know why Lt. Col. Carl Haddox had been relieved as the division maintenance officer. Lieutenant Colonel Haddox had always managed to come up with parts for our vehicles when the supply system couldn't produce them. We valued his ability and connections and treated him royally whenever he visited the squadron. Then, all of a sudden, he was transferred out of the division.

Jim said he knew exactly why Haddox was fired. He explained that a couple of months earlier several battalion commanders had complained to Major General Dupuy about vehicles being deadlined and their inability to get repair parts. The division inspector general's office investigated the matter and found that fifteen vehicles had been cannibalized for parts in an effort to make other vehicles operational. The inspector general determined that Haddox had acted without the general-officer authorization that was necessary in order to begin cannibalizing vehicles. The danger in starting this process was that it often got out of control. Units quickly discovered it was easier to take parts off a deadlined vehicle than to go through the time-consuming process of ordering replacements and then waiting for them to trickle down through the supply system. Eventually all that is left is a naked hull or chassis. Jim said the fifteen vehicles in question had been stripped pretty clean.

I shared with him a related incident that involved one of my vehicles.

For various reasons—rotation, wounds, and R and R—my platoon's strength at one point fell to thirty soldiers present for duty. That left me with just three men per vehicle, the minimum needed for effective operation. I had a man who was getting ready to go on R and R and contacted our executive officer, who was serving as acting commander, for advice. He offered me two choices: I could either cancel the man's R and R or place one of my vehicles in administrative storage. He said he preferred the former. However, because the soldier had been looking forward to this leave for many months and certainly had earned it, I argued strongly on his behalf. The XO finally agreed to allow the soldier to go and told me I could place one of my ACAVs, with everything detachable locked up inside, in the 3d Brigade's motor pool at Lai Khe.

A couple of weeks later, after my men on R and R had returned and with the arrival of some replacements, I was ready to recover my tenth vehicle. We made a special trip to Lai Khe to pick it up. When we arrived, we found the vehicle still securely locked up, but it was sitting on blocks. All of the road wheels had been removed and one complete track was gone! I immediately notified the troop commander, who made a formal report of the theft and discovered that Lieutenant Colonel Haddox had authorized another troop to take all twenty of my track's road wheels to keep three of their vehicles operational. Two days later I received a call that my vehicle was serviceable and that I could pick it up.

Jim listened to my story and said that Haddox had probably sent his mechanics out to strip another vehicle in order to get mine running again, starting a vicious circle. He agreed that there was no way they could have gotten all the parts through the supply system that quickly.

Whenever a vehicle was declared a combat loss we always stripped it for repair parts. That was SOP and not the same as cannabilizing. The large number of destroyed vehicles should have provided a large supply of parts flowing to the rear. Apparently, though, these didn't completely satisfy the need for repair parts.

Everyone agreed that Lieutenant Colonel Haddox was a fine officer who got the job done. However, he had broken the rules in the process and the division commander decided he had to go.

Jim completed his M16 inspections at dusk and we ate dinner together under a mahogany tree near my command vehicle so I could monitor the radios. He had agreed to spend the night and go with us in the morning to test-fire our weapons and ensure that the problem had been solved.

Sitting there in the dark and talking about old times was enjoyable. We had been cadet officers in the same ROTC battalion and both of us had chosen to be commissioned in Armor Branch. He recalled in great detail our elaborate commissioning ceremony and our trip to Fort Knox, Kentucky, following graduation.

Neither of us had any great interest in the military when we started college, but at the time the Selective Service had required us to enroll in ROTC in order to qualify for an educational draft deferment. We had not considered it a hardship or inconvenience, we had simply accepted it as the cost of citizenship in our great nation.

We made the decision to branch armor while we were at ROTC summer camp at Fort Sill, Oklahoma, between our junior and senior years. We were given an orientation on the various branches of the army, and all of the presentations were rather bland except for the one on armor. Five tanks came charging out of a wood line in front of the class firing blank ammunition. As they converged on the bleachers we were seated in we could feel the ground tremble beneath us. The instructor, a young lieutenant wearing strap-on tanker boots, made a superb impression as he told us how the firepower and shock action of his tanks made enemies run in terror and decided the outcome of most battles. His presentation sold us on Armor Branch.

Our training course at Fort Knox lasted about ten weeks and was what I would call hands-on fun. It consisted of two hundred young lieutenants learning how to drive, shoot, talk on the radio, and command a platoon of five tanks.

I still have fond memories of that training: driving my tank too fast through a large mud hole and being covered from head to foot with thick, green mud. Out on a firing range one morning just as it was getting daylight, a few moments before the command to open fire was given, a large buck deer with a nice set of antlers wandered in front of our tanks. Fifteen tank guns with young lieutenants at the controls zeroed in on the hapless deer and it evaporated at the command, "Commence firing!"

Neither of us had any regrets about choosing armor as our specialty branch when we finished our training, and both had looked forward to our first duty assignment.

I left Fort Knox with orders assigning me to Baumholder, Germany, with a delay en route to attend the airborne training at Fort Benning, Georgia. Jim went directly to Fort Hood, Texas, where he became an assistant personnel officer.

Those were fine memories, but now it was time to get some sleep. I had borrowed a cot from nearby the artillery unit for Jim, and with me on one side of the vehicle under my shelter half and him under a poncho on the other, we settled down for the night.

The next day the men test-fired their M16s and only one continued to have problems. The soldier had damaged the bolt with a screwdriver while trying to clear a jammed cartridge in the heat of the ambush. Jim gave the man his own rifle and took the damaged one back to division with him when he departed on the evening resupply helicopter.

Although it took some time to regain our confidence in the M16, Jim's visit had apparently corrected the mechanical problems with the rifle. It also provided a morale boost for me and the platoon.

The Worst Day

Any danger spot is tenable if men, brave men, will make it so.
—John F. Kennedy

Our departure from our night defensive position was delayed by thirty minutes as we awaited the arrival of our new troop commander, Capt. Bill Yarborough. I stood at the edge of a small clearing with the other officers and the first sergeant and watched the helicopter carrying our new CO land. Captain Yarborough jumped out as soon as it was firmly on the ground and came over and shook hands all around. He was an older captain with a heavy Southern accent. We stood in a small circle as he asked each of us platoon leaders to brief him on our personnel strength and the current day's mission. Then, after a few words of greeting, we mounted up and the platoons moved out in three different directions to begin our day's assignments.

My platoon was tasked with clearing mines from and opening up an unused section of plantation road just south of Quan Loi, then searching the area of thick jungle directly to the east of it

We began the mission with all three tanks on the road following two men using minesweepers. I deployed the two scout sections on either side of the road at the edge of the tree lines.

No American units had been in the vicinity for several months. However, its reputation for being a rough and dangerous area was well known. We were warned before moving out to pay close attention to what was hanging from nearby trees. The last unit through there had lost four men decapitated by huge command-detonated mines that had been hung in the trees about eight feet above the ground. There was something terrifying about the thought of decapitation that immediately got our attention, and I could see that this warning had not been wasted on the scouts, who were keeping their distance from all large trees.

The platoon had been moving in this formation for about an hour, with me walking just in front of the lead tank and directly behind the minesweepers, when suddenly there was a large explosion. The lead scout vehicle on the right side of the road had been hit and thick black smoke billowed up from it. I clambered up the front slope of the tank following behind me and shouted at the driver to head in that direction. When we arrived on the scene I discovered that the vehicle had hit a large mine buried in an unlikely spot some distance off the road. The enemy had apparently anticipated our tactics and buried the mine where we were most likely to deploy security vehicles.

Three men on the track were slightly wounded, and the driver, Specialist Jones, had been killed instantly. The mine exploded directly under him in a focused blast that came up through the floor of the vehicle and shredded the entire right side of his body.

Specialist Jones was a fine soldier, humorous and a real asset to his crew. He always had a funny story or joke to tell to brighten the day. When I first joined the platoon it was the accepted practice for each vehicle to carry five cases of beer and five cases of soft drinks on every operation. Each vehicle also carried an ice chest stocked with ice we purchased from the many Vietnamese trucks plying their trade on the roads that we performed outpost duty on.

On one of my first operations with the platoon, at about two in the afternoon Jones's scout section reported finding a tunnel, so I moved to their location to see what they came up with. As we finished our inspection and started to return to the road, Jones fell backwards off his vehicle. When I jumped down to see if he was injured, he grinned broadly and offered me a cold beer. He was obviously drunk.

This colorful incident resulted in my first policy: While we were in the field, which was almost constantly, no beer would be consumed before 5 P.M. This was a real hardship for some of the men, but they learned to live with it. Often we would still be out deep in the jungle on a search-and-destroy mission when, at the appointed time, someone would radio me and ask for a time check. Then, after I had verified that it was after five, a regular happy hour began. Up and down the line I would see men pulling cans of beer from their coolers. However, vehicle commanders maintained control of their crews and intoxication was a rarity.

As we removed Specialist Jones's mutilated body from the vehicle, I noticed that the little finger on his right hand was dangling by a tiny thread of skin. The memory of it is crystal clear to this day.

I wrote a short letter to Jones's family explaining how much we thought of him and how much he would be missed. For five years thereafter I received a Christmas card from his devoted family.

The vehicle was a total loss and, with one dead and three wounded, I had lost one-tenth of my fighting strength. After evacuating the wounded and detailing another crew to recover the vehicle for spare parts, I continued the mission of clearing the road with the rest of the platoon.

When we reached the end of our sector of the road, I called in the scouts and loaded up the minesweepers. Then, with two tanks leading the column, we turned east and began moving out into the jungle for the remainder of our mission. I was behind the lead tanks, followed by the other ACAVs. The third tank brought up the rear.

As my vehicle turned and moved off the road, I heard a tremendous explosion directly behind me. We were showered with rocks and other debris. When the smoke cleared we could see that the One-Three track, which was carrying the survivors of Jones's crew, had hit a large mine and was lying upside down in a crater created by the blast.

I ordered the scout sections out for local security and raced back with the medic to help. It looked very bad for the crew: Four men had been blown free of the vehicle, one was partially pinned under the left rear with only his legs sticking out, and the driver was still trapped inside.

The engine was smoking and there was a strong odor of raw gasoline. We hurriedly began to dig the trapped soldiers out. Within a few minutes we were able to pull the man pinned under the rear of the vehicle out. A horrible sight greeted us as we dragged him clear: The blast had ripped him open from the middle of his chest to the top of his knees. In the midst of the bloody red pulp I could see that his genitals had been crushed to one side and that his heart was still pumping furiously, forcing out more blood and causing his entire body to shake. Suddenly the shaking stopped and the soldier's body lay still. We continued to pull him out. His head emerged with eyes wide open, and his mouth was frozen open as if he had been trying to scream. It was a sickening sight. All of us, the medic included, recoiled from it.

I walked to the front of the track and looked closely at the smoking engine and badly ruptured fuel tank, expecting it to burst into flames at any moment. A second crew member came up to me with tears in his eyes and told me that Private First Class Williams, the driver, was still alive and that we had to get him out. I got on the radio and started jockeying vehicles around in an effort to get a cable on One-Three in order to pull it over so we could remove the driver. The new troop commander, who had been monitoring our situation, radioed me that no vehicles should move in the immediate vicinity without minesweepers out front. Realizing there was little time left, I grabbed a fire extinguisher, ran to the front of One-Three, and tried to get the engine-compartment door open. The latch was extremely hot and wouldn't open.

I went to the back of the vehicle and prepared to enter the combat hatch while several men dug feverishly trying to get to the driver's hatch. It was a time-consuming process and the vehicle appeared to be ready to explode at any moment. So, with fire extinguisher in hand, I opened the combat hatch and crawled in. Black smoke billowed out and I could smell raw gasoline all around. With the vehicle upside down, everything—weapons, C rations, personal clothing—was on the ceiling. I clawed my way through the mess trying to reach the injured driver. It was dark inside and my spraying the fire extinguisher made it even harder to see. Finally, after groping around I found the driver's compartment. Williams, a small black soldier who was proud of his ability to skillfully maneuver his large armored vehicle, was unconscious. I reached under his armpits and dragged him back to the combat hatch. I crawled through the opening and then reached in and lifted Williams out and placed him on a waiting stretcher. Soon a medical evacuation helicopter arrived and the dead and wounded were transported back to the nearest field hospital. We later heard that Williams died of his wounds.

Two crewmen from the One-Three vehicle who had not been wounded now requested permission to ride on one of the tanks which, because of their thicker armor, provided greater protection from mines. I agreed and then turned the vehicle recovery operation over to our troop maintenance section, which had just arrived. They would clean up the area and evacuate the destroyed vehicles. My immediate objective was to get the platoon away from this deadly area as quickly as possible.

We continued on with our sweep of the jungle east of the road. At the first rest break I visited each vehicle and spoke briefly with the crew to make sure that everything was all right after our losses that morning. Later in the day, as we neared our boundary with 2d Platoon, one of the tanks developed a transmission leak and, rather than take it farther from the road, I left it with two scout vehicles for protection. I then crossed a large open area covered with tall grass with the rest of the platoon to investigate the tree line on the far side.

Unknown to me, our 2d Platoon had moved into the area, spotted my vehicles guarding the tank with the transmission leak and, because of the heavy foliage, assumed they were looking at my entire platoon. They then moved to the edge of the clearing and, not knowing that five of my vehicles were on the other side, formed up on line and began to recon the tree line by fire.

Reconnaissance by fire was an accepted practice when in an area cleared of all friendly forces. The idea was to fire into areas where you suspected the enemy was hiding. Normally, if any enemy were there, they would fire back and thus give away their positions.

When 2d Platoon began firing my initial reaction was that we had been ambushed. However, because of the large volume of heavy weapons fire, I decided it must be on one of our own units. I ordered everyone to cease firing and take cover, that we were receiving friendly fire, and then made an urgent call on the troop radio net, reporting that we were receiving heavy fire and asking that all units cease firing immediately.

The firing soon stopped and I asked for a platoon status. We were very fortunate: There were no casualties, although two of our ACAVs had been hit by machine-gun fire.

The new troop commander made a net call demanding to know the exact location of each platoon. After studying the map he determined that 2d Platoon had strayed out of its sector. The CO proceeded to chew out the 2d Platoon leader on the radio, using some rather novel profanity in doing so.

It was still early afternoon and a large portion of our sector still needed to be covered. I deployed the tanks in a central location for security and directed the scouts to continue clearing the area. Not long after that I received a radio call advising me that a squadron helicopter was inbound with a message for me and needed the grid coordinates for my location.

I moved the platoon to a cleared area and we watched the sky for the helicopter's arrival. It soon appeared and, as requested, we placed identification smoke in the center of the clearing.

The helicopter was a Korean War–vintage two-seater with a large Plexiglas bubble. I ran over as the chopper settled into the clearing and the warrant officer pilot handed me a large, brown envelope. Then, without a word, he gave me a thumbs-up and was gone.

I stood there in the clearing, sheltering my eyes from the rotor wash, and wondered what might be inside the envelope flapping violently in my hand. When the chopper was clear of the area I opened it and pulled out a letter from the squadron commander that read:

Dear Lieutenant Walker:
On this, your twenty-fourth birthday, the officers of the 1st Squadron, 4th United States Cavalry, convey to you their sincere wishes for continued success in the future.

I was dumbfounded! How, in the midst of the war, could anyone justify using a squadron helicopter to run birthday greetings out to the field? It was just unbelievable. I held the letter up to the sun thinking there might be a hidden message in it but I could find none. I finally decided that someone back in the rear knew I was having a particularly bad day and had ordered the greeting sent out in an effort to cheer me up. Still, it seemed odd, especially since my birthday had been the day before.

Later that evening we rejoined the troop in a night defensive position. It was only after finishing dinner—the ubiquitous chili over rice—as we sat there going over the day's events with the CO, that I realized just how tired I was.

After the CO's meeting I went back to the platoon area and met with my vehicle commanders, who were sitting on ammo boxes and a fallen tree awaiting my return. They were a sad and frustrated group. We had suffered three killed and seven wounded that day without ever seeing the enemy and then had been shot up by our own unit.

I let each vehicle commander voice his concerns. I generally agreed with them. Nevertheless, I assured them that we were being treated fairly by troop headquarters and that, although it might seem like we always got the dirtiest and most dangerous missions, things would soon even out.

Before dismissing the sergeants I told them that we would be departing an hour later the next morning to allow time for sandbags to be placed on the floor of the driver's compartment in each vehicle to protect our drivers from mines. This directive produced an outburst from a sergeant who was particularly upset about Specialist Jones's death. He said it was a waste of time and wouldn't do any good. I asked him to stay and sent the others back to their vehicles. I then spent an additional hour talking with the sergeant, who had been doing a good job since joining the platoon three months earlier. It was obvious that the day's events had gotten him down, as they had all of us.

This operation was one of the rare occasions when our mess hall accompanied us to the field, and the next morning, as my men filed through the mess hall, I made a special effort to talk with them to bolster their morale.

As I was visiting with crewmen from the One-Three track, whose vehicle had been destroyed the day before, one of them explained

to me that although he was an infantryman, he had always wanted
to learn how to drive an armored personnel carrier. He then asked
if there was any chance of him ever being allowed to do that in the
platoon. I told him we always needed drivers because of the large
turnover in the unit. Then I looked at the man's vehicle commander, caught his eye, and said, "If you explain this to Sergeant Mills,
I'm sure he'll give you a shot at it."

The sergeant picked up on my comment and said, "Sure thing,
Sir. If he wants to be a driver, he can start this morning."

After filling sandbags and covering the driver's compartment
floor in all our vehicles, even the tanks, we lined up outside the
perimeter wire and moved out on the day's mission. Our orders
were to conduct a road march back to Phu Loi, pick up a resupply
convoy, and escort it back to our base area in the field prior to nightfall.

As we moved along an old jungle roadway that was half dirt and
half asphalt, we came to a place where the road curved around what
had once been a large mahogany tree. All that remained of the tree
was a three-foot stump sitting right next to the road. We were rolling
along at about twenty-five miles per hour when I received an urgent
call from the rear of the column informing me that One-One had
just been involved in a serious accident.

I immediately stopped the platoon, swung my command vehicle
around, and raced to the rear. As we approached One-One I could
see that it had run head-on into the tree stump. The medic and I
dismounted and found Sergeant Mills, the track commander, standing in the midst of the wreckage with blood pouring down the side
of his face. He was shaking his head and swearing at the man I had
spoken to at breakfast. It was obvious he would never drive for Mills
again. The man had apparently been distracted somehow or had
lost control of the vehicle, causing him to run into the stump.

Sadly, three men were injured in this freak accident. One suffered a broken arm, Sergeant Mills had been thrown into the gun
shield and suffered a deep gash on his face and a possible skull frac-
ture, and the third individual had injured his knee and was limping
badly.

After examining the injured, I decided to call for a medevac to
take them to the 24th Evacuation Hospital. I then called the troop

commander and gave him a full report. His immediate reaction was, "You've got to be kidding!" Then he said, "Let's get that driver out of the troop." He explained that our unit had been tasked to attach one soldier to squadron maintenance for an indefinite period of time, and said, "Regardless of his training, he's our man."

I agreed with this arrangement and told the CO, "I'd even waive a replacement to get rid of this fine soldier."

When I examined the vehicle closely, I discovered that the impact had split the vehicle's hull in three places and broken off the right sprocket. It would have to be declared a combat loss and towed back to base by one of my tanks.

It was hard to believe that we had not seen a single enemy soldier in two days of combat operations resulting in three killed, ten wounded, and three vehicles destroyed

Thinking again about the accident, I recalled that when I had first taken command of the platoon, eight soldiers from the Project 100,000 program were assigned. To date, four still remained, and they continued to account for more than their share of casualties and accidents such as the one just described.

When the program was first explained to me, I figured that the men had been rated low on ability because of their difficulty with the English language. However, the longer I worked with them, the more I realized that some were virtually untrainable and should never have been allowed into the military, and certainly not sent into combat. Their presence made my job more difficult, and every vehicle commander who had one of these soldiers assigned to his crew had to work a little harder in order to compensate. Private Borgos was the notable exception.

No one ever asked me to evaluate this program, which someone once explained was necessary because so many draftees failed to report for induction. However, if someone had asked for my opinion I certainly would have enlightened them.

Later, while back in the squadron base camp at Phu Loi, we picked up four new men who had just arrived in country, and I signed for a new armored personnel carrier. Then, with a little encouragement, the squadron mechanics set about transferring One-One's machine guns and gun shield onto it.

While we were there the men were able to shower, put on clean uniforms, and eat a hot meal using real silverware and metal serving trays, rather than plastic forks and paper plates, and, finally, to visit the spartan little base PX.

When I picked up our mail I found orders promoting two of our soldiers from Private First Class to Specialist Fourth Class. So, just before heading back, I held a platoon formation and promoted those individuals. I also took the opportunity to tell the men a little bit about our new troop commander and to explain that we would be moving back into an area that we were more familiar with and where we might even be able to do some tiger hunting.

The Vietnamese People

What the United States wants for South Vietnam is not the important thing. What North Vietnam wants for South Vietnam is not the important thing. What is important is what the people of South Vietnam want for South Vietnam.

—Richard M. Nixon

Although I spent an entire year in Vietnam, I had few face-to-face encounters with the people. This was because we operated in remote areas far removed from the populated areas and most of the Vietnamese we encountered were enemy.

One of the first things I did after receiving my orders for Vietnam was visit the Baumholder post library to learn about that strange and faraway land. The post library had several books about the current war, the French experience, and the Vietcong, but little about the Vietnamese people or their culture.

I did manage to find a slender volume about a twelve-year-old Vietnamese girl that described day-to-day events as she grew up. This little book provided the only information that I would receive on the people of Vietnam prior to my arrival there. The book offered a brief look at Vietnamese society, including the emphasis on the family and ancestral worship, the Buddhist religion, and the indecisiveness of the people. In Vietnam, yes could mean no, a decision might be to make no decision at all, and the people were generally unwilling to offend or to always agree with you.

Armed with this bit of information, and having heard war stories about terrorists who tied bombs to little children, street vendors who sold Coca-Cola with shaved glass in it, and drug dealers who sold battery acid as heroin, I was wary and suspicious of all Vietnamese.

My first morning in Vietnam, as I sat in the mess hall enjoying a hot breakfast, I noticed an older Vietnamese man enter the building with a ladder and a toolbox. He came over near our table, set up his ladder, and climbed up into an access panel in the ceiling. My immediate and paranoid reaction was that he was a Vietcong terrorist who was putting a bomb in the ceiling to blow us all up. I quickly finished my breakfast and left the building, fully expecting a blast to destroy the building and kill dozens of unsuspecting Americans. During my twelve months in country I never completely overcame this mistrust of the people.

The children were like children everywhere: Babies clung to their mothers, older children played games in village streets, and teenagers gathered around our armored vehicles. Most of the soldiers were friendly with the children, letting them approach their vehicles while on outpost duty and giving them candy or other items from their C rations.

When I arrived in Lai Khe to take over my platoon, Sergeant Cowhig explained how our laundry was handled by introducing me to an old, stooped Vietnamese woman with gray hair and rotten teeth who put her hands together and bowed deeply. Every morning, he said, the woman would come into camp, pick up dirty laundry, and then return it clean later that afternoon. The cost was thirty-five cents per set of jungle fatigues. With much grinning and bowing we arranged for her to pick up and deliver my uniforms.

What Sergeant Cowhig *didn't* tell me was that this nice woman washed our jungle fatigues in a slime-covered irrigation ditch and hung them up to dry on a barbed-wire fence running along an unpaved portion of Highway 13. Often, as we moved out on our morning mission, I'd see my uniforms hanging on the fence as the road dust boiled around them. When I got them back the perspiration smell was gone, replaced by a strong swamp odor, and the light green color had taken on a pinkish tinge from the road dust.

Sometimes the troop moved out on short notice and I wouldn't get my laundry back in time. Upon my return I would inquire of the old woman, through her interpreter, what had happened to my missing uniform. She would shrug her shoulders and turn her palms up. I lost three sets of jungle fatigues this way and assumed that either the Vietcong were wearing them or she had sold them on the black market. The real cost of my laundry thus was much more than thirty-five cents per washing. The innocent-looking old woman was, in fact, a pretty clever thief.

Once, while pulling outpost duty on a road south of Lai Khe, I had my platoon set up with about two hundred yards between vehicles. I positioned my command vehicle near a small Vietnamese army outpost. The road went over a small hill, and the top of the hill provided good observation for several miles in all directions.

The Vietnamese position was a typical French triangle fort with ten-foot walls. The walls were dirt mounds in the shape of a triangle, about fifty feet long on each side. At each corner was a low, sandbagged fighting position, and the outside perimeter was covered by barbed wire to about fifty feet beyond the walls. The ground under the wire was sown with several hundred land mines. Manned by fifteen to twenty soldiers, its primary purpose was observation and early warning. The enemy knew of these positions but rarely bothered them.

On this particular day, as we sat in our vehicle about thirty yards away from the fort observing the road and monitoring the radio, a group of six to eight little kids gathered around us on the dusty ground. The kids laughed, waved, and made faces at us as we threw them candy and other items from our C rations. They had a mongrel dog with them and, as they started to leave, one of the kids threw a stick inside the barbed-wire perimeter and the dog sprinted in after it. There was a small explosion and the dog was blown up in the air. It hit the ground and took off running as fast as it could go. We all watched in amazement as the dog raced out into a nearby rice paddy as though the devil himself was chasing after it. The dog then circled back around toward our location and ran right back into the barbed-wire enclosure, where he detonated a second mine. This time, the dog was killed. Its mutilated body landed near the edge of the barbed wire, and the Vietnamese kids, with the soldiers now hollering at them, picked up some long sticks and pulled the dog's body out from under the wire.

The little group came over to our vehicle with their dead dog and I told one of the men to let them borrow a shovel to bury their pet.

As the soldier handed down the shovel, the kids shook their heads and yelled something that I didn't understand. My driver, who understood a little Vietnamese, finally said, "They said they're going to eat it."

That explained why they didn't shed any tears over the dog.

Most Vietnamese traveled by bicycle, motor scooter, bus, truck, or Lambretta (a three-wheeled scooter outfitted with a bed like a pick-up truck that seated six to eight people). There were few private automobiles. The real people movers, though, were the equivalent of our old yellow school buses loaded to the breaking point. A luggage rack usually extended the length of the roof, and a platform supported by chains hanging off the back normally held chickens or hogs. Running boards extended along both sides of these vehicles. I often counted more than a hundred people on those buses, which seemed to run on some sort of schedule known only to the drivers. Nevertheless, they did provide a valuable service to most villages. The Lambrettas were more expensive and carried passengers to remote villages or made special runs, much like taxis.

The motor scooter was like the family car. One day I counted seven people on one—a mother, a father, and five children. I also saw a huge hog weighing three hundred pounds or more slung over the back of a motor scooter being taken to market. Vegetables were often hauled to market in large baskets fastened to the back of small motor scooters.

Trucks of all descriptions, with brand names I didn't recognize, moved the nation's commerce.

The bus and truck drivers were always very friendly to the cavalry because we kept the roads open and allowed them to make a living. We also reduced their overhead by eliminating Vietcong "tax collectors" who set up roadblocks and charged each vehicle a small fee to pass. These lowlifes also boarded buses and robbed passengers at gunpoint. We considered it a major accomplishment when we caught any of these bandits.

I have vivid memories of seeing logging trucks or buses stalled beside the road. The drivers would invariably be perched up front on the fender, covered with grease and oil, tools and parts spread everywhere as they tried to get their old, worn-out vehicles running again.

Generally, women rode bicycles and men rode motor scooters. Bicycles were also used to carry heavy loads of farm produce and animals to market. The bicycle frame was loaded with counterbalancing bags or baskets, and the Vietnamese would walk along beside the bike, pushing it.

Given the variety and quantity of commerce that moved on the roads, there appeared to be some real potential for development and free enterprise in Vietnam. When we operated in the remote areas near the Cambodian border we were especially impressed by the work ethic of the loggers and charcoal producers in the region. There is no telling how much they had to pay the Vietcong to permit them to operate, but it certainly must have cut into their profits.

The water buffalo was a fixture of Vietnamese life and has often been referred to as a Vietnamese tractor. These animals were used to pull wagons, plow fields, cultivate rice paddies, and, on special occasions, for food.

Large animals weighing eight hundred to a thousand pounds or more, they were gentle and easy to train. It was common to see small children riding on their backs as they pulled wagons or powered irrigation pumps.

I never found water buffaloes out by themselves; they were always being watched or protected by their owners, whose wealth was often determined by how many they owned.

One of my tank commanders had painted a miniature water buffalo on the turret, much like fighter pilots in World War II would paint swastikas or iron crosses on their planes to depict the number of enemy planes they had shot down.

This kill happened when our executive officer was serving as troop commander. The troop arrived late in Phu Loi one evening and the XO was bringing up the rear with the maintenance section and three nonfunctioning vehicles. He was about thirty minutes behind the main column. As the platoons entered the squadron area and began shutting down, topping off their fuel tanks, and cleaning weapons, a frantic call came in over the radio announcing that the

XO's little group of five vehicles had been ambushed about eight miles from base. As one of the few still monitoring my radios, I immediately let the XO know that I'd received his message and that we were on the way.

I yelled at my platoon to mount up and quickly explained the situation to my vehicle commanders. I led the way as we moved through the compound at top speed, mud flying from our tracks; my column was spread out more than usual, and 2d and 3d Platoons were slow to round up their troopers to follow.

In similar situations, as soon as reinforcements arrived, the enemy would break contact and disappear. Furthermore, because we were so close to base I figured all we needed to do was show up and the battle would be over, so speed was very important.

Along with calling the troop for help, the XO had also contacted squadron headquarters, and soon we had the squadron commander overhead in a helicopter directing our movement. He came down on my platoon frequency and told me to stop the column, wait for all my vehicles to catch up, and put my two tanks up front. It took about five minutes, but we were soon in textbook formation and back on the march to rescue the XO and his people.

As we entered a small village a large water buffalo wandered into the path of the lead tank and, although the driver tried to avoid him, the right track struck the animal and knocked it down. The water buffalo fell forward, spun around on the muddy ground, and then slid back out in the roadway, where the second tank ran over its neck and head. My vehicle also ran over it before we had time to react. I radioed the remainder of the platoon to go around the carcass.

As we approached the XO's column we learned that two of his vehicles had been hit by RPGs. One track was still burning and three men had been slightly wounded. Seconds before we arrived they were still receiving enemy fire. The XO was glad to see us, and my medic immediately began treating the wounded. In the fading daylight my men hooked the disabled vehicles to my second and rear tank, and then we began the slow march back. The squadron commander had already ordered the 2d and 3d Platoons to turn around and return to base.

As we approached the small village on our return, we saw a mob of people gathered in the street around the dead water buffalo. The crowd blocked the narrow street and it looked like we might have trouble getting through. They clearly were not happy.

When the column stopped, I could see a wrinkled old man kneeling over the dead animal. His face was wet with tears and his hands were trembling. I didn't really know what to expect, so I took three men armed with M16s forward with me to clear the road. As I approached the crowd, I could see they were not threatening or hostile, just grieving for the dead animal. Seeing this, I told one of the soldiers to get an empty sandbag and take up a collection from the platoon. After a few minutes the soldier returned with the bag almost full of C-ration cans, cigarettes, Vietnamese piastres, and our own military payment certificates. I personally put twenty-two dollars in the kitty.

Carrying the bag of conscience money, I approached the old man, who was still kneeling over his treasured animal in the headlights of the lead tank. Someone nearby got his attention and helped him stand up. At the same time my attention was drawn to the large quantity of dark red blood that had run out on the road.

The old man, still weeping, put his hands together and bowed deeply. I stepped forward and handed the bag to him. He took it and then smiled weakly and bowed again. At this point, my riflemen and I each grabbed one of the dead animal's hooves and dragged it out of the roadway as the villagers quietly looked on. That done, we climbed back on our vehicles and the column once again began to move. As my command vehicle passed by the crowd, the adults stood silently, most still looking at the dead animal. However, the children, as always, gave us big smiles and waved.

The U.S. Army provided very little information about the Vietnamese armed forces. What little information I had was gained firsthand, and this lack of information almost cost innocent lives.

About two months after I arrived in country my platoon was escorting truck convoys about twenty miles north of Saigon on Highway 13. As we moved along the dusty road at the same speed as the heavily loaded trucks, one of my vehicles radioed me that there was a group of Vietcong no more than a hundred yards away, marching along the tree line in plain view. I asked why he thought they were Vietcong and his response was, "They're all dressed in black pajamas, they're wearing conical straw hats, and each of them is armed." It sure sounded like they were the enemy.

Finally, I was able to see them clearly. They appeared just as he had described them. I was sure they must be Vietcong marching in the open. I deployed my scout teams, one in front and one behind, and surrounded the enemy troops. I accompanied the second scout team and told them to hold their fire as we raced over the dry rice paddies and blocked the little group of about twelve men armed with old M1 rifles and carbines. I expected them to run or shoot at us, but they did neither. The Vietnamese simply ignored us and continued on their way, walking right through our little circle of vehicles.

I called headquarters to ask if there were any friendly forces operating in the area. I was told there were none and that I should go ahead and take them under fire.

The enemy soldiers were walking in a file along the wood line with my five armored vehicles no more than thirty yards away moving in column over the dry rice paddies, shadowing them.

I hesitated to open fire on these men, who showed no fear of us and appeared to be older. Some were even limping.

Our armored vehicles followed along with guns trained on them. Then the enemy soldiers began to move into the brush. My immediate reaction was to order my men to open fire before they could escape. However, despite repeated requests from my vehicle commanders for permission to fire, I allowed the enemy to escape.

This episode bothered me for several days. I was unable to explain to the CO why I'd let the enemy escape. Then one day, as I was reading the *Pacific Stars and Stripes,* I came across an article about a new village defense force controlled by the village chief and dressed in the local garb, black pajamas. The article explained that the men were armed with old U.S. Army surplus weapons and were called Civilian Irregular Defense Groups (CIDG). Their mission was to provide local defense. I realized that we had come very close to wiping out one of those CIDG groups.

• • •

On a routine road-clearing operation in May of 1967, one of my vehicles was destroyed by a command-detonated mine that our minesweeping teams had missed. Mine detectors would only detect metallic mines, and this one consisted of an explosive charge placed in a wooden box. The blasting cap was made of metal, but it was too small to be picked up by the detector.

The mine blew off the vehicle's track and damaged two road wheels but did not injure the crew.

The unusual thing about this mine was that it had been placed in the road directly in front of a brick Vietnamese home. As soon as the mine exploded, about twenty villagers who had gathered behind the house emerged and went on their way. The TC of the damaged vehicle was very upset that none of the Vietnamese tried to warn him about the mine. He concluded they were all Vietcong or at least VC sympathizers.

After inspecting the damage and calling for a recovery vehicle, I moved on down the road behind the minesweeping team. A few minutes later, the platoon leader behind me called and reported that when he passed my disabled vehicle, it looked like my sergeant had gone on a rampage and was tearing up the nearby brick house.

I turned my command track around and moved back to the disabled ACAV. When I arrived I could see the sergeant and his crew throwing furniture out of the windows of the house. We pulled up out front and I entered the house and ordered the sergeant to stop. I then tried to convince him that the owners, an elderly Vietnamese couple huddled in one corner of the house and obviously frightened, were not responsible for the mine. I explained that if they'd tried to warn him about it, they probably would have been killed by whomever put it there.

The sergeant didn't want to hear it, so I ordered him and his crew to gather up everything they'd thrown out of the house and put it back exactly as they'd found it. This was done under protest. As I waited to make sure it was done, I found a chair and deer antlers in the sergeant's vehicle. I got his attention and made sure that they were also put back.

Finally, when I was sure everything was in place, I reentered the house to look around. The old couple saw me and came over. They pressed their hands together and bowed. Then they broke out in big smiles as the old man handed me a small bunch of grapes.

The maintenance vehicle arrived and the sergeant in charge of the maintenance team assured me the vehicle could be repaired and running within an hour. I warned my sergeant to stay out of the house and told him to rejoin us as soon as his track was operational.

That night at our vehicle commander's meeting I mentioned the looting incident and reminded them all that the Manual for Courts-Martial specifically prohibited that sort of thing.

Most of the people in the villages were uneducated, and efforts by the government to communicate with them were normally accomplished through what were called cultural drama teams. These teams were groups of Vietnamese actors who normally visited remote villages in the company of Vietnamese soldiers who surrounded the village to ensure that the enemy did not interfere. The villagers would all be assembled and the head of the cultural drama team would make a short, progovernment speech and then introduce the actors.

The actors' job was to perform a play depicting the Vietcong as the bad guys and the government as the good guys. This was all presented in the context of a historical drama with which most of the villagers were familiar. Two or three musicians usually accompanied the production.

The cultural drama team visits were popular with both children and adults and won many converts to the government's cause.

Many Vietnamese line officers were trained in the United States and knew a bit about our country and its government. They also spoke at least a little English.

On one occasion, while we were helping to clean up after a mine destroyed a crowded civilian bus, I picked up some propaganda leaflets that had been dropped by the enemy. The leaflets were directed toward the Vietnamese people and blamed the United States for bringing misery and suffering to their country. The leaflets proclaimed that the Vietcong were trying to restore peace and security to the land and rid the country of the American imperialists and their Saigon lackeys.

Returning to the front of the bus, I saw a young Vietnamese lieutenant standing nearby with a handful of the leaflets, reading them. I went over, reached out my hand, and said, "Let me have those. I need them for evidence."

"I'm not finished with them," said the lieutenant, jerking his hand away. As I stood there waiting, he deliberately took his time. Finally he said, "Have you ever been to Georgia?"

"Yes," I replied, "I went to airborne school there."

"I attended the infantry school at Fort Benning," he responded.

"Did you like America?" I asked.

"Oh, yes! America is a great country," he said with a smile.

After this brief exchange he handed me all the leaflets but one, saying, "I need one for my report."

With the arrival of other Vietnamese soldiers, I loaded up my men and allowed the lieutenant and his soldiers to finish the cleanup operation.

After my encounter with the Vietnamese lieutenant I gave the Vietnamese army credit for being better trained and professionally led than I had previously thought. It obviously had some leaders who had received some quality training.

Pilots in the Vietnamese air force were all trained in the United States and spent a minimum of three years there. These airmen, particularly the helicopter pilots, were great showmen who often wore brightly colored helmets and silk scarves. They were heroes to the local people. Occasionally they gave villagers rides in their aircraft to generate goodwill.

On at least one occasion, the planes that responded to our request for tactical air support were propeller-driven World War II–era fighter-bombers piloted by hard-charging Vietnamese officers. Because of their excellent training and the planes' slow speed, they were able to put all of their bombs on the target.

An incident involving Vietnamese civilians on Highway 13 near An Loc has caused me some concern over the years. After setting up a night defensive position near the highway we set out on the road with a minesweeping team in front clearing the road in the direction of An Loc.

As the minesweeping team was busy clearing the road, I looked up and, about a mile away, saw a Lambretta headed toward us. As I watched the vehicle close in on us I saw a bright orange flash and then heard a loud *BOOM!* The Lambretta had hit a mine. My first reaction was to forget sweeping the road and rush to help the injured passengers. However, I controlled the urge and had the minesweeping team continue its efforts. In about five minutes we reached the destroyed vehicle. It had hit an antitank mine, turning it into an unrecognizable, twisted mass of junk. Pieces of bodies were scattered over a fifty-foot radius around the mine crater; it was obvious there were no survivors. The gory sight was sickening and the peculiar smell of death settled over the area. We were able to determine from the visible body parts of men, women, and children that there had been twelve people riding in the vehicle.

I had just radioed Sergeant Cowhig to organize a burial detail when my attention was drawn to another civilian vehicle traveling at a high rate of speed over the same stretch of uncleared road. Not knowing what to expect, I drew my pistol and prepared to jump into a nearby ditch. As the vehicle drew closer I could see it was an old, gray Land Rover with just one man inside. The vehicle stopped about ten yards short of the crater and a large, bearded man wearing a flowing tan robe, leather sandals, and a silver cross around his neck got out.

Putting my pistol back in its holster, I approached him. The man, who had a heavy French accent, introduced himself as Father Navarre and explained that the unfortunate souls in the Lambretta were his people.

I gripped his hand, introduced myself, and told him what we were doing on the road. The priest, with tears in his eyes, walked around the area making the sign of the cross and mumbled the same prayer over and over. We reverently stood back and gave him some room. I had heard of these courageous priests. They had been in Vietnam since the colonial period and would most likely remain there for the rest of their days, ministering to their flocks.

After a few minutes, I approached the priest and informed him we had planned to bury the victims there next to the road. I asked him if he thought that was appropriate. He held up his hand and shook his head. He then pointed to a poncho rolled up on the side of my vehicle and said that if we would help gather the body parts into several of our ponchos he would see that the remains were given to the victims' families.

We spread six ponchos out on the road and began the grisly task of picking up heads, arms, legs, torsos, and other bits of human flesh. Finally, when the priest was satisfied, we folded up the ponchos and placed them in the back of his Land Rover. As the priest turned the Land Rover around and slowly headed back to An Loc, we continued with our mission. Although two vehicles had already traveled over the road, I was still concerned about the possible presence of command-detonated mines.

Later, our troop interpreter told us the priest had been a fighter pilot in World War II and had spent time in a German prisoner-of-war camp. After the war he had gone to a Catholic seminary. He had been in Vietnam since the late 1940s and the Vietcong didn't seem to bother him.

Enemy Base Camp

History teaches that wars begin when governments believe the price of aggression is cheap.

—Ronald W. Reagan

The morning dawned crisp and clear, like a spring morning in Utah—clean air with just a little bit of a chill. Our mission that day was to clear and outpost an abandoned section of asphalt road near the Minh Thanh rubber plantation a short distance from Highway 13. This plantation was the source of many rumors as our helicopter pilots often reported sighting beautiful young French girls sunbathing around a swimming pool outside the sprawling plantation house. However, the reports were always second- or thirdhand, and thus difficult to verify.

Invariably, the stories went something like this: Helicopters out on a tactical mission, normally with young warrant officers at the controls, would detour from their flight plan to make a pass over the house and see two or three young Caucasian girls wearing bikinis sunbathing around the pool. The girls would smile and wave enthusiastically as the pilots circled the house, but there was no place to land. It was reported that at times the air was so thick with helicopters that an air traffic controller was needed to keep them apart.

This story provided material for many daydreams and much wishful thinking. If true, of course, the enemy was receiving an advantage by allowing the plantation to operate and the French family to remain. I never saw any workers gathering raw rubber, but there was evidence that someone was etching the trees and gathering the rubber on a regular basis in spite of the war.

An additional part of our mission was to provide local security to two Rome plows that would be improving the road. These bulldozers had a standard front blade for pushing trees and brush back from the road so the enemy could not get in close enough to ambush a supply column. The bulldozers also had a fishhook-like device attached at the rear that penetrated the ground about ten to twelve inches, cutting any electrical wires the Vietcong might have connected to explosives buried in the road. The VC would allow regular traffic to pass freely by. Then, when a lucrative target, such as a truck loaded with soldiers or a bus packed full of civilians, came along, the enemy, from a hiding place a hundred yards or so off the road, would detonate the mine and destroy the target.

On this particular morning, my platoon cleared the road without incident. I then placed vehicles on either side of the road about a hundred yards apart. When the Rome plows arrived and began their work, I moved up the road in my command track to visit with the troop commander. During my brief visit Captain Yarborough asked about the M14 rifle that I still carried in my vehicle. While demonstrating the accuracy of the weapon by shooting at some birds in a distant tree, I heard heavy gunfire and several large explosions coming from the direction of my platoon.

While attempting to contact my platoon without success, I discovered a radio was stuck in the transmit position, jamming the platoon radio net. I assured the CO that I would call him with a situation report as soon as possible, loaded up my crew, and raced at top speed back to the platoon's outpost area. Off in the distance I could see armored vehicles on both sides of the road firing into the jungle. Unable to sort out what was happening I swung my track in beside the closest platoon vehicle and asked the TC what was going on. He replied that one of our vehicles farther up the road had been ambushed.

Looking ahead through the thick, black, billowing smoke, we could see the crew of the destroyed vehicle on the ground, returning fire from behind several trees that had been knocked down by the Rome plows. The burning vehicle was only about two hundred yards from my position, so I decided to take my medic and radio operator on foot to investigate the situation. The enemy fired on us as we dodged and leaped from one log or fallen tree to another. Upon reaching the crew of the disabled vehicle I learned that two RPGs had hit the rear of their track, one setting the fuel tank on fire and the other ripping through the hull into the crew compartment.

The TC, Staff Sergeant Miller, and a machine gunner were badly wounded. After determining the exact location of the enemy fire, I called for artillery and a medevac for the two wounded soldiers. Soon, accurate artillery fire was blasting the target area and I moved one of the nearby tanks across the road to fire directly into the enemy positions. About this time the artillery forward observer called and informed me he had two jet fighter-bombers on station ready to drop their ordnance. He instructed me to move my vehicles back at least a hundred yards farther from where the artillery was landing.

Everything was clear of the target area except the tank I had moved across the road. Its radios were still malfunctioning. I looked up and saw the two jets circling, getting into position for their bombing runs. Jumping out of the protective cover of some tree stumps, I ran across the clearing to the exposed tank, which was firing its main gun off to one side. I climbed onto the tank's front slope, crawled up to the driver's hatch, got the driver's attention, and shouted at him to start moving right now!

With me hanging onto the tank's headlight guards, we bounced and leaped over the rough terrain back to the road. Within seconds, the two jets began their steep bombing runs, firing their cannon and dropping napalm as they approached the target. We could feel the heat as the flaming jellied gasoline spread through the jungle to our front, silencing the enemy guns. I began waving frantically, signaling the other vehicles to cease firing. Next, I ordered my crew to move up the line without me and notify all of the TCs to switch their radios to our alternate frequency so communications could be reestablished.

After looking over what remained of the burned-out track, my radio operator, Private Borgos, ran over and told me that the medevac chopper was in-bound and wanted us to pop smoke to mark our location. We located a smoke grenade on the tank and I tossed it out onto the road. Within seconds, we were loading the two wounded men on board. As I helped lift Sergeant Miller into the chopper and assure him that he was going to be all right, he told me that while he and his crew were lying there wounded and pinned down behind the tree stumps, he knew I would eventually come and get them out.

I watched as the helicopter disappeared from sight and then ordered what was left of the crew of the disabled vehicle to gather up anything that might be of use to the enemy. I then distributed them among the shorthanded crews. Finally, I repositioned the platoon along the road and we continued to provide security for the Rome plows. By then it was almost lunchtime.

It was close to 2 P.M. when the plows completed their work and began their snaillike journey back along the road to the nearby artillery fire support base. The plan was for them to return with enough daylight left so they could spend two to three hours expanding the base perimeter.

The mission outlined by our CO earlier in the day was that when the plows had completed their work, each platoon would form into column and make a final sweep along the north side of the road. We were to head out about a kilometer to the north, then go west for another two kilometers, then return to the road. I enjoyed these off-road expeditions because we usually found trails, streams, and, occasionally, buildings not shown on the map.

We made our way off the main road in a close column with the tanks leading. The ground was solid and thickly covered with small trees ranging from one to three inches in diameter. Occasionally we encountered a large teak or mahogany tree. We made good progress through the heavy brush as the lead tanks smashed down the small trees, making it a relatively smooth ride for the ACAVs.

As we approached a narrow stream depicted on the map, I halted the column and organized a five-man patrol to investigate. After going only a short distance through the thick brush we came upon a heavily used footpath leading directly to the stream. With the tanks still in sight, we cautiously followed it. I led the way with an M16 in hand and Private Borgos directly behind me with the PRC-10 radio. The footpath ended at the stream, and I knelt down at the edge of the water to take a closer look at the area. It had not rained all day, but the stream bank was wet, as if water had been dipped out to fill large containers. I could also see footprints and a few rice kernels scattered along the bottom of the stream, indicating that cooking pots may have been washed here.

Realizing that the enemy was probably close by, I turned the patrol around and headed back to the safety of the platoon.

After reporting our findings to Captain Yarborough, I ordered the platoon to continue northward another two hundred yards. As the lead tank made the turn onto the western leg of our sweep, some of the broken and twisted trees became caught in its sprocket and the track slid off, immobilizing the vehicle. It couldn't have happened at a worse place, and the driver compounded the problem jockeying the tank bank and forth in an effort to work the track back onto the sprocket.

I ordered the TC to stop in place and then I dismounted and moved forward. Assisted by the tank commander, I checked the damaged track. It was about six inches off the sprocket and I figured we might be able to jump it back on by having the driver execute a neutral steer, which would cause the tracks to move in opposite directions.

With the tank commander in front relaying my instructions to the driver, we jumped the track one way and then the other a number of times. It quickly became apparent that this was not going to work. The only solution was for us to break the track, separating it at a single point and then laying the track over the sprocket and reconnecting it. If everything went right, the procedure would take about an hour.

I gathered the platoon's vehicles around, forming a makeshift circle of men and vehicles to provide security for the tank crewmen as they worked on the track. I instructed each TC to leave one man behind the .50-caliber machine gun on his vehicle and to send out a dismounted patrol approximately fifty yards to the front but within sight of the rest of the platoon. I didn't want the enemy moving in and sniping at us.

As the patrols were going out, I moved over to assist the tank crew and monitor the radio.

Within five minutes one of the patrols returned and reported finding another trail nearby with fresh footprints on it. I immediately called in four of the patrols and organized a larger fourteen-man patrol armed with M16s and an M60 machine gun for extra firepower. I told Sergeant Cowhig that, in the event of trouble, he was to bring at least one tank and two ACAVs to the rescue.

We moved out, picking our way through the tall grass and heavy brush. I was third in line with Private Borgos and his radio directly behind me. I had brought two sergeants along and organized the patrol into two teams of six men.

My intent was to stay off the trail so as to avoid mines and booby traps, and we made our way parallel to it, one team moving ahead covered by the other in a leapfrogging fashion. This may sound good, but the noise we were making in the thick brush could have been heard a mile away. After covering a little over a hundred yards I ordered the patrol to halt. I moved over onto the trail to take a look around. I could see that the trail opened into a clearing maybe thirty yards ahead.

We crouched down close to the earth and moved quietly forward. After allowing the point man to enter the clearing, I whispered for him to move an inch at a time so as not to trip anything. He was soon back, reporting that it appeared to be an abandoned enemy base camp and that he had checked the perimeter of the clearing and it looked safe to move forward.

I radioed Sergeant Cowhig about the enemy camp and told him as soon as the damaged track was back together to bring the entire platoon to my location. He indicated they were just about finished and could be moving in a few minutes. Then he asked where we were. Rather than try to explain, I sent a sergeant and two men back to serve as guides. I then ordered the rest of the patrol into the clearing and started putting men around the edges for security.

The clearing was sheltered from aerial observation by the branches of four large mahogany trees, and heavy brush grew up all around. As Private Borgos, Sergeant Green, and I moved around the area, we were able to get some idea of its size. Four footpaths led into the thirty-yard-wide clearing. One area had been set aside for cooking. A pile of charcoal was scattered among a group of large stones near which were cooking pots and an ancient single-barreled shotgun. Another area appeared to be a classroom, with a small blackboard, chalk, and logs set up in rows. A wire tied between two trees had a bandana draped over one end. I guessed that it had been used for drying clothes. Five yards outside the clearing was a series of well-hidden bunkers, complete with overhead cover. Farther out from the clearing I found triangular shaped holes that were about four feet on a side and neatly cut into the ground to a depth of approximately ten feet.

Sergeant Cowhig arrived with the platoon's vehicles within minutes of this last discovery.

I called the troop commander and made a full report. The CO was extremely excited and wanted to know exactly where the enemy camp was and what size unit I thought had occupied it. My guess, based solely on the size of the cooking pots and the classroom setup, was that it must be at least a regimental-sized base camp (an enemy regiment consisted of one thousand to fifteen hundred men). The CO accepted that estimate and passed it along to higher headquarters. Later, in an official report and a newspaper article, our discovery was described as a regimental base camp.

The CO ordered me to set up local security and continue to search the immediate area.

I again organized four three-man patrols and, after providing very detailed instructions about trip wires and booby traps, sent them out with instructions to stay within sight of the clearing. Soon, two of the patrols reported finding clearings that were similar to the first one, complete with cooking areas and classrooms. While searching the bunkers we found about fifty rounds of rifle ammunition and an opening leading into a large tunnel.

While all this was going on, I received a call saying that the CO was en route to my location with the Rome plows to cut a path in from the main road. I reorganized my vehicles into a better defensive position, moving the platoon off to one side of the original clearing and into a tight circle about twenty yards in diameter with all vehicles pointing outward.

While waiting for the CO, a helicopter appeared overhead and circled the area. The CO called to inform me that the squadron commander wanted to land and take a look around. He instructed me to throw a violet smoke grenade to mark the spot where I wanted him to set down. I had my vehicles pull forward another ten yards while the helicopter hovered above the circle formed by our vehicles. However, the chopper was unable to land because of the mangled trees and uneven surface. So, with the helicopter hovering a couple of feet off the ground, the squadron commander and four other men jumped out. As soon as they were clear of the chopper I motioned for the colonel to come in my direction and the helicopter departed.

After returning my salute, the colonel explained that he had brought two tunnel rats and a cameraman to search the tunnel complex and instructed me to lead the way. Private Borgos remained glued to me with the radio as I took the colonel on a tour of the base camp and told him how we'd found it by following the trail leading from the stream. He was particularly interested in the triangular ventilation shafts, and told me this usually indicated a large tunnel complex.

The tunnel rats wasted little time entering the tunnel we had found inside the large bunker. They had lights like the kind surgeons wear strapped to their heads and were armed with .38-caliber revolvers fitted with silencers. They were back on the surface within fifteen minutes, one dragging a case of Chicom hand grenades, and the other a bag of rice.

I was showing the colonel the ventilation shafts when, seeing the tunnel rats emerge, he hurried over to hear their report. The two men described going into a narrow passageway and then down into a large eight-by-ten-foot room that appeared to be a sleeping or hospital area. They then followed a larger passageway that led to a series of storage rooms. One room contained hundreds of grenades and mortar rounds, and another was stacked from floor to ceiling with bags of rice. They indicated the tunnel was quite extensive in size and suggested we look for other entrances, perhaps as far away as a hundred yards.

The squadron commander told me to form a detail and see how much of the rice and weapons we could bring to the surface. He also told me to extend my patrols out another hundred yards and see what we could find.

Within minutes my men had formed a human chain and begun passing rice, weapons, and ammunition up out of the underground bunker. Soon they had sizable stacks of materiel piled up in the clearing.

Leaving the squadron commander to supervise the stacking of captured weapons, ammunition, and other supplies, Private Borgos and I moved out to see how the patrols were doing. One sergeant had located another large bunker and was in the process of searching it for a second tunnel entrance when I arrived. While I was talking to him, I heard another helicopter circling and received a call from Sergeant Cowhig saying that the squadron commander wanted me back at my vehicle ASAP.

Returning to the platoon, I could hear the roar of the Rome plows as they broke through the trees and brush. The squadron commander met me back at my track and told me the division commander would be landing in about five minutes and that I should stand by to escort him through the base camp.

While we were waiting, I had my tanks flatten out the center of the perimeter so the general's helicopter could land. While his chopper was making its final approach, the squadron commander spotted the Rome plows entering the area and yelled, "Walker, get over there and stop those bastards before they plow up your base camp!"

As I flagged down the Rome plows and reported to my CO, who was directly behind them, the general landed and the squadron commander took him in tow. I stayed there with Captain Yarborough and brought him up-to-date on what we had found. Since daylight was fading fast, I recommended that we expand our perimeter and remain in the area overnight in order to protect the captured materiel and to finish cleaning out the tunnels.

I led him down the original trail to where Major General Dupuy and the squadron commander were standing. The tunnel rats were briefing the general, who was listening intently and didn't look up when we joined their group. They were describing the size of the complex, the types of supplies and equipment found. They added that they had also found an underground radio room. The general asked about other entrances to the complex and the men said they had found only two more, but that there was still a main tunnel that they hadn't fully explored.

The general finally acknowledged our presence and said to me, "You've really stumbled onto something here."

"Yes, Sir," I replied. "The men tell me it might take a couple of days to get all the rice out of there."

Captain Yarborough spoke up and said he wanted to keep at least one platoon in the area overnight to secure the area and finish unloading the tunnels the next day. The squadron commander agreed, and we fell in behind the general as he walked over to the center of the large clearing. Surveying the large pile of rice and mortar rounds, the general observed, "We're going to need a Chinook to get this stuff out of here tomorrow." The general exchanged a few more remarks with the squadron commander and then, motioning to his aide to get the helicopter started, departed the area.

After the general left, the squadron commander explained to the CO and me what he wanted in the way of security. He said that the tunnel rats would be attached to the troop for the next two days and he instructed them to make a map of the complex and document the find with photographs. He was very concerned about the enemy infiltrating back into the area after dark, and he made eye contact with the CO as he said, "Bill, I think you ought to stay here with Lieutenant Walker tonight. He might need a few extra guns."

The colonel's chopper arrived about fifteen minutes later to transport him back to the nearby fire support base.

I could tell the CO had not intended to stay the night by the way he began asking about my plan to defend the perimeter. Since the plows were going to remain with us, I suggested we use them to expand our little perimeter, giving us some standoff room from the thick brush. He agreed, and I sent Sergeant Cowhig over to get them moving and keep them moving until it was too dark to operate.

I mentioned that, with all the tunnels and ventilation shafts leading into the area, we probably should not include the enemy bunkers inside our perimeter. I added that I would place an ambush patrol at the entrance to the main tunnel complex. The CO agreed and said I could use four of his six vehicles to beef up the perimeter. He added that he would keep his command and control vehicles in the center. When I asked about the bulldozers, he told me to use the operators for guard duty and park their equipment in the center next to his vehicle. Finally, he said the tunnel rats would stay with him.

I called in the Rome plows at dusk and took stock of the situation. Our little perimeter had grown to about a hundred yards in diameter, with the vehicles located about twenty-five yards from the thick brush. I ordered all concertina wire out and instructed each crew to put out three trip flares for early warning.

After a quick meal of hot C rations in the fading light, the CO and I led Sergeant Moore's ambush patrol through the wire and out to the enemy base camp. We halted about fifty yards from our closest vehicle and rigged a trip flare in the bunker to warn of the enemy's return and made sure the patrol was set up in a tight position for all-around defense.

On our way back to the perimeter, the CO and I paused briefly next to the large mound of rice that had been removed from the tunnel complex. There appeared to be well over a ton of it. Nearby the men had also stacked numerous boxes of grenades and mortar rounds.

The little area under the mahogany trees had grown pleasantly cool and peaceful as the sun set and, with a light breeze blowing in the trees; it reminded me of a small park.

After returning inside the wire, the CO and I walked the perimeter, talking to the men on their vehicles and checking security. The soldiers appeared upbeat and enthusiastic about our day's work. Pride of discovery came through as they talked about finding such a large trove of enemy materiel. It was good to see everyone in an upbeat mood again after our recent heavy losses.

As darkness closed in around us, there was almost a total blackout and, except for the hiss of radios, absolute silence.

I was awakened at about 2:30 A.M. by my driver, Specialist Weaver, who was on guard duty. "The ambush patrol says a flare went off to their front," he whispered.

Jumping up to look, I radioed the ambush patrol for a report. Sergeant Moore explained in a hushed voice that the patrol had first heard digging or clanking sounds, then the trip flare went off, and it was still burning. I told Sergeant Moore to wait until the flare burned out and then throw a grenade into the bunker. He complied and, after the explosion, there was no further activity. I next told Sergeant Moore to pull his patrol back closer to the perimeter wire and out of grenade range of the bunker.

I contacted the rest of the platoon and we went on 100 percent alert for the next hour. The remainder of the night passed uneventfully.

The next morning, after breakfast, the Rome plows continued their work. However, this time I put a rifleman aboard each of them to act as a lookout for tunnels and bunkers. The tunnel rats returned to the tunnel to make sure it was clear and to finish mapping it.

I was standing near the entrance when one of the tunnel rats stuck his head out and said, "Sir, could you come over here for a minute?"

I had no desire to enter the tunnel. I was afraid it might cave in and that I would suffocate. Nevertheless, when the young soldier motioned for me to follow, I stuck my head in and crawled through the tiny opening. After crawling about ten feet on my hands and knees, my back scraping the ceiling, we reached a small, roughly eight-by-ten-foot room. Inside, the other tunnel rat was holding a canvas bag as he knelt there, pointing to some footprints in the loose dirt. He said it appeared that three enemy soldiers had returned during the night, tripped our flare and, in their haste to get out, had left behind the canvas bag.

After speculating on what they might have been doing there, I stayed and watched the tunnel rats work as they carefully checked every inch of the tunnel, searching carefully for booby traps and tripwires the enemy might have left behind. After what seemed like an eternity, I crawled back outside and into the fresh air. With the tunnel again clear, I got together another detail to help bring out the remaining rice and ammunition.

Around noon, just as the tunnel rats were completing their rough sketch map of the complex, we brought up the last of the rice. I had asked Sergeant Cowhig to put together three large demolition charges to blow up the complex and he, along with Sergeant Denison, set about placing the explosives inside the main passageways close to each of the three entrances.

Our morning resupply helicopter had brought a hot breakfast and two cargo nets, plus a photographer from division PIO. We loaded everything we'd brought out of the tunnel into nets and sat around waiting for the arrival of the Chinook helicopter to wrap up the operation. At the last minute, the CO received a call from division G3 informing him that they would be picking up only the rice and that we should destroy the weapons and ammo.

Throughout the morning I had observed several of the men having their pictures taken next to the large pile of captured materiel. Some had even asked if they could take my picture or stand next to me while Private Borgos took our picture with the captured weapons and supplies in the background. The division photographer was also helpful in this effort.

The Chinook finally arrived and we hooked the cargo net up to it. Then, with its big, dual rotors straining and its downdraft creating a miniature tornado, it lifted the load of rice out of the clearing, over the trees, and back to Dian, where it would be used in a division-level pacification effort.

Next, with one of my tanks attached for extra security, the CO departed with his six vehicles and headed back to the artillery fire support base.

With all of the straphangers gone, I ordered the platoon to pull back a ways and then we poured three .50-caliber ammo cans full of gasoline over the pile of captured enemy weapons and ammunition, which was minus twenty-two Chinese SKS assault rifles that the CO had carted off.

I instructed Sergeant Housh to wait until everyone was safely hidden behind something solid, before torching the cache. When we were set, he ran forward and threw a lighted sandbag onto the mound of weapons and ammo piled in a ditch, then sprinted back to where we were taking cover. The gasoline ignited with a powerful *swoosh* and, with much loud popping and cracking, the ammunition began to explode.

The final tally of captured materiel was thirty pounds of salt, fifty-one hundred pounds of rice, 624 Chicom hand grenades, 114 82mm mortar rounds, twelve thousand rounds of rifle ammunition, two large claymore-like antipersonnel mines, two rolls of electrical wire, thirteen RPGs, two ancient shotguns, and twenty-two Chicom SKS assault rifles.

After an hour of pyrotechnics, the fire began to die out and the bulldozers filled in the still-smoldering ditch.

I ordered the platoon to form up in a column facing in the direction of the main road, and then gave Sergeant Cowhig permission to destroy the tunnels. We soon heard three muffled explosions and felt the ground shake. The tunnels were no more.

We moved out with the Rome plows in the middle of our column, forcing us to limit our pace to their top speed of about seven miles per hour.

The return trip was long and uneventful. My men and I had enjoyed the two-day operation, and it was our hope that our efforts would put a small dent in the enemy's activities for a while.

The Elvis Presley Club

There are always three choices—war, surrender, and present policy.

—Henry Kissinger

By the halfway point of my tour, even with our constant operations and numerous battles with the enemy, it was difficult to say how much progress we were making in the war. It seemed that enemy contact and sightings were actually increasing as the huge American buildup continued.

It was the fourth day of a two-week operation in and around the Michelin rubber plantation, which was located near some of the roughest terrain in South Vietnam. Our mission that day was to report signs of enemy activity and to destroy any enemy supplies and equipment found in the sector.

The platoon was moving on line through rows of old rubber trees that had four-foot-high underbrush growing around their trunks. We were moving slowly, looking for signs of the enemy, when a TC on the far right announced on the radio that he had spotted a tiger about thirty yards to his vehicle's immediate front. I stopped the platoon and asked how big the tiger was and what it was doing. The response was that it looked like a large, black-and-orange-striped dog and that it appeared to be eating something. I next asked the vehicle commander if he could get a good shot at the animal, and he said he would try. We all watched as the sergeant stood on top of his vehicle, took careful aim, and fired. A couple of seconds later, the sergeant's RTO excitedly reported that the tiger appeared to have been hit and was moving toward the center of the platoon. I immediately ordered each vehicle to put a man on top, armed with an M16 set on semiautomatic. I then had the two end vehicles move forward about fifty yards before ordering the rest of the platoon to begin a slow advance. The tiger soon appeared, running through a small clearing about twenty yards out. Two of our marksmen fired and missed, and the tiger disappeared. We sighted it several more times that afternoon but were unable to bring it down.

Some months previously we had discovered the Vietcong also had an interest in tigers.

While operating in the more populated areas near the Saigon River, I had the platoon establish a night defensive perimeter near the river and set up an ambush patrol on a trail leading to a small village. With a curfew in effect, it was reasonable to assume that anyone out on the trail after 10 P.M. would be working for the enemy.

The man pulling guard heard movement on the trail at about 1 A.M. and alerted the rest of the men in the ambush patrol. As the enemy walked into the kill zone, one of the VC tripped a flare and our patrol opened fire with all weapons, including a claymore mine. Three Vietcong were killed outright; their bodies were found on the trail the next morning, along with two blood trails leading away from the ambush site.

While examining the bodies, I found a twelve-inch square of what appeared to be tiger skin tied to one of the enemy's legs. I removed the piece of hide and carried it with me as I entered the village.

Normally, village dogs would crowd around and bark when strangers entered their village. However, this time the dogs ran in the opposite direction and didn't bark as I approached. Finding a dog sleeping between two huts, I walked toward it waving the skin. Startled from its sleep and seeing the tiger skin, it shot under the nearest building. I tried the tiger skin on two other dogs and got the same reaction. The Vietcong obviously had learned that wearing a piece of tiger skin kept the dogs quiet as they entered and departed from villages at night. Perhaps that was another reason why there were so few tigers left in the area.

The tiger sighting was the topic of conversation for several days, and many of us even began to visualize a tiger-skin rug on the family room floor back home.

In western Vietnam, particularly along the Cambodian border, many areas have never been settled or fully developed. These areas have not changed for hundreds of years and they contain some very rare and exotic animals. Monkeys were common, as were deer and armadillos. Tigers and black bears were present but considered rare, and we sighted only one of each during all of our operations in that region.

We were moving slowly through a village on one of my first combat operations when I noticed small monkeys tied to poles or stakes in front of some of the huts. My first reaction was that the cute little animals were children's pets. Later, I learned the Vietnamese consider them a fine delicacy and that, since they didn't have refrigerators, they kept the monkeys alive until they were ready to eat them. After this revelation, I noticed a few monkeys for sale in one of the local village markets right there next to the live chickens. I had eaten monkey while attending the Jungle Warfare School in Panama and found it pretty tasty, especially after it had been smoked for several hours.

Later in the afternoon of the day we sighted the tiger I received an urgent call from troop headquarters advising me that our resupply helicopter had crashed nearby. I was ordered to move my platoon along a particular compass heading until we found the helicopter, secure the crash site, and be prepared to evacuate any casualties.

This was not a complicated assignment as the enemy was not involved and the aircraft had gone down due to engine failure. The helicopter was our lifeline on all operations. We depended on it to maintain a constant flow of supplies, food, and mail to the men in the field. Our troop was authorized one helicopter delivery per day to bring out supplies and repair parts. Our executive officer, cooks, and supply personnel, all of whom were stationed in the rear, would collect the requested items when we called them in and load them into the resupply chopper along with a hot evening meal. This system worked very well and we were always glad to see the helicopter arrive at the end of a long day.

The compass heading I had been given led us through row after row of rubber trees and waist-high underbrush. Finally, up ahead, we saw several broken trees and the tops knocked out of about a dozen more. There, under broken limbs and leaves, we could see the wreckage of the helicopter lying on its side. There was no sign of life.

I sent the scout sections out to set up a security perimeter and then dismounted and moved forward with two men to investigate. About twenty feet from the wrecked chopper we saw someone move on the ground next to it. A young enlisted soldier stood up and said, "Boy, are we glad to see you!" He was the door gunner, and he had set up his machine gun under tree limbs for local defense. There were four of them lying there close together a few feet from the wreckage. The pilot, a warrant officer, had leg injuries and couldn't walk. The copilot, also a warrant officer, had rib and chest injuries. The door gunner who had greeted us had a deep gash on his head, and the other door gunner, partially wrapped in a poncho, was dead. He had been crushed on impact.

My medic treated the injured as best he could while I radioed the CO a full report of the situation. He instructed me to search the air- craft for our shipment of supplies, food, and mail, as well as any- thing else of value such as weapons or ammunition and then move to our night defensive position. He said the aviation unit would come out the next day and recover anything still usable from the he- licopter. I didn't think they'd find much. The rotor blades had been destroyed, the tail section had broken off, and the entire front was smashed in. Perhaps the instruments and engine were salvageable, but I doubted it.

While the medic treated the wounded and supervised loading them and the body into the scout vehicles, Sergeant Cowhig and I took a detail of six men and searched the wreckage for our supplies. We found the insulated food containers, both upside down. We opened them expecting to find steaks with baked potatoes but were disappointed to discover the usual chili and rice, which was still ed- ible. We put the food and mail on my vehicle and the chopper's ma- chine guns and other items on Sergeant Cowhig's.

It was here, while poking around in the wreckage, that Sergeant Cowhig acquired an aviator's helmet, which he wore proudly for the rest of his tour. The aviator's helmet, with its huge adjustable sun visor, large earphones, and a more comfortable fit, was plush compared to our combat vehicle crewmen's helmets. It was white but he promised to paint it olive drab if I would allow him to keep it. I did, and he cut a dashing figure with that helmet—Flash Gordon on a tank.

With the wounded and dead securely inside our vehicles and darkness fast approaching, we made our way to where the rest of the troop was setting up for the night. Twenty minutes later we broke out of the rubber trees and into a clearing the size of a football field. The other platoons had already deployed their vehicles facing outward around the edge of the field, leaving a small section open for us. A medevac helicopter waited at the far end of the clearing to evacuate the injured aviators.

After loading the casualties into the helicopter, I took my track over to the CO's vehicle and unloaded the food and mail while Sergeant Cowhig maneuvered the platoon into their night fighting positions. When I had completed my report of our day's activities, the CO called the other platoon leaders and the first sergeant over to explain the next day's mission and give us our assignments. As the meeting ended, the CO went around the circle and asked for additional comments.

When it was the first sergeant's turn he cleared his throat and said, "Gentlemen, you need to make sure all of your men know the following: A group of whores has set up back here in one of the plantation buildings and they've been doing a terrific business. However, there's a problem. They've got a strain of gonorrhea that penicillin won't kill and if somebody catches it, they won't let 'em go home. They call the whorehouse 'The Elvis Presley Club.'"

We looked at each other and burst out laughing. The CO motioned for us to be quiet and added, "This is serious, Gentlemen. Make sure your men get the word. I don't want to hear of any of your men being over in that area tonight."

I returned to my platoon and briefed the vehicle commanders on the next day's mission, adding the warning about The Elvis Presley Club.

It was almost dark when we finished setting out our trip flares and putting up barbed wire. Later, as I was sending out the listening post, a messenger ran up. He said there were two lieutenants back at my track and that they wanted to talk with me. The other two platoon leaders, both young lieutenants, were there to invite me to pay a visit to The Elvis Presley Club with them, "just to make sure none of our soldiers have wandered over."

After much persuasion, I grabbed my M16 and a couple of hand grenades and followed them over to the other side of the perimeter. There I alerted two vehicles on the line that we were going out through the wire and would return in about thirty minutes.

A wide dirt path led from our area to a group of buildings about fifty yards away. As we approached the buildings we could see that one of them—an old, wooden garage with its doors closed—had a half-dozen or so small tables out front with small candles on them. Seated at the tables were Vietnamese women and some soldiers from our unit. The faint sound of American music was coming from inside the garage. A Vietnamese man, probably in his fifties, was serving cold beer to the men seated at the tables. The three of us stood in the shadows and watched for a few minutes. We wondered how a place like that could operate way out here in the middle of nowhere with a war going on.

The answer had to be that the enemy was getting some kind of a payoff. Perhaps they were getting part of the take from the girls. Maybe they were getting information gleaned from the GIs about unit strength, future operations, and the type of units involved. Or maybe it was as something as simple as the whores had a killer type of gonorrhea and the enemy thought that every GI who passed through the place would soon become a casualty, the same as if he'd been shot with a rifle. Whatever the arrangement, we knew that the enemy was somehow involved and receiving a payoff.

The women were wearing tight American skirts and they had puffed-up hair and wore thick makeup. Even from thirty feet away we could smell their cheap perfume. Women with old faces and few curves led the soldiers through a side door into the garage, where they plied their trade.

We watched for a few more minutes and then walked up to the group of tables and announced that the place was off-limits and that the men were to return to their units. The four GIs still sitting with girls at the tables got up and I immediately recognized Private Borgos. Pretending to be upset I said, "Jorge, you're not supposed to be here! Get back to the platoon!"

He grinned sheepishly and headed back down the darkened path toward the troop with the other three men. We decided to wait for a few minutes and see who else was inside.

We were standing there with about a dozen whores all around us talking in excited tones and the bartender offering us beer, when up out of the dark walked the first sergeant. He stared at us with a look of disbelief and said, "What are you sirs doing here?"

We answered his question with one of our own: "What are *you* doing here, First Sergeant?"

He said that the CO had been checking the perimeter and had discovered that all three of his platoon leaders were over at the whorehouse in violation of his orders and had angrily ordered him to "go over there and bring them back before they catch something."

We all laughed and then the first sergeant went into the garage and brought out two more of our soldiers. The whores yelled obscenities at us as we headed back to the perimeter with the two men in tow.

Once we were safely inside the perimeter we chased the two GIs back to their platoons and the four of us found the CO and reported to him on why we had ventured over to The Elvis Presley Club. It was, as we explained, to enforce the CO's order and to bring our soldiers back safely. The CO accepted our explanation. After some ribbing about our real motives, we chatted for a few minutes and then headed back to our platoons for an uneventful night's sleep.

That was the only night we spent near The Elvis Presley Club. The CO believed that maintaining security there was simply too great a problem, so we never went back.

Our concern about the men's safety was well founded considering that an armored unit much like our own had had one of its men shot by a village whore. The unit had been pulling outpost duty on a road passing through a small village. One of its vehicles with a five-man crew was stationed at the edge of the village.

It was a hot, boring day with little traffic passing on the road. Children, as they normally did, came out from the village to beg for candy. After being given C-ration chocolate, they soon left. Later, in the hottest part of the afternoon, a very attractive woman in her thirties emerged from the village to tempt the crew with the old offer of sex for sale. She offered to take them back into the village one at a time and conduct business in a cool hut where no one would bother them. The vehicle commander, a sergeant, took the bait, paid his money, and went back to her hut.

About ten minutes later the crew heard a shot and they immediately started up their vehicle. They drove into the village and called out the sergeant's name but got no answer. Finally, they dismounted and searched every building but they still couldn't find their TC. As they made one last sweep through the village, one of the men happened to look down a nearby well and there was the sergeant, with a bullet in the back of his head and his pants down around his boots.

The Graves Registration report filed on this "suspicious death" indicated the soldier had been shot with his own .45-caliber pistol. Incidents like that made us particularly cautious when our soldiers were around people who were obviously working for the enemy.

One final comment on this incident: About five days after our visit to The Elvis Presley Club our daily supply request included a requisition from the troop medic for six applications of penicillin to be sent out over the next five days. The first sergeant had been only partially right about The Elvis Presley Club: All six of our men recovered completely within two weeks.

The lead element of an armored cavalry platoon, preparing to escort a truck convoy through enemy territory. This is a mission we often received.

Platoon leader (author on right) and platoon sergeant Graff inspecting the perimeter. For weeks at a time, we slept and worked in our uniforms; they got washed only when it rained, but here we appear fairly well groomed. (Author's collection)

Moving vehicles massed together on a road was like a rolling fortress, with guns bristling in every direction. Just the appearance of these columns should have been enough to scare off the enemy, but they were attacked on a regular basis.

After numerous maintenance problems with my assigned vehicle, "16," I loaded up my radios and the medic along with George Borgos and moved over to vehicle "13." Shown here is the "13" track commander, Staff Sergeant Bletcher, a very formal old army NCO, with Borgos and me. (Author's collection)

The enemy had little fear of ACAV's, but tanks were another matter. When tanks joined the battle, the enemy would run. Crews realizing this would dress the tanks up with monster eyes and mouths to heighten the effect.

The commander of *Birth Control*, Staff Sergeant Ovitt and crew were proud of their newly arrived tank. After a few days in the bush, fenders were gone, large chunks missing out of treads, and the shine was replaced by dirt and mud.

I am seated in the position where I ran the platoon, top left, rear of "13" vehicle, with a radio mike in one hand and a map in the other. (Author's collection)

We lived in our vehicles; they were our homes. Shown is a machine gunner firing his weapon, while a soldier writes a letter. It was not unusual to see guns being fired as men ate C rations, shaved, or even took a nap.

Shown is an exterior mounted .50 caliber machine gun, which made tank commanders easy targets twelve to fifteen feet above the ground, resulting in many casualties before gun shields were finally installed on all tanks.

While checking out a woodline, a scout team encounters enemy fire and responds. These teams were the workhorses of the platoon and suffered the majority of casualties.

An MI Team Visits

The military don't start wars. The politicians start wars.
— Gen. William C. Westmoreland

One day, while squadron fuel trucks were refueling our vehicles along Highway 13, the troop commander called and directed me to remain at my present location near the Minh Thanh rubber plantation. He said he was en route there to discuss a new mission for my platoon.

Within twenty minutes, six armored vehicles appeared from the south, moving up the road in a cloud of dust. As soon as the CO had maneuvered his command vehicle next to mine, we both climbed down. As I approached him I glanced up at three strangers who sat perched atop his track.

The CO steered me over to a stand of rubber trees about fifty feet away so we would be out of earshot of the vehicles. After briefly discussing maintenance and ammunition resupply matters, he said, "The three men who came out here with me are from Military Intelligence. I really don't know why they're here, but squadron sent them out to spend a week with us, and I want them to accompany your platoon."

"Sir, this really sounds unusual," I replied, "Can't you tell me anything more?"

"All I know is that they've got radios and recording equipment," he said. "I'm not sure what they plan to do with it, so be careful. They might be recording both your transmissions and the enemy's."

With that, the CO and I moved back to his vehicle. "Gentlemen," he said as we approached the trio of MI soldiers, "I want you to meet Lieutenant Walker. You'll be spending the next week with his platoon."

The three men, dressed in jungle fatigues with no visible rank, jumped down from the CO's vehicle and shook my hand, introducing themselves as Mr. Smith, Mr. Wilson, and Mr. Barnes. They appeared to be in their thirties and forties, and all were a little overweight. Each was armed with a .45-caliber pistol and carried a small black equipment box, much like a large typewriter, and a duffel bag. I instructed them to get into my vehicle. They climbed in through the combat hatch and stood in the open cargo hatch as we moved out.

Fearing the presence of three extra bodies on my track might attract the enemy's attention even more than the extra radio antennas already did, I suggested to Mr. Smith, who appeared to be their leader, that it would be better if we spread his team out on three different vehicles. I explained that the enemy might single us out because of their being on board and blow us up with a command-detonated mine.

"No," he replied flatly, obviously unimpressed with my reasoning. "We can't do that. It's just not possible."

Not wanting an argument, I allowed all three of them to remain on my command vehicle for the time being.

I first learned about command-detonated mines one day when the platoon was clearing Highway 13 south of Ben Cat several months earlier. On that particular day I was out on the road following behind the minesweepers. Our troop commander was always pushing us to clear the roads as quickly as possible because there was generally a convoy waiting to make a run over the road and the minesweepers would move faster with me walking behind them.

Although they checked every chuckhole and broken place in the road, the minesweepers apparently missed a mine, which damaged the fifth vehicle in the column of tracks moving behind us. No one on board was injured by the small mine's blast. However, it did break the track on one side and damaged four road wheels.

While checking the area where the mine exploded, we found wires buried in the ground leading about a hundred yards away to a tree line. To make sure it wouldn't be used again, we pulled up as much of the wire as we could.

I left a scout section with the damaged vehicle while we finished clearing the road. A maintenance team soon arrived on the scene and, within an hour, the track was operational again and rejoined the column.

Later, while trying to figure out why the enemy had allowed the minesweeping team and four other vehicles to pass before detonating their mine, I remembered that the One-Nine vehicle was carrying eight people—its regular crew of five, plus three new people who were being given an orientation by Sergeant Denison. I reasoned that the VC saw that track as a more lucrative target because of the number of men on board.

From then on I tried to keep the crews looking the same, allowing nothing that would make one vehicle stand out from another and make it a prime target. All of the vehicle commanders were very cooperative in this effort, for good reason.

Whenever we stopped for at least ten or fifteen minutes after the MI team joined us, they would take out their monitoring equipment and go to work. They kept to themselves and seemed very defensive and secretive about what they were doing.

During our initial briefing at division headquarters by Lt. Col. Alexander Haig, the subject of intelligence-gathering operations was covered with just a few short remarks. I can recall being shown a map of our division area that was covered with small dots. Each of the dots was supposed to represent the location of an enemy radio transmitter. Haig explained that this was one tool the intelligence officers used to determine enemy movement and to predict where the enemy was most likely to attack.

I had never given much thought to how the information was gathered. I simply assumed that someone sat behind a powerful receiver with a large antenna at one of our bases and intercepted enemy radio transmissions. The idea that they sent men equipped with simple equipment out to the field to gather this information by working in close proximity to the enemy had not occurred to me.

However, my guess about the MI team's mission could have been completely wrong. They might not have been gathering anything at all on the enemy. They may have been sent to monitor our radio transmissions to determine how well we were following our own policies and regulations.

Adding to the mystery, they wore no rank insignia. Nevertheless, it appeared that the older man was an officer and the other two were either warrant officers or sergeants. We determined this by the fact that the three brought no food with them but were constantly rummaging through our C-ration cases looking for their favorite meals. The two younger men always cooked the food and deferred to the older man, giving him their food if he showed the slightest interest in it. My men also noticed that our visitors had bottles of Tabasco and A-1 Sauce to season their food, but never offered to share it with the rest of the crew.

At exactly nine each night, the MI men would set up their Special Forces hammocks in nearby trees and bed down for the night. This prompted Sergeant Jones, one of my TCs who had only three crewmen, to ask at a vehicle commanders' meeting if I would order the MI men to pull guard duty like everyone else. He added that his crew was badly overworked and needed help. I told him I'd think about it and get back to him.

We were holding our meeting in the open when it began to rain hard. I abruptly ended the meeting and, after sending the sergeants back to their vehicles, headed back to my track. Private Borgos had taken my shelter half and set a lean-to for me on the side of the vehicle. I made a beeline for it and, when I ducked under the wet canvas, I found the three MI men huddled there. Shocked at their brazenness, I snapped, "This is my hootch, you're going to have to find your own."

They just sat there, staring at me. I angrily grabbed hold of the closest one to me and said, "C'mon, let's get moving," as I pulled him out into the rain. As the other two crawled out from under the canvas shelter dragging their duffel bags with them, I heard the older one say, "These sorry bastards don't know what hospitality is." With that they climbed in the back of my vehicle through the combat hatch. I could hear more grumbling and swearing as they attempted to hang their hammocks up inside the cramped crew compartment, where the rest of my crew had already settled down.

As I lay there listening to their whining and complaining through the remainder of the night, I decided to make them perform regular duties, just like the rest of the platoon. There would be no prima donnas here. I'd become fed up with their air of superiority and with the condescending way in which they responded to my men's simple attempts to make them feel welcome.

Early the next morning I radioed the troop commander and explained the problem I was having with the MI men. I asked for permission to make them pull radio watch, guard, ambush patrols, and other regular duties.

"Sure," he replied. "Treat them like any other member of the unit. They're soldiers just like you and me."

After thanking him, I called the three MI soldiers over to my track. I sat them down on the back ramp and told them what my CO had just said about their status.

"Lieutenant," said the older man, "we are exempt from extra duties. We have our own mission to perform."

"There's nothing extra about these duties," I replied, "it's what we do to stay alive." I further informed them that starting that evening they would pull guard duty and that Mr. Barnes would be going out with the ambush patrol.

They began complaining that I couldn't do this and I couldn't do that and that I was overstepping my authority. I cut them off by saying, "We're all subject to the Uniform Code of Military Justice and you're going to start pulling your own weight around here."

With that I assigned the MI team to Sergeant Jones's vehicle and told him that he should let me know what he wanted them to do and I'd see that they did it.

After that we continued our search-and-destroy operation near the Cambodian border as part of a task force that included the 1st Battalion, 16th Infantry, and a separate artillery battery.

We spent an uneventful day that included leading a twelve-man foot patrol over a small creek to investigate thick jungle on the other side, and then settled into a new night defensive position. While the platoon was preparing the perimeter, I attended a meeting with the infantry battalion commander.

The battalion S2 briefed the enemy situation at this meeting. He reported that there had been several sightings of large enemy units moving around and near our location. The S3 then outlined the next day's mission and directed each unit to send out one ambush patrol and one listening post within its sector of responsibility. The battalion commander ended the meeting by saying that the task force would probably see heavy fighting over the next few days and that he wanted subordinate commanders to ensure that their soldiers were fully prepared for a maximum effort.

After picking up a case of apples from the mess tent, I returned to my platoon and called for the track commanders to assemble by my vehicle. When they were all gathered around the back of my track, I relayed the information I had received from battalion, the key part of which was that large North Vietnamese units had been sighted just a few kilometers to our west. I also advised them that one of our infantry battalions had been in contact with a large enemy unit of unknown size almost the entire day and that casualties on both sides were high.

I placed Staff Sergeant Richardson in charge of the platoon ambush patrol and tasked each crew to provide one man, with vehicle One-Three furnishing an M60 machine gun. I exempted the tanks from this requirement because they needed their entire crew to fight the vehicle if the enemy decided to attack us during the night. There was a large mahogany tree about a hundred yards to our front, and I directed Sergeant Richardson to set up his ambush patrol at the base of that tree at about 8 P.M.

I next directed Sergeant Weeks, the TC of vehicle One-One, to set up a two-man listening post just outside the wire in an area where the brush came very close to the perimeter. I wanted them in position no later than 9 P.M.

Our part of the perimeter covered approximately one hundred yards, and we cleared fields of fire by running our vehicles back and forth to knock down the brush and small trees for about seventy-five to eighty yards to our front. The area was heavily wooded, covered by large teak and mahogany trees, some of them as much as 150 feet high, with thick brush at ground level.

We finished our C-ration meals and tied the platoon in with adjoining units as darkness began to fall. Sergeant Richardson came over as the last light faded away and let me know that the ambush patrol was ready to move out. I inspected his seven-man patrol in the gathering gloom and assured myself that they were well prepared, with each man carrying two hundred rounds of ammunition, two grenades, one trip flare, and every other man carrying a claymore mine. Sergeant Richardson carried the radio. He had briefed all patrol members thoroughly and given them individual assignments.

I watched as the ambush patrol filed out in front of tank One-Four. As the men started moving through the barbed wire, the tank commander made a routine call on the platoon radio net to alert everyone that we had friendly troops moving across our front. The tank commander's message was simply, "Dragoon Charlie One, this is Dragoon Charlie One-Four, be advised, the alpha papa is now going out to my front."

Within seconds, Mr. Smith was at my vehicle. He got right up in my face and announced that my tank commander had committed a security violation by broadcasting the location of our ambush patrol in the clear. He said I would have to move the patrol in order to protect the men.

"You must be kidding," I said. "We've been doing this as long as I've been here. No radio security has been violated." Smith insisted that the enemy was more sophisticated than we thought. He said he often sat outside our perimeter and watched us while monitoring our radio transmissions. The enemy could easily have seen and heard the sergeant on tank One-Four make his call, thus pinpointing the patrol's location.

I told him that his theory was an interesting one and that I would consider his suggestion to move the patrol, but right now he needed to get back to his vehicle.

As he started to leave, he turned and said, "Lieutenant, are you going to move the patrol?"

"The patrol's staying right where it is," I replied.

"Then I'm going to write up a formal report of the incident and turn it in to my higher headquarters!" he said petulantly, like a small child who hadn't gotten his way.

"Get back to your vehicle!" I said sharply. I was convinced that his sudden hysterical interest in the ambush patrol was because one of his team members was out there.

After Sergeant Weeks positioned the men in the listening post in front of his track, I checked the perimeter one last time. By 9 P.M. it was so dark that I couldn't see my hand in front of my face, and I slowly made my way back over fallen trees and brush to my own vehicle.

It was a very dark night and unusually quiet, with the normal reports coming in from the platoon every hour. Just after midnight we heard a series of loud explosions close to our rear. I checked in with the infantry battalion and was told that it was incoming enemy mortar fire.

About the same time, Sergeant Richardson called in to report movement in the vicinity of his ambush patrol. With the enemy mortar fire continuing at a rate of fifteen to twenty rounds per minute, Sergeant Richardson called again and reported that they had exploded two claymore mines and fired up what appeared to be an enemy patrol. I told them to sit tight and listen for further signs of movement.

I called the infantry battalion operations center and reported our enemy contact. I then requested artillery fire two hundred yards out from the ambush patrol. The supporting battery quickly complied, and Sergeant Richardson reported no further enemy activity to his front.

While I was sitting there in the crew compartment of my track monitoring the radios I heard the combat hatch open and looked back to see who it was. I saw Sergeant Weeks standing there with the two men from the listening post. I asked him who had given them permission to come in and Sergeant Weeks said, "No one, Sir, they just got scared and came in on their own."

I stared at the two young men. They were probably no more than nineteen years old and looked pitiful, but I could not let them get away with abandoning their post without permission. Not only did that threaten the platoon, but they could have been shot by our own men as they came back in unannounced.

I loudly informed Sergeant Weeks that what they had done was a court-martial offense and that unless they were back out in position within five minutes, I would have them court-martialed. I told him that if the court didn't sentence them to be shot by a firing squad, I figured they would at least spend a long time at Fort Leavenworth. The two soldiers, who must have heard every word, which is exactly what I intended, vanished. Soon I heard one of them asking for a radio check on the platoon net.

After they left, Sergeant Weeks told me they were both good soldiers and that they'd probably just gotten rattled out there in the dark by themselves while all the shooting was going on. I agreed. However, I still ordered him to speak with the two men about the seriousness of what they had done when they came back in the morning. I added that I would accept his recommendation on what to do with them.

Around 4:30 A.M., about an hour before daylight, the ambush patrol again reported movement to its right flank and front. The men in the patrol threw four grenades and I requested artillery at the same coordinates as before. Again, no further enemy movement was reported. However, this time one of the men in the patrol was wounded by grenade fragments in the right hand and arm. It was nothing serious. His wounds were bandaged on the spot and he walked back unaided when the patrol came back after dawn.

The next morning, Sergeant Richardson and Sergeant Weeks briefed me on their patrols' activities during the night. It was obvious to me that the enemy had been probing our position in preparation for an attack.

A short while later I attended a meeting with the battalion commander. Units all around the perimeter had been probed, and one of the infantry companies reported killing three enemy soldiers who had made their way inside the perimeter wire. The enemy soldiers were unarmed except for a twenty-pound satchel charge each had strapped to his back.

The battalion commander reported that another battalion from our division, located eight kilometers away, had been attacked during the night and suffered heavy casualties. It was his opinion that the enemy, finding our defensive perimeter well defended, decided to attack the other battalion's position instead.

Since we would be staying in the area for three more nights, the commander outlined additional defensive measures for each unit. The infantry companies were instructed to dig more bunkers, set out more mines, and adjust their sectors so that my cavalry platoon could be pulled off the line and placed in reserve. No matter where the perimeter was attacked, he wanted my platoon free to rush there and bring the full force of its big tank guns and .50-caliber machine guns to bear.

When the infantry first moved into their positions, they had hastily dug foxholes around the perimeter, adding just a few sandbags around the edges for protection. Now, with a major battle looming, they pulled out all the stops. Truckloads of sandbags arrived and groups of men everywhere were busy filling them.

Since we fought from our vehicles, there was no need for us to fill sandbags. But some of the vehicle commanders did position eight or ten sandbags on the rear of their vehicles to better protect the men who were manning the two M60 machine guns back in the cargo hatches.

Our only unprotected area was the latrine, and I had two men build a low, four-sided sandbag structure around it so that when you sat down you could just barely see over the top.

We watched the infantry to our front construct bunkers that looked like little sandbag houses, complete with overhead cover. The bunkers, which were about four feet tall and ten feet wide and had firing ports at the forward corners, were located every thirty yards and had a shallow trench connecting them. The plan was for M60 machine guns to be placed in the firing ports of each bunker, giving us interlocking fields of fire all around the perimeter. These fighting positions, which later became known throughout the army as "1st Division bunkers," did a fine job of protecting the men and normally resulted in considerably fewer casualties. I also believe it helped morale by putting five or six men together in one strong position with plenty of supporting firepower. To complete this picture, one man would usually take cover behind the bunker and fire high-explosive rounds from an M79 grenade launcher into the enemy formations.

We spent the remainder of the day escorting supply vehicles to and from An Loc and constructing a makeshift road just inside the perimeter defenses that encircled the task force area.

The battalion commander was quite proud of his defensive plan and kept repeating at every opportunity that the cavalry was his "ace in the hole." Furthermore, he said he hoped that the enemy would be stupid enough to attack so we could rip them to pieces.

Two nights later, what we believed to be an NVA regiment attacked the south side of the perimeter and we were able to implement our unique plan. About ten minutes before the ground attack, the task force was hit by a heavy mortar attack that wounded several men. After the mortar barrage we saw tracer rounds arcing overhead and heard the sound of heavy firing coming from the south side of the perimeter. Frantic calls on the radio confirmed that an attack was in progress.

By the time we received the word to move out, I had all my vehicles lined up with their machine guns charged and ready to fire. With tanks leading, we inched toward the south end of the perimeter. The battalion commander personally radioed and encouraged me to "get in there as quickly as you can and blast the hell out of them!"

We raced around the rough perimeter road with most of the vehicles buttoned up. When we reached the designated spot, I ordered the tanks, which were less than twenty feet apart, to make a sharp right turn. They slowly advanced toward the line of friendly bunkers with their .50-caliber and coaxial 7.62mm machine guns blazing. The tanks opened up with 90mm canister rounds when they reached the bunker line, and at that point I ordered the crews of the ACAVs to unbutton and move up behind them with all machine guns firing.

I was able to make out movement in the brush to our front in the eerie light of artillery flares bursting overhead. I ordered the platoon to move slowly forward with the tanks spreading out as they advanced. Two RPGs hit the tank on the far right, which ground to a halt, although its crew continued to fire. The rest of my tracks continued to creep forward, firing their weapons all the while. Reaching the edge of the thick brush, I ordered the platoon to hold up and fire controlled bursts in order to conserve ammunition.

Private First Class Adams, who was standing next to me in the cargo hatch manning a machine gun, was killed and two men on a vehicle twenty yards away were seriously wounded by enemy small-arms fire.

We soon silenced the enemy to our front, but the NVA continued to press the attack with great effect to our left. Leaving two vehicles with the disabled tank, I moved the rest of the platoon about fifty yards in that direction. As soon as we reached what I believed to be the center of that enemy attack, I had the vehicles turn outward again and increase their volume of fire.

One tank reported a direct hit by an RPG on its turret, but the TC said there was no internal damage. Shortly after that the battalion commander called and ordered me to cease firing. As our firing died down the only thing we heard from the enemy side was the sound of our own artillery hitting about a hundred yards beyond the edge of the tree line.

The surprise and shock effect of the tanks had worked. The attack had been stopped in its tracks and the enemy was withdrawing from the southern end of the task force perimeter.

The battalion commander asked if we could "tell Charlie goodbye with some direct fire high-explosive."

"Yes, Sir," I replied. "Would five rounds from each tank be enough?"

"That ought to be enough to burn their asses," he answered.

After firing that mission I had the platoon back up to the line of infantry bunkers and prepare to stay there for the remainder of the night.

Meanwhile, I had One-One police up the dead and wounded and take them to the aid station located with the artillery battery.

Private Adams lay on the floor of our crew compartment. He had been hit by a bullet just under the left arm, and died as I was putting a field dressing on his gaping wound. As I removed his shirt, he held firmly to my arm. A few seconds later his grip loosened and he whispered, "I can't . . ." That was it. He died in my arms there on the floor of the darkened vehicle.

With darkness again blanketing the area, I supervised the recovery of the disabled tank. The crews of the two vehicles protecting the tank attached tow cables to it and dragged it back into our defensive line with their tracks. A sniper had shot the tank commander in the leg while we were attaching the cables, and I ordered our four vehicles at that position to open fire and keep firing until the tank was safely back inside the perimeter.

The sergeant had received a serious wound, high up on the left thigh, and was losing blood fast. We carried him back to my vehicle and turned on the interior lights so the medic could work on him while we raced back to the aid station. As soon as we arrived I put in an urgent request for an immediate medevac. Only after confirming that the helicopter was en route did I return to the perimeter to ensure that my vehicles were properly tied into the infantry positions on either side of them.

My medic radioed soon after we dropped them off at the aid station and informed me that, despite his best efforts, SSgt. James Ward was dead. Sergeant Ward was one of my original vehicle commanders; a quiet man who could always be counted on to get the job done. When I first joined the platoon and went around to meet all the vehicle commanders, Sergeant Ward had proudly pointed out the twelve bullet holes in his tank's searchlight cover. He thoroughly enjoyed telling me how the damage occurred, and I was impressed with his professionalism. He died less than a month before he was scheduled to go home to his wife and two children.

Remembering the helicopter, I radioed the aid station and canceled the medevac. I then told my medic to stay there and get a good night's sleep. Later, as I sat there in the darkness waiting for dawn, I promised myself that we would be more cautious in the future. These types of losses could not continue.

At first light we were able to sort out the damage. The casualty toll in the infantry battalion, which had more than eight hundred men engaged, was four killed and seventeen wounded. My platoon, with only fifty-eight men present for duty, had suffered three killed and eight wounded. We also had two vehicles slightly damaged.

The battalion commander recommended me for an award for heroism. However, since I saw nothing really exceptional about my performance, I always believed he did it because he was embarrassed by our high casualty figures and thought we had carried more than our fair share of the battle. However, that was the nature of life in the cavalry, particularly when we were attached to an infantry unit. We were always being rushed to the hottest part of the battlefield or brought in at the last minute to rescue a unit that was in danger of being overrun. Even though our casualty toll that night was high in comparison to the infantry's losses, considering the amount of movement we made on the line, the heavy fire we attracted, and the large number of enemy attacking, I didn't think it was unusually high.

Later that morning, infantry patrols sweeping the area found seventy-two dead NVA plus numerous blood trails indicating many more had been wounded or killed. They also picked up thirteen abandoned weapons.

Two of my eight wounded returned to duty within three days, and I wasted no time in putting in a request for personnel replacements, using my long-range radio to reach our troop headquarters. I again requested a platoon sergeant, which I had been operating without, a new tank commander to replace Sergeant Ward, and four experienced cavalry scouts or tankers. Given the dangerous missions we were expected to perform, we couldn't afford to operate shorthanded.

While I was supervising the repair of tank One-Four, Mr. Smith, the MI team leader, informed me that their work was finished and that they were going to spend some time with the artillery battery located in the center of the perimeter. I asked if he wanted me to coordinate anything for his team and he said, "No, Lieutenant, it's already been taken care of." Then he turned around and walked away without so much as a good-bye or a thank you.

Smith himself was scheduled for the next ambush patrol, so I've always believed that was what hastened their departure. The previous night's attack, which they were right in the middle of, almost certainly helped.

Late one night about two weeks after the MI team's departure, I received a call on the radio saying that our squadron executive officer wanted to speak with me. We arranged to meet at the main intersection in An Loc at ten the next morning. I had no idea why he wanted to talk with me. I figured it might be to discuss a change of assignment since I'd been on the line for so long.

The next day, after an uneventful night, I organized a convoy and moved out of the perimeter escorting sixteen empty supply trucks headed for the town of An Loc. When we arrived, I found Major Moore sitting alone in his jeep in an unsecured area waiting for me.

I sent the remainder of the platoon on ahead to the supply point with the trucks and then pulled my track up next to the XO's jeep.

"How's the war going?" he asked, greeting me with a broad smile.

"Fine, sir," I yelled back as I jumped down, saluted, and then shook his hand.

"We've been hearing some good things about you back at squadron," he said. "Sounds like you're giving Charlie a hard time up here."

As I climbed into the jeep on the passenger side he turned to me and said, "The squadron commander and I both think you're doing a fine job, Paul. We certainly have no complaints about your performance. But anytime a complaint comes in from a higher headquarters, we've got to look into it. That's why I'm here today." He paused and handed me a very official-looking document from the Military Intelligence Command in Saigon. He told me to read the document and then asked me to tell him what I knew about it.

The document began: "On 16 May 1967, three of our agents [it then listed their names] were present and witnessed 1LT Paul D. Walker of the 1st Squadron 4th U.S. Cavalry, 1st Infantry Division, openly and flagrantly violate published security procedures established by this command for the safe transmission of information regarding the location of friendly units. . . ." The document continued on in that vein for eight pages, basically restating the events that occurred when the now-deceased Staff Sergeant Ward alerted the platoon over the radio that an ambush patrol was going out in front of his tank.

The document painted me as a monster, responsible for needlessly exposing the ambush patrol to extreme danger and directly responsible for the patrol being attacked and two good men being wounded. The report upset me considerably since I believed we were doing the MI team a favor by allowing them to come along and share our piece of the war.

I sat in the jeep for nearly an hour explaining to the major what had actually happened on 16 May 1967 while he took detailed notes. When I finished, Major Moore said, "I've had a few run-ins with these bastards myself. They were supposed to be listening to enemy radio transmissions but instead they were monitoring and recording your transmissions. You know, you probably pissed those guys off by treating them like regular enlisted men and putting them on guard duty, ambush patrols, and other details. For all we know, Mr. Smith may be a major or lieutenant colonel. Their more senior officers also go to the field occasionally."

"Yes, Sir," I replied, "but my instructions were to treat them like any other crew member, and that's just what I did."

"Lieutenant Walker, you did *exactly* what we wanted you to do." Finally, Major Moore said, "I'm going to write up the response to this report and say that I've investigated the facts concerning the allegations against you and that I found you were operating in complete compliance with all squadron policies and procedures pertaining to communications security. Furthermore, I will let them know that I found the accusation that you needlessly endangered the lives of your men to be malicious, slanderous, and totally false."

As I left, Major Moore apologized again for having sent those "low-life bastards from Military Intelligence out to make your tough job even harder."

That ended the incident with the MI team. Later, we heard through the grapevine that whenever a member of the squadron staff would foul up or get into trouble, Major Moore would threaten to send them out to work for me for a couple of weeks to straighten them out.

One final note: About two weeks later, I had an opportunity to sit down with my CO and discuss the MI complaint. Major Moore had briefed him about his visit with me, and the CO also apologized. As strongly as I felt about the incident, it would have been easy for me to get out of line with the CO. However, I opted to say little, except to ask him to never send anybody out again to joyride with the platoon. I told him I was convinced that the MI team had only wanted to be chauffeured around and take a vacation at our expense. When I made them perform as members of a regular crew they resented it and tried to cause trouble. Sergeant Jones, the TC on their track, told me that all three of them cowered on the floor of the crew compartment in the heat of battle and refused to fire their weapons as ordered. Aside from being a nuisance factor, I told him they had actually endangered the lives of Sergeant Jones and his crew.

The CO agreed and, figuring I'd said enough, I let the matter drop.

Friendly Fire

Although war is evil, it is occasionally the lesser of two evils.
—McGeorge Bundy

The army in Vietnam conducted combat operations seven days a week and there were no weekends or Sundays off. Nothing distinguished one day from another. Occasionally, however, there would be some indication that the day was a special holiday or a Sunday, but we rarely altered our operations because of it.

On one particularly rainy and humid day, my platoon was escorting supply convoys between Dian and Phu Loi. We'd just dropped off about thirty supply trucks at Phu Loi and were turning around to pick up another convoy going south when I saw a hand-lettered sign next to the road that read: "TODAY IS SUNDAY, PLEASE JOIN US FOR CHURCH AT 10:00." I looked at my watch and saw that it was five minutes to ten. Directly behind the sign, a chaplain's assistant was setting up a field table covered with a purple cloth and silver candleholders.

Realizing that we would be there for only a few minutes waiting for the next convoy to line up, I got on the radio and called for all personnel to assemble with me in the field next to the road. We parked our tracks alongside the road next to the church sign and my reluctant crewmen trudged over and gathered around the chaplain's field table. About fifteen soldiers from other units joined our group.

The chaplain, an older captain wearing a black cloth draped around his neck, pulled up in a jeep and got out. Beaming from ear

147

to ear, he welcomed us and blessed us with a short prayer. The chaplain's assistant turned on a small tape player and led us in singing several traditional hymns. Finally, the chaplain launched into a short sermon.

Private Borgos wore a PRC-10 radio on his back so we could monitor our platoon frequency. While the chaplain was talking he came over to where I was sitting on the ground and whispered, "Sir, they want you on the radio." I took the handset and listened as the caller advised me that the convoy we were to escort was ready to go.

The chaplain was still in the midst of his sermon when I stood up and said, "Excuse me, Sir, but my men and I are going to have to leave now. Our unit's moving out."

"Please wait," he replied. He walked back through the group, put his hand on my shoulder, and offered a prayer for our safety.

When he finished, I shook the chaplain's hand and issued orders for everyone to mount up. As we headed to our vehicles, what was left of the little congregation began to sing "Onward Christian Soldiers."

That was the first church service I had attended in almost a year and, even there in that muddy field, dressed in dirty jungle fatigues, it was impressive. Later in the week several of the men told me it had been an inspirational event for them, too.

We escorted two more convoys that day before we finally settled down for the night in a defensive position near Phu Loi. As we were putting out our barbed wire and trip flares, the resupply helicopter landed with our evening meal—chili and rice again—and our mail, which included a typed note from the CO.

The note stated that we were to rejoin the troop in the morning and begin preparing for a large-scale operation that would be conducted up north and last approximately a week. This massive operation was to include the 173d Airborne Brigade and would be conducted in the vicinity of where Highway 13 enters Cambodia.

The concept was for the 1st Infantry Division to serve as a hammer and the 173d Airborne Brigade as an anvil. The 173d moved into a strong blocking position along the border while our division consolidated about ten kilometers to the south and began conducting sweeps that hopefully would drive the enemy into the 173d's positions so the airborne soldiers could destroy them.

The first phase was to get the blocking units into position, with some of the units parachuting in and the remainder being airlifted in by helicopter. The second phase involved trucking in some of our infantry units and starting the hammer moving toward the anvil. Our cavalry squadron was to provide flank security by occupying a series of blocking positions along the division's western flank.

During the operation, we were constantly being ordered to move in echelon to a new blocking position and wait. To help pass the time, I periodically switched my long-range radio to our brigade or division frequencies to see if other units were making contact with the enemy. Throughout the day, the only type of activity being reported was numerous sniping incidents and, on one occasion, an exploding booby trap that resulted in three casualties.

On the first day of the operation, we moved through three abandoned villages which, according to our briefing, had been demolished and the people resettled. As we rolled through each of the villages, it was obvious that, despite our best efforts, someone was still living there. Chickens and pigs roamed the abandoned streets, and wells had been uncovered and cleaned out. Some of the houses had even been rebuilt. A close examination of the rice paddies revealed that someone was working them.

As we moved through our sector, some of the men asked whether the people living in the area were enemy or just unhappy villagers who had become homesick and returned. We never resolved that question, but I knew the official policy was that no one was supposed to be there, and that we were to treat anyone we encountered as the enemy.

Many of the villages had fruit trees laden with bananas and mangos, so whoever did live there certainly wasn't going hungry.

The primary reason for the resettlement program was to get the villagers away from the Vietcong and North Vietnamese. The Vietnamese all looked the same to us and spoke the same language, so it was very easy for soldiers trained in the north to enter villages in the south and blend right in without fear of detection. An additional reason for moving the people out was that the villages supplied the enemy with support, either willingly or unwillingly.

The strategy was to move the villages back away from the Cambodian border and then conduct the kind of large-scale military operations our military forces were so good at. Any Vietnamese found in these free-fire zones after the B-52s had done their work were considered enemy and received our full military effort.

During May and June of 1967, as we traveled throughout War Zone C, it was obvious that more and more of the remote villages had been resettled closer to Saigon. This massive pacification effort, sometimes referred to as "The Other War," was prompted by the mixed results of the Rural Development Program. That program, initially sponsored by the U.S. State Department, involved placing teams of Vietnamese civilians in selected villages. They built schools, improved sanitation, and introduced modern farming practices. While the team was there, an ARVN unit was sent in to protect it.

Those administering the program had, in most cases, received little training and were often heavy-handed in their dealings with local officials. And, more often than not, these young cadres were sent into areas where they received little or no support from the local ARVN or U.S. forces. Since many of the teams were frequently on their own, when harassed or terrorized by the Vietcong, they simply left the areas or quit and disappeared into the population.

Those who showed courage and stayed, regardless of the conditions, were the most effective. Unfortunately, these same people were often found with their throats slit by the local Vietcong. During one seven-month period in 1966, more than three thousand Rural Development Program personnel were murdered or kidnapped by the enemy.

By the end of June 1967, more than 25 percent of South Vietnam's people had been driven out of their native villages either by our or the enemy's military operations. As a result, we often would see teeming masses of people in the larger villages and cities who were there, in most cases, because they had been forced out of their native village or it had been destroyed and they refused to live in one of the shabby refugee camps. Because of the failure of the Rural Development Program, a large portion of South Vietnam's population was left rootless and hostile, and the refugee camps became a breeding ground for Vietcong sympathizers.

It was my experience that the advance preparation and reconnaissance normally required for major operations alerted the enemy to our plans and, by the time an operation commenced, he had flown the coop.

That was the case with this operation. Our only effective contact with the enemy was through night ambush patrols set up well clear of friendly positions. The three-day operation ended when we linked up with the 173d Airborne Brigade along the border. Some two hundred enemy soldiers were reported killed compared to about thirty Americans killed or wounded. Even so, the operation was called highly successful. However, one incident occurred during the operation that caused many of our soldiers to lose confidence in our supporting artillery.

On the second night of the operation, 1st Infantry Division units began to close up and our troop moved into a large night defensive position with two artillery batteries, a battalion of infantry, and several support units.

That evening, as the troop moved into a large clearing, there was much activity as the perimeter was divided up and sectors assigned to the platoons, which were just now finishing the final positioning of vehicles. At dusk we began to put out our concertina wire and trip flares. We'd chosen a beautiful clearing with tall mahogany trees scattered around it and virtually no brush, just short, green grass. The clearing was about three hundred yards across and allowed for good fields of fire.

To our rear, some of the men in the artillery battery, who had arrived earlier, were eating a hot meal and others were starting to dig in their guns. It was the busiest and most exciting part of the day for me, with all the activity of setting up the perimeter and requesting ammunition, C rations, and repair parts for the next day, plus organizing and sending out an ambush patrol.

I had just finished checking a maintenance problem on one of my tanks and was returning to my command vehicle when, not more than thirty yards behind me, there was a deafening explosion. Everyone hit the dirt and someone yelled, "Incoming!" Flattened out on the ground, we were braced for the next round when I heard a weak, muffled cry for help from someone who sounded like he'd had the breath knocked out of him. Without a second thought, I raced toward the pleading voice.

When I reached the tank where I'd been standing not more than three minutes before, I dove behind it and then low-crawled around to the side. There, a terrible sight greeted me: Sergeant O'Leary lay in a pool of blood. He was so badly mangled that I didn't recognize him at first. His skin was blackened and mud spattered, punctuated with little red streaks that were getting bigger as I watched. He was obviously critically injured. I hurriedly stripped off his flak jacket and tried to find the major wound so I could stop the bleeding, but the blood was coming out from several places. He stirred slightly and coughed, then he lay there very still with his eyes open. I felt his neck but there was no pulse. Hearing voices inside the tank, I yelled angrily for someone to "Call for the medic on One-Six!"

Stunned by the grisly scene in front of me, I stumbled to the front of the tank and, there, about ten feet away, was a large crater with loose dirt scattered around it. While examining the size of the crater, I heard moaning and saw movement to my front. I ran forward and found the tank's loader grimacing in pain, holding his bloody left arm. He was drawn up in a tight fetal position and rocking slowly back and forth. The wound in his arm, which was serious, was the only one I could find.

Hearing movement behind me, I looked up and saw the medic staring at Sergeant O'Leary. I waved at him to join me and he ran over and immediately began to treat the loader's arm.

I patted the man's good arm and told him we'd get a medevac and evacuate him ASAP. The medic said a large shell fragment had entered the man's arm and nearly severed his bicep muscle but he was certain the doctors would be able to save his arm. That news brought a weak smile to the loader's lips.

Sergeant O'Leary still lay in the grotesque position where I'd left him. I climbed up on the tank and switched the radio to the troop frequency, reported the incident to the CO, and asked him to please call for an immediate medevac for the loader. Next, I switched back to my platoon frequency and tried to energize the vehicle closest to me to get two stretchers and a four-man detail to my location ASAP.

As I headed back to help the medic, I was again struck by the size of the crater. It was more like a bomb crater than a mortar or artillery crater. Within minutes of my call, the medevac helicopter landed and we loaded the injured tanker and Sergeant O'Leary's body on board.

Sergeant O'Leary, who had been with the platoon only about a month, was a feisty, gray-haired man who loved to argue with everyone, including his platoon leader. He reminded me of a little leprechaun whenever I saw him standing on top of his tank.

During his first week with the platoon we were all going in ten different directions preparing to move out on a two-week operation. I was busy making all the necessary last-minute coordination prior to departure when Sergeant O'Leary walked up and said, "Sir, I refuse to take my tank out on this operation. It's unsafe."

Caught by surprise, I asked, "Why is it unsafe?"

"The hydraulic power is out in the turret and none of the gauges work," he replied. "It's just not safe."

I was aware of the problems with the One-Four tank and had already requested parts and a repair team. As soon as the parts came in, squadron maintenance would fix both problems. Until then, the crew could use the tank, manually traversing and elevating the main gun. Furthermore, the tank weapon we most relied on was the .50-caliber machine gun at the TC's position, which operated independent of the turret. We also relied on the vehicle's psychological effect on the enemy.

I explained all that to Sergeant O'Leary, but he turned his lower lip inside out and kept insisting that the tank was deadlined and unsafe and that he wasn't taking it out. I further explained to him the number of times Sergeant Ward's old tank, which was now his, had been blown up by mines and its main gun knocked out of alignment by ramming it through the jungle, yet we didn't worry about its accuracy.

Finally, I said, "Look, we're not fighting Soviet tanks, we're fighting guerrillas armed with AK-47s."

When he started to protest, I called him off to the side and, in a more serious tone, told him that the platoon needed his tank's firepower on this operation and that even without hydraulic power, his tank still had many times the firepower of the armored personnel carriers. Seeing he still wasn't convinced, I finally said, "Sergeant O'Leary, you're going out on this operation, so get on that tank over there and get ready to move out. I don't want to hear any more about this. Do you understand me?"

"Yes, *Sir*," he said grudgingly.

He was a good soldier, but being newly arrived from a stateside unit, he hadn't adjusted to the sorry state of maintenance of most of our vehicles.

The sound of the medevac chopper departing brought my thoughts back to the present. I returned to One-Four's position just as the CO and first sergeant began to examine the crater.

The first sergeant was almost hip deep in the crater collecting bits and pieces of metal. He climbed out a few minutes later and the three of us examined the fragments. We were able to make out some numbers on one. Another had "155mm" plainly stamped on it. The CO, suspecting the round was one of ours, radioed our supporting artillery unit and asked the battery commander to come join us on the line.

After examining the fragments, the artillery unit's CO confirmed that they were indeed from an American 155mm round. After further discussion, the artillery commander told us he would report the incident to his battalion commander and that an investigating officer would be appointed.

"That's fine," said our CO, "but call that one-five-five unit and make sure they know we're here so it doesn't happen again."

The artillery captain left and the CO turned to me and said, "Paul, you've got a tank here with only half a crew, what are you going to do with it?"

"Sir," I replied, "Sergeant O'Leary is the second TC killed on this tank in the last three months. I think it's jinxed. I'd like to get rid of it."

He smiled and said, "Do you have any trained tankers left?"

"Only me," I responded.

"That settles it, then," he said. "Start moving your command radios over and I'll see how soon I can get you a replacement for Sergeant O'Leary."

One-Four's driver, who had been inside when the shell landed, told me he had been trained as an armored personnel carrier driver and was learning about tanks as he went along. He reminded me that the turret hydraulic and wiring harness problems still had not been fixed, but added that the engine was running fine.

I radioed my command track and told the crew to move over next to One-Four so Private Borgos and I could transfer our equipment and the command radios to the tank.

Because of my practice of being out on the ground with patrols, directing fire, or walking with the minesweeping teams, I didn't like the idea of being tied down to one vehicle. I had no other choice, though. Borgos and I would just have to deal with it until a replacement TC arrived.

The night quieted down. I made a lean-to by tying my shelter half to the side of the tank after the troops were fed and the ambush patrol had gone out. Laying there on my cot listening to the radio, I felt almost at home. Borgos and the driver, like most tankers, had chosen to sleep on the back of the tank over the engine compartment. Their cots were six to eight feet above the ground, and they looked very comfortable.

The driver took the first guard shift. I'd just begun to doze off when the platoon medic tapped on the canvas. He'd forgotten to give me my mail. He handed me a packet containing several letters from home and a large, strange-looking, dog-eared envelope. I thanked him and we visited for a few minutes. Normally the medic was at my side in my command track, so he was particularly interested in where I wanted him to ride while I was on One-Four. Due to the limited space on the tank, I told him he would have to stay on One-Six and that I'd make sure they were always right behind me in the order of march. I also told him not to wait for my call if we took casualties but to go where he was needed.

After he left, I put the mail in my map case and made a mental note to read it in the morning when I wasn't so tired.

It was an uneventful night. The next morning life was back to normal, with the CO assigning sectors for the platoons to patrol and the troop moving out in column. The big difference was that now I was perched about ten feet up in the air with the tank's

90mm main gun tube bobbing up and down in front of me like a limp noodle. The good thing about being in the lead vehicle was that you got to breathe clean air; there was no dust or diesel fumes to fill your lungs and sting your eyes. The big drawback was that being in the lead vehicle was like walking point on a patrol: You were the first to hit a mine or run into an ambush. It thus came as no surprise that nobody argued with me when I offered to take the lead in One-Four.

After we arrived in our flanking sector, I began to check out the old tank to determine its limitations while simultaneously cross-training Borgos and the driver. We practiced crew drills, with first Borgos and then the driver serving as loader. Then I brought the rest of the platoon on line with us and notified troop headquarters that we were going to test fire our weapons. After getting the okay, I started with the most familiar weapon—the externally mounted .50-caliber machine gun. It was surrounded by a heavy gun shield and not affected by the hydraulic problem. After firing twenty rounds, I climbed out of the cupola and told Private Borgos to load and fire the weapon. A small man, he was easily able to yank the charging handle back, load the weapon, and, thumbing the butterfly trigger, fire off twenty rounds. The driver, also a small man, had some difficulty with the charging handle, so I demonstrated how to use both hands and put his whole body into it. He quickly mastered the technique and sent another twenty rounds ripping into the trees to our front.

Firing the 90mm main gun was a little more complicated. The damaged hydraulic system would not hold the gun steady, so when traversing or elevating, Borgos had to reverse the hand crank to stop the gun's travel; this made for sloppy aiming. I fired a high explosive round at a tree a hundred yards away and missed it by fifty feet. I had Borgos crank the tube a little to the right and then I fired a second round. That one hit within five feet of the target, plenty close enough for the type of fighting in which we usually engaged.

I slid down into the turret and took a turn as loader so that Borgos and the driver could take turns firing a canister round at an anthill about twenty-five yards to our front. It boosted my spirits to see how much they enjoyed firing the main gun. When they were finished, I knew we could hold our own as a crew.

Our test firing completed, we moved out to our first blocking position. By late afternoon I found riding high up on the tank to be quite comfortable. My fear of being a prime sniper target faded as I focused on other problems.

That evening we rejoined the troop in a position similar to the one we'd been in the previous night. The troop commander called a meeting after supper and outlined the next day's mission. After briefly mentioning the friendly fire incident, he explained that the officer in charge of the 155mm unit's fire direction center had been reprimanded for the erratic round. The FDC officer blamed the gun crew, and we were probably lucky that they acknowledged their mistake. The artillery unit apparently was treating the death of Sergeant O'Leary and the wounding of the loader as a minor incident. That didn't sit well with our CO, who told us that he was registering a formal complaint with division artillery, for whatever that was worth.

Later, after sending out the ambush patrol and checking the perimeter, I retrieved the mail I'd put in my map case the previous night and, using a red-filtered flashlight under my lean-to, opened the large, dog-eared envelope. It had at least six different addresses on it. Inside was a heavily soiled manila envelope with eight more addresses on it. The return address on that envelope was from my former unit in Germany: B Company, 2d Battalion, 68th Armor. The envelope had followed me to the Jungle Warfare School in Panama, then to Fort Dix, New Jersey, then to San Francisco, and, finally, over to Vietnam. It had taken nine months for it to reach me from Germany. What could it be?

Inside the battered envelope I found an equally battered photograph of me marching at the head of my tank platoon just prior to departing for Vietnam. The inscription written across one corner read, "Hope you've found a good pair of boots in Vietnam. Best of luck," and was signed by my former battalion commander. There was nothing else inside the envelope.

The photograph reminded me of a portion of my life about which I had completely forgotten. As I sat there in the darkness under my shelter half, my thoughts returned to what seemed like the distant past, some twenty months before, when I was en route to Germany for my first duty assignment.

The 2d Battalion, 68th Armor, was located in Baumholder. We had been housed in an old brick barracks built in the early 1930s and used by the Wehrmacht in World War II. I commanded a platoon of five M60 tanks, a newer version of the M48s we had in Vietnam. They were equipped with a 105mm main gun and had better optical sights.

My platoon sergeant there was a grizzled World War II veteran who'd had the tip of his nose shot off and his feet frozen during the Battle of the Bulge. He was a real professional whose vast knowledge of tanks would have been a great help to me in Vietnam. As it was, he taught me a lot during the time we spent together in Germany.

I had been detailed to Germany on a thirty-six month tour, and I would have been more than happy to continue in that pleasant assignment for the entire three years. However, during the first week of June 1966, I was in the motor pool helping a tank crew replace a road wheel when a runner came down from the orderly room to inform me that the battalion S1 had an urgent message for me. I rushed to the personnel office, where a sergeant handed me an envelope with my name on it. Inside was a blurred teletype message advising me that I would be leaving for Vietnam within sixty days, with a delay en route to attend the Jungle Warfare School. Official orders would follow in regular mail. This was such a shock that I had to sit down and read it again to make sure they had the right Walker. Only one other soldier in the battalion had received orders for Vietnam. He had gone into a deep depression, treating it like a death sentence. My tour suddenly went from thirty-six months to seven months, but that often happens in the army. I began the familiar process of clearing post, getting plague and yellow fever shots, and arranging for transportation to Panama.

Upon hearing the news, my company commander, who had been in Germany for almost three years himself, insisted that I take leave and see as much of Europe as possible before I left.

I had recently bought a 1955 Volkswagen from a warrant officer in our maintenance section, so I loaded it with a pup tent, sleeping bag, extra fuel, and a case of C rations and set off on a two-week tour of Europe. My itinerary included Luxembourg, Paris, Italy, Switzerland, Austria, and southern Germany. Of all the places I visited,

Bavaria was my favorite, particularly the beautiful little town of Berchtesgaden and the village of Obersalzberg, where I explored the bombed out ruins of Adolf Hitler's house.

Upon my return to Baumholder, I discovered that a military parade had been scheduled, not in my honor, but for our division's annual Organization Day celebration. My company commander asked me to participate in it as my last official act.

All went well on the day of the parade. The weather was beautiful and many family members and local Germans were present. As I marched onto the field at the head of my platoon, I noticed the sole of my right boot, a pair that I'd had since starting ROTC, was beginning to separate and flap with each step. When we finally assembled in mass formation in front of the reviewing stand, I sent one of my tank loaders out the back of the formation to the nearest building to find some tape. He returned with a huge roll of green tape. During a particularly long round of applause, I wrapped a large strip of the tape around the toe of my boot. Later, as we passed in review, I hoped no one would notice. However, sitting there in Vietnam, I could see from the photograph that somebody had.

At a small reception after the parade, I shook hands all around, said good-bye, and then had the soldier who bought my Volkswagen drive me to the Frankfurt airport for the flight back to the States.

The sudden sound of my driver's voice announcing that one of our vehicles was not answering a radio check brought me back to the present. The soldier on guard was probably asleep but I felt compelled to go over and investigate. I tossed the photo into my map case and headed out into the darkness.

I eventually was asked to provide a statement to the office investigating the friendly fire incident. Later, I learned that the lieutenant in charge of the fire direction center had been relieved of his duties and reassigned out of the artillery. Even that seemed insufficient punishment. However, as time passed, I began to look at the incident as more of an accident of war than a criminal act that had to be punished.

Ambush Patrol

In this age when there can be no losers in peace and no victors in war, we must recognize the obligation to match national strength with national restraint.

—Lyndon B. Johnson

One day we spent an hour recovering a tank that had bellied up on an anthill, its tracks spinning helplessly, rather like a man straddling a fence with neither foot touching the ground.

Occupying anthills like the one our tank had gotten stuck on are some of the most aggressive red ants in the world. The ants, a breed closely related to South America's fire ants, were one-half to three-quarters of an inch in length and had extra large, powerful jaws. They also very cleverly built nests in trees, forming them with leaves held together with a substance much like the silk strands in a spiderweb.

Whenever one of our vehicles drove under low tree branches, which was quite often, the radio antenna would whip through the leaves and hundreds of red ants would rain down on the unsuspecting men and their vehicle. The vicious creatures would immediately grab hold of any exposed skin with their powerful jaws. It was not unusual to see vehicles skid to a stop and crewmen scramble to the ground, throwing off helmets, flak jackets, and shirts as they swatted wildly at the ants. It was an amusing sight if it was someone else fighting the ants. When no trees were present, the ants would burrow into the ground and create giant anthills as hard as rock, some as big as six feet tall and four feet wide at the base. It was one such anthill, which had been obscured from view by heavy brush, on which our tank had become stuck.

Our SOP in such a situation was to bring up an ACAV, attach tow cables to the stuck track, and pull it free of the obstacle. The procedure normally took only a few minutes. Today, however, the method didn't work. I ordered another tank forward from the rear of the column, hooked up its tow cables, and pulled the stuck tank off the anthill.

While these efforts were underway, I had the two scout teams out checking the edges of the clearing, providing security for the disabled tank and the men on the ground.

Just as the tank was being pulled free, I received a call from one of the teams. They had discovered something and wanted me to come over and see it. Leaving the rest of the platoon in place, I moved my command track a hundred yards or so to where the two scout vehicles were stopped. Expecting to see the entrance to a tunnel or some other evidence of an enemy base camp, I was surprised to see the two track commanders standing beside a small creek. One of them was poking a stick into the water.

As I stepped down and walked over, the one with the stick said, "Sir, how about a bath today? We've found the perfect spot." They surely had. The water was about three feet deep with a sandy bottom and the banks were about six feet high to protect against snipers.

"Sure," I said. "Have your crews go first; then we'll start rotating the others in."

We rarely had a chance to take showers because of the policy of keeping us in night defensive positions away from the fire support bases, so we had become adept at finding streams and bathing on the run in the field. When no creeks or rivers were available, the platoon had two three-gallon canvas buckets with plastic showerheads fitted on the bottom and equipped with rope handles for hanging them up. These would be passed from vehicle to vehicle so those who were desperate for a shower could use them.

When it was my crew's turn to use our field shower, I would position our track in a prominent spot with good all-around observation and wedge my folded stretcher across the .50-caliber machine gun's armored shield so that the handles extended about three feet over the side. Then, dragging along a five-gallon can of water and one of the shower buckets, I would climb up on top of the vehicle, hook the bucket over the end of the stretcher, and fill it with water.

Next, after laying a clean uniform out on the back ramp, I would walk naked around to the side of the vehicle with soap and shampoo in hand. Finally, while standing on a .50-caliber ammunition box, I would unscrew the showerhead, allowing a fine spray of water to wet me down. As soon as I was soaked down I would turn the water off and then lather up and shampoo my hair. The rinse lasted about a minute. Two people normally could shower out of a single bucketful of water.

However, I rarely got through a shower without being interrupted by at least one radio call or having a packed Vietnamese bus go by with the driver honking and the passengers whooping and waving. On one occasion, during a hard rain, I thought I could strip off, lather up, and get a good rinse before the rain stopped. Unfortunately, I was wrong. I stood there coated with a layer of soap and a sticky head of hair and the sun shining.

Getting the tank off the anthill and then bathing in the stream had taken us about two hours. When we finished, we continued on our search-and-destroy mission west of Lai Khe, not far from the Saigon River.

The division intelligence section had reported that enemy equipment and supplies were being brought down the Ho Chi Minh Trail and into Vietnam not far from us. The enemy was believed to be hauling the stuff just north of Tay Ninh and over to the Saigon River, where it was loaded aboard sampans and distributed to various points along the river all the way down to Saigon.

Helicopter gunships fitted with searchlights had been patrolling the river at night in an attempt to intercept the little boats, but without success. The enemy could hear them coming and would quickly glide under the heavy brush lining the river's banks. Our search-and-destroy efforts were intended to interdict the supplies arriving by way of the river.

The squadron was working the western side of the river, with C Troop operating in the northernmost sector. We had found and destroyed a number of small enemy supply dumps. It appeared the enemy was stockpiling materials for an offensive of some kind.

Later in the afternoon we rejoined the troop and moved into our night defensive position a short distance from the Saigon River. There, we set up in our standard circular formation, with the vehicles spaced about twenty yards apart and facing outward. The men quickly laid out the perimeter barbed wire and set out trip flares and claymore mines while the platoon leaders met with the CO to review the day's reconnaissance and receive the next day's mission.

The troop commander told us that a patrol had found a sampan landing site about a mile north of our position and that our troop had been tasked to place an ambush patrol near it. My platoon was given the assignment, and each of the other platoons was tasked to furnish five additional men. The CO spread out his map and pointed out the exact coordinates for the patrol. The patrol was to set up where a foot trail following the edge of the river intersected a trail leading from the river and to an abandoned village about five hundred yards from the water's edge. There was a slight depression where the two trails met, and then the ground sloped steeply down to the river.

The CO instructed me to use my vehicles to run the patrol out at dusk and try to disguise the drop-off by making several stops, just in case someone was watching. He and the artillery FO had selected some targets so that if any enemy ran into the ambush we could call in preplanned artillery fires all around the ambush site. If it looked like the patrol had more than it could handle, my platoon would go out with guns blazing and rescue it.

The CO dismissed us after instructing the other platoon leaders to have their men at my command vehicle no later than 7 P.M. with face camouflage, seven magazines of M16 ammo, three fragmentation grenades, and one claymore mine each.

We often discussed the kind of people we didn't want to send out on patrols: guys with two left feet, little guys with Coke bottle glasses, or any of the Project 100,000 guys who didn't understand English.

I can remember guiding an ambush patrol out one night through the trip flares and barbed wire and, as we reached the last trip wire, putting my hand on the wire and telling each patrol member to step over my hand. One of the men stepped on my hand, setting off the trip flare and starting a fire that took about thirty minutes to put out.

Some patrol leaders would go out shorthanded rather than take certain individuals along. I could not blame them and insisted that we put our best men on ambush. We'd find equally challenging duties for the rest. Other valid reasons for not sending a man on ambush patrol included having a bad cough or cold or diarrhea.

As soon as I got back to the platoon area I assembled the necessary equipment and ammunition for the patrol: an M60 machine gun, a radio, a compass, a map of the area, a poncho for warmth, and two cans of C-ration cookies with jam in case I got hungry.

As the rest of the patrol members arrived, I checked them over and directed them to where I had scratched out a rough map on the ground depicting the trail junction and the depression in which it was nestled. When all of the men had gathered—five scouts or infantrymen from each platoon, plus my medic and me—I began my briefing. I suspected the men believed that higher headquarters considered these patrols expendable and that whoever went out was simply another early warning device, like a trip flare, to warn the main body of an enemy attack. This may have been true in some units, but I always had a rescue plan if any of my patrols got in too deep.

I explained that we would set up about ten yards from the trail junction with teams covering all four approaches, and then broke the men down into the various teams. My medic and I, along with four men armed with M16s and the M60 machine gun, would cover the trail to the river. All members of the patrol would be positioned within ten yards of the trail junction, mutually supporting each other.

There were not many questions, except a request to be on 50 percent alert with two-hour shifts to allow the men to sleep. I agreed to that and then answered questions about the rescue plan I'd devised if we made heavy contact.

Members of the platoon goofed off and clowned around a lot, but when their names came up for an ambush patrol they became very serious. Few things in this war pitted them against the enemy on a more equal basis than did an ambush patrol. They were out there on the ground in the enemy's element, far from their armored vehicles and knowing full well that, late at night, there would be no fighter-bombers or helicopter gunships available to bail them out.

The most vulnerable time for the patrol was going out and setting up in position. Booby traps were always a problem. Sometimes the enemy would be waiting for us along the route, or they would detect us as we moved in and set up, and then later mortar us or throw grenades into our position.

I still marvel at how men could go out, lay down, and go to sleep right next to a heavily traveled enemy trail. Getting by on six hours' sleep every night certainly contributed to their fatigue, and they were becoming used to the presence of danger and could only stay keyed up for so long. But don't get the wrong impression. They were always in a light sleep, so all it took was a gentle pat or nudge to bring them instantly awake and ready for action.

Twenty minutes before departure, with daylight fading fast, the CO and first sergeant came by as they were checking the perimeter. When I greeted them, the first sergeant started stomping the ground. The two had apparently disturbed a large bamboo viper that was thrashing around in the grass while the first sergeant was stomping on its tail. The snake, which had alternating bands of black and sand coloring, soon disappeared.

"Didn't you know that was a deadly bamboo viper?" I asked the first sergeant.

"Naw," he replied, "It was just a little ol' grass snake."

The CO asked how the patrol was coming along and I told him we were just about ready to go out. He casually asked who the patrol leader was. When I said, "I'm taking it out," there was a long pause.

"No, you're not!" he snapped after glaring at me for several moments. "I need you here to run this platoon. Send someone else." With that he spun on his heel and, followed by the first sergeant, continued around the perimeter.

As soon as the CO left the area I started looking for Sergeant Cowhig. He was on top of his tank with his boots off sipping a beer when I climbed up and asked him how things were going.

"Just fine," he said, smiling.

I told him about the CO's visit and that our patrol was now leaderless. "Sergeant Cowhig, I want you to take the patrol out."

Turning pale, he stood up and said, "Sir, I'm a tanker. I don't know anything about patrolling." I took hold of his arm and said, "Sergeant, you'll do just fine." Then I told him he had about fifteen minutes before departure and to follow me over to the map I had scratched out on the ground so I could explain to him how I had intended to run the patrol.

At the appointed time, and with Sergeant Cowhig still in a slight daze, I gathered the patrol together and told everyone that he had asked to go along so I had decided to let him be in charge. I asked for questions and, when there were none, we mounted up and headed out through the wire. As we moved along, I helped Sergeant Cowhig apply camouflage paint to his face, gave him my cookies and jam, and, for good luck, hooked two grenades on his flak jacket.

With two tanks leading our ten-vehicle column, we moved about half a mile beyond the drop-off point, turned around, and then headed south, trying not to be too obvious about our real purpose. As we approached the drop-off point the column slowed to a crawl as the patrol members jumped down and disappeared into the tall grass in the direction of the depression. I gave Sergeant Cowhig a thumbs-up. He responded with a very sour expression.

As we headed back to our night defensive position, I made a commo check with Sergeant Cowhig to ensure that his radio was working properly. He whispered that he could hear me "loud and clear."

Back inside the perimeter the platoon's vehicles pulled into the line again with my command track twenty-five yards to the rear. It was my policy to ensure that each vehicle had at least four men for guard duty/radio watch, so that with four two-hour watches between 9 P.M. and 5 A.M., each man could expect to get six hours of sleep. With naps during the day, this generally was enough for young, healthy men to function.

My vehicle maintained only a radio watch and every hour on the hour all vehicles and the ambush patrol called in with a situation report. Normally the reports were routine: "This is One-Two, negative contact. Over." If for some reason a vehicle didn't report, my man on watch went over to the vehicle to find out why. Ninety-nine percent of the time the soldier on duty would be asleep. He would be awakened, his name taken, and the next morning I would speak to his vehicle commander. There was always the danger that while a man on guard slept the enemy could sneak up and cut his throat or blow up his vehicle. Not quite as threatening, but equally real, was the possibility that I would have him court-martialed for dereliction of duty. Probably the most effective punishment was myself or Sergeant Cowhig venturing over to a sleeping guard, slapping the back of his helmet, and then chewing him out for about five minutes.

I had the first watch that night, nine to eleven, and everything was quiet. A report from the ambush patrol indicated that they were in place with trip flares and claymores set up and everything normal.

At a little after eleven I lay down on my stretcher and covered up with a poncho liner. I told the man taking over on radio watch to wake me if the ambush patrol reported any activity.

Shortly before 2 A.M. Private Borgos nudged me awake. "Sir," he whispered, "the ambush patrol is in trouble."

I shook my head clear and got on the radio. It took me about five tries to raise Sergeant Cowhig. Still unruffled, he explained in a slow, measured tone that three sampans had landed at the end of the river trail and that there appeared to be twelve individuals manning them. I asked if the enemy was moving up the trail. He said they were busy unloading the boats. I told Sergeant Cowhig that I would alert the artillery to be ready for a fire mission and to keep me informed.

About five minutes later I heard three large explosions off in the distance, followed by the rattle of small-arms fire. Sergeant Cowhig called on the radio and, in an excited voice, told me the enemy had begun moving up the trail and had walked into their ambush. The explosions were their claymore mines going off. He asked for artillery fire and said his patrol was going to "move forward just a little bit" for a better field of fire. I notified troop headquarters and soon artillery fire began pounding the river's edge where the sampans had landed.

Artillery coming in at night often seems closer than it really is, and being in a ground depression would make it seem even more threatening. Few things in war are more terrifying than being ambushed, and a night ambush was even more so. The victims were always caught by surprise, their minds not focused on danger. Most ambushes usually begin with an explosion. In this case there were three. The enemy must have felt a tremendous sense of disorientation and terror as they realized that someone was trying to kill them.

One's first reaction is to take cover and then, as you realize what is happening, to get up and crawl or run from the killing zone. Ambushes are set up with that in mind. Patrol leaders must select the best fields of fire and position men and weapons where they will have the greatest likelihood of cutting off the enemy's escape. An effective ambush is one that leaves no survivors. That's why it's so terrifying.

Sergeant Cowhig again called me on the radio. "Stop the artillery!" he shouted. "It's coming in on top of us!" I got on the command radio and, within seconds, I was able to stop the artillery. That done, I called Sergeant Cowhig on the platoon net and asked if they'd suffered any casualties. He said one man was slightly wounded.

I explained the situation to the troop commander, and we decided to move the patrol up the village trail to the top of the depression and then call for more artillery fire. I relayed this information to Sergeant Cowhig and he and his men were soon moving. Within a few minutes, the artillery fire resumed.

After ten minutes of intense shelling I called and asked that the big guns cease firing. I then called Sergeant Cowhig and asked for a situation report. He said that they could neither see nor hear anything in the direction of the river. "Since everyone in Vietnam knows we're out here now, can we come back in?" he asked when he'd finished his report.

I agreed that his night's work was over and said I'd clear it with the troop commander.

It was 2:45 A.M. when we moved out under a full moon to bring in the ambush patrol. For safety I ordered everyone to turn their lights on. As we neared the pick-up point I had my gunner fire the .50-caliber into the abandoned village to keep any enemy there down in their holes.

I had earlier informed Sergeant Cowhig that we would halt the column, turn off our lights, and load the patrol as quickly as possible. This was to ensure that he and his men weren't silhouetted, thus making them a tempting target for any sampan survivors.

When we were safely back inside the wire I checked on the wounded soldier, who was from 2d Platoon. His injury was a small but deep gash in his back at about waist level and maybe six inches over from his backbone. My medic said it was not serious and that we could wait until first light to evacuate the man.

After telling the patrol members what a fine job they had done and thanking them, I sent them back to their vehicles. Within about thirty minutes the area was quiet again. The CO then came over and wanted to debrief Sergeant Cowhig with me.

As we sat there in the moonlight on my vehicle's back ramp, Sergeant Cowhig explained what had happened. He said he had been asleep when a patrol member shook him and said he could hear voices coming from the direction of the river. Unable to see anything, Sergeant Cowhig and another man moved down the trail to where they could see the three sampans and count twelve men. The enemy started unloading the boats and one of the men turned on a flashlight and began shining it into the brush as if he was looking for something. Afraid of being discovered by the man with the flashlight, the two men rejoined the patrol.

From their position at the trail junction, the patrol was set up to attack anyone coming from the abandoned village to get supplies or to engage the men from the sampans if they moved up the trail toward the village.

A few minutes after Sergeant Cowhig returned to his position, they spotted four men—maybe more—carrying heavy boxes up the trail. While members of the ambush patrol watched from their hiding places, the enemy soldiers drew even with the first claymore mine. Sergeant Cowhig let the men advance another couple of yards and then signaled for his men to spring the ambush. All three mines were detonated at the same time and the patrol members opened up with their M16s and the M60 machine gun. It was then that Sergeant Cowhig had requested artillery fire.

I asked the CO if we could continue to hit the landing site with intermittent artillery fire for the rest of the night so that the enemy wouldn't disturb the area. Also, I asked for permission to send out a patrol in the morning to determine the extent of enemy casualties and collect any weapons or equipment that might still be there. The CO agreed and, after a few more questions, departed.

Sergeant Cowhig announced that he was going to go back to his tank, smoke a cigarette, fix some coffee, and then eat the cookies I had given him. There was still an hour or so before stand-to, so I returned to my stretcher and tried to sleep.

The man pulling the last radio watch woke me up at five minutes to five. There was a flurry of activity as we loaded up our gear, then, while we waited for the medevac helicopter, I had one last meeting with the CO. As the helicopter departed with our wounded patrol member on board, a pleasant young man whose condition had improved dramatically from what it had been earlier, we moved out with the troop headquarters vehicles following behind us. The CO wanted to inspect the ambush site and determine for himself the extent of the damage we'd inflicted.

As we approached the western end of the depression, I sent one scout section to the north and one to the south to secure the trails leading into it.

I had Sergeant Cowhig put together a five-man patrol and, with Private Borgos at my side carrying the radio, the seven of us entered the depression with Sergeant Cowhig leading and Borgos and I bringing up the rear. It was obvious the trail had been heavily used. It was well worn, dusty, and had no vegetation growing on it. We cautiously made our way down the hundred yards or so of trail to the ambush site. There we found the bodies of three men who had been killed instantly when the ambush was sprung. Two were lying in grotesque positions, eyes and mouths open, their bodies riddled with numerous bullet holes. The ants and flies were already starting their work and the stench of death filled the depression. The boxes they had been carrying contained hand grenades and land mines and were scattered along the trail. A fourth enemy soldier had apparently been wounded, crawled behind some brush, returned fire, and then bled to death. We found several shell casings near him. Nearer to the river we found the badly mangled body of a fifth enemy soldier who most likely was killed by the artillery fire.

Scattered along the trail were six more cases of rifle ammunition and RPGs, along with a large plastic bag full of salt and some documents. One of the sampans had been hit by artillery fire and lay half submerged, its hull split in half. Another sampan, apparently undamaged, was floating a few yards farther downstream, caught in some tall grass just a few feet out in the water. Expecting to find live enemy or booby traps, we proceeded cautiously while searching the area. Although we found no more bodies or supplies, there was much evidence of the damage caused by the artillery and many blood trails, indicating that the enemy had suffered more wounded.

I radioed the CO and told him the area was now secured and reported our tally of enemy dead and captured materiel. Within minutes he and the first sergeant arrived on the scene. Sergeant Cowhig gave them a blow-by-blow description of the night's events as he led them around the ambush site.

Meanwhile, Borgos and I continued to look for the third sampan. The CO came over and told me to load the captured materiel on his maintenance track and bury the enemy soldiers where they had fallen. I told Sergeant Cowhig to use my radio to round up a detail to dig the graves and carry the captured supplies back to the maintenance vehicle.

While I watched the detail going about its business, Private Borgos handed me the radio handset and said the CO wanted to speak with me.

I put the receiver to my ear and listened as the CO advised me that he would be leaving in a few minutes to take the captured materiel over to squadron headquarters and make a full report. He told me to give Sergeant Cowhig a "pat on the back for his good work" and then continue on with the day's mission as soon as we finished burying the enemy dead.

I told him that I planned to throw grenades into the still-floating sampan to ensure it was on the bottom before we left. He said that was fine with him and that he would see me that evening.

Fortunately for the burial detail, the ground was soft. Using the standard army D-handled shovels from our tracks, the men were soon down to a depth of four or five feet. Sergeant Cowhig instructed them to dig the graves next to the bodies so they wouldn't have to be carried.

I was a short distance away from the gravesites when Sergeant Cowhig called me. "Sir," he shouted, "there's something different about one of these guys." The bodies of the five men had been blown, twisted, or bent into grotesque, awkward positions. Now, as they lay there stretched out next to the open graves after having been searched for documents and identification, it was plain that one soldier was larger than the rest, looked healthier, had more meat on his bones, and wore a uniform that was a different shade of green. His face was full and round but obviously Asian. We knew that Chinese advisers accompanied regimental-sized NVA units, but this was a small Vietcong unit.

I recalled overhearing members of the MI team that rode with us talking about a radio intercept of someone speaking Mandarin Chinese in this same general area. I also knew that Gen. William Westmoreland, the MACV commander, was extremely sensitive about the Chinese entering the war and would reprimand commanders for even suggesting that Chinese advisers might be accompanying North Vietnamese units in the South. General Westmoreland, who had commanded an airborne regiment in Korea, no doubt remembered the Chinese intervention in that war and the fate of General MacArthur shortly thereafter.

We searched the dead man's uniform but found only a pistol magazine with five 9mm bullets in it, some string, and a small writing tablet with several sets of numbers on one page.

I marked the ground at his feet and at the top of his head and, using my boots to measure with, determined that he was more than six feet tall. I sent a man back to my vehicle for my camera and then took a dozen pictures of the big man—front, side, face, feet, items from his pockets—before we rolled him into the shallow hole and covered him with the rich Vietnamese soil.

After sinking the sampan, Private Borgos and I were walking back up to my command vehicle when Sergeant Cowhig came hurrying up the trail behind us. He was excited.

"Look what we found under one of those little gooks," he announced as he held out a French submachine gun with an adjustable wire stock and "1952" stamped on it. It was a weapon normally used by the French Foreign Legion, and it was in excellent condition, a handsome reminder that this war had been going on for a long time. A closer look revealed the letters "TU"—a Vietnamese name, probably that of its last owner—carved into the receiver.

I told Sergeant Cowhig I'd take care of it and went on back to my vehicle. Sitting on the back ramp examining the weapon, I started to call the CO and report our new find but instead decided that rather than providing another souvenir for some colonel back at division headquarters, I would give it to someone more deserving.

I taped two empty sandbags around the gun and when Sergeant Cowhig came by to report that everything was done and that we were ready to move out, I put the weapon in his hands and said, "See if you can get this thing home." We never mentioned the gun again; however, I heard later that he had sent pieces of the weapon home inside a stereo and in a camera box. Perhaps it found a special place on his family room wall, a reminder of a very successful ambush patrol he once led.

Later that evening when I reported my suspicions about the possible Chinese adviser to my CO, he showed an almost total lack of interest. His only comment was, "Not all Vietnamese are the same size."

The Leprosarium

You have a row of dominoes set up, you knock over the first one, and what will happen to the last one is, that it will go over very quickly.

—Dwight D. Eisenhower

During the middle of April 1967, an air force reconnaissance plane flying along the lush, green, serpent-like Vietnamese border photographed what appeared to be large numbers of North Vietnamese soldiers moving in a southerly direction along Highway 13. Our cavalry squadron was familiar with the area because we had conducted three previous operations there in the past six months. Furthermore, because the Ho Chi Minh Trail had many distribution points there, it was considered an enemy-controlled area.

To take advantage of this fresh information, our squadron was alerted and ordered to move to the vicinity of the Cambodian border within twenty-four hours. Our squadron commander was given overall charge of the operation and the following additional units were placed under his command: an infantry battalion, a 105mm artillery battery, a platoon of four M42 twin-40mm "Dusters," and a company of tanks.

We felt a sense of urgency during the road march from Phu Loi to Loc Ninh, as if the enemy might escape if we didn't catch him on the run. We arrived just as it was getting dark, with only the artillery battery and Duster platoon accompanying the squadron; the infantry and tanks would join us the next day.

The air cavalry troop's aerorifle platoon had secured a large open field about three kilometers north of the town and a short dis-

174

tance from the road. Ground guides met us when we arrived and we could see infantrymen scattered around the edges of the field securing it, which allowed us to quickly move in and begin setting up our defenses.

Later that evening, the troop commander told us squadron aircraft had made several enemy sightings and, because contact with the enemy was likely, all units were to remain on 50 percent alert until further notice.

All was quiet until about 1 A.M. However, from then until first light, the perimeter was subjected to repeated probes consisting of sniper and mortar fire, hand grenades thrown into our barbed wire, and a loudspeaker being turned on and off. Those manning the perimeter responded with M79s and artillery fire but had little effect on the enemy. Units inside the perimeter suffered no casualties and, as far as I could determine, we inflicted no damage on the enemy. There was no doubt the enemy was there and in large numbers.

Our squadron headquarters and attached units were set up a short distance from Highway 13, almost at the point where it crossed into Cambodia. Working from there each day, the cavalry troops were assigned sectors to patrol and then moved back into night defensive positions from which they could easily be supported by the artillery battery that was colocated with squadron headquarters.

One day, as I was studying my map, I noticed a cluster of buildings identified as a leprosarium inside our sector. Being curious, I worked out a compass heading to it and we moved off in that direction. After traveling a short distance I saw several mud-colored buildings grouped closely together with what looked like a barbed-wire fence stretched around them.

Throughout history, leprosy has had a very dark and sinister reputation. Many believed the disease was God's punishment for the wicked. Furthermore, because there was no known cure for it and because it was highly contagious, those who contracted the disease were driven from the local community for fear of contamination. In college I had read about the famous leper colony in Hawaii and the Catholic priest who devoted his life to caring for the lepers there. I can still recall the vivid descriptions of victims whose fingers, toes, ears, and noses fell off as the disease ran its course.

I decided it wasn't a good idea to move right in and check out the buildings, so I picked up my binoculars and ordered Sergeant Cowhig to bring his tank over. As soon as he pulled alongside, I stepped over onto his track and climbed up on the very highest part of the turret for a clear view. Through my binoculars I saw about fifty individuals with what appeared to be burlap cloth wrapped around various parts of their ulcerous and wasting bodies. They all seemed to have great difficulty walking or moving around. Sergeant Cowhig, always one for detail, pointed out that the wind was blowing from the direction of the leprosarium and wondered if leprosy germs could be falling on us as we stood there. I returned to my vehicle without delay and quickly ordered the platoon to move off in the opposite direction.

As we moved through the tall grass we could see large craters created by recent B-52 bombing runs. The craters were thirty to fifty feet in diameter and up to fifteen feet deep, and looked like small ponds when filled with water.

I was looking ahead as the column was passing through a small clearing with Sergeant Cowhig's tank in the lead when, just as the last vehicle reentered the brush, his tank vanished. I radioed the second tank in line for a status report and the commander replied, "Sergeant Cowhig's tank went into some kind of tiger trap."

I moved my command vehicle forward and ordered the scout sections to move out and provide local security. When I reached the head of the column, all I could see through the brush were the grill doors of Sergeant Cowhig's tank.

I dismounted with Private Borgos and made my way to the far side of what could only have been a huge bomb crater. I pulled the grass away for a better view and saw the brush-covered tank with its front slope and gun tube buried deep in the muddy water.

Sergeant Cowhig and his crew were nowhere to be seen. When I called to him, he finally stuck his head out of the hatch and, with a frantic look on his face, shouted, "I can't get my driver out! He's about to drown!"

Startled by his comment, I ran around to the rear of Cowhig's tank, yelling instructions to Sergeant Jones in the following tank to hook his tow cables up and start trying to pull Sergeant Cowhig's tank out of the water.

The dirt around the edge of the hole was loose and, with Sgt. Cowhig's tank almost vertical, it was difficult to climb onto it. I finally managed to crawl around to the driver's hatch and, lying mostly in the water, started pulling brush and small trees away from the main gun and the open driver's hatch. Water had filled the front of the driver's compartment, almost closing off access to the hatch opening. In order to see what was going on inside, I had to put my face in the water. Looking in, I could see that the driver was unconscious. Sergeant Cowhig, who was reaching through the turret basket, struggled to hold the driver's face out of the water so he could breathe. When I asked how badly the driver was hurt, Sergeant Cowhig answered that he had been knocked unconscious by the impact. "If the tank settles any more," he added. "I'm not going to be able to hold him." The look on Sergeant Cowhig's face told me the situation was desperate, and it was clear to me he couldn't stay in that position much longer.

It was an extremely hot, humid day, and I'm sure it must have been at least ten degrees hotter inside the tank. I again yelled for Sergeant Jones to get the tow cables hooked up as I climbed back on to solid ground. As he moved his tank forward, the edge of the bomb crater started to give way and I waved at him to stop. I motioned for Private Borgos to come over to me. I took the portable radio handset from him and ordered the tank at the rear of the column to move forward at top speed.

While I was talking, Sergeant Cowhig's loader stuck his head out and yelled, "The tank's sinking lower!"

I radioed the mortar track and ordered it forward as fast as possible, instructing the crew to break out their shovels when they arrived.

As soon as the One-Seven tank arrived and the mortar crew began shoveling down the near side of the crater, we got the two tanks connected with cables. Sergeant Jones then came forward to hook up Sergeant Cowhig's tank. I radioed the disabled tank and told the crew we were again going to try to pull them out. I told them they might sink slightly but to hold on because I knew we were going to succeed this time.

After ordering the men with the shovels away, I radioed instructions for the two tanks to inch forward. As the ground settled under the first tank, Sergeant Jones hooked the tow cables to the up-turned tank and then signaled his tank and the One-Seven tank to reverse direction. Ever so slowly, Sergeant Cowhig's tank eased out of the crater and leveled off. I ordered everyone to stop. I climbed onto the front of the tank with my medic's and Sergeant Jones's help and began pulling the unconscious driver out of the hatch. He was overweight and difficult to get through the small hatch, but we soon had him on the stretcher. The medic took over. He removed the driver's shirt and began pouring cold water on him. When the driver failed to respond well to cold water or smelling salts, I called for a medevac helicopter.

Sergeant Cowhig, totally exhausted, climbed down off the tank. Although he had not been in the water, he was completely soaked with perspiration. He kept shaking his head as we examined the crater where his tank had just been. He started wiping the driver's face with a cool cloth and said, "I don't know how in the hell this happened."

Soon the medevac chopper was overhead requesting smoke to identify a landing site. Calling for Private Borgos to get me a smoke grenade, I had Sergeant Jones and the medic grab the stretcher and the three of us ran back the hundred yards or so to the small clearing we'd passed earlier. I expected to find a scout section posted there but we were all alone. I drew my .45-caliber pistol, threw a smoke grenade into the clearing, and then we waited for the helicopter to land. When the chopper was about fifty feet off the ground, we heard shots in the distance. The pilot settled into the clearing, and as we were putting the driver on board, the door gunner leaned out toward me and shouted, "Sir, we're taking enemy fire! You guys better get out of here!" With that the helicopter lifted up and the door gunners began hosing down the area outside the clearing with their M60 machine guns. With only my .45-caliber pistol for protection, the three of us wasted no time running back to the safety of the platoon.

As soon as my breathing returned to normal I contacted troop headquarters and made a full report of the bizarre incident. Soon afterward the CO radioed to say he didn't know how something like that could happen if the crew was paying attention. He then asked if my men had been taking their salt tablets. Each man was supposed to take one a day. He said it sounded like my driver was suffering from heat exhaustion brought on by a lack of salt. I reminded him that the man was my acting platoon sergeant's driver and, although I hadn't observed him taking his salt tablets every day, I was confident that he had. That was the extent of the CO's concern.

Sergeant Cowhig removed his tank's escape hatch and drained out most of the water. Then, with his loader driving and Private Borgos to round out the crew, we continued our mission for the day.

My infantry track had developed an oil leak around the transmission seal and required about five gallons of fluid each day to operate. Shortly after reporting the problem to squadron maintenance I received a radio call to send the vehicle back to base camp.

Through rotation home, killed, and wounded, I had lost most of my experienced sergeants and so was forced to operate with inexperienced junior NCOs or specialist fours as vehicle commanders. The vehicle with the oil leak was commanded by one of my most inexperienced sergeants, so I sent along another vehicle with what I considered an experienced crew to serve as escort.

After checking to see that the TCs had a compass and map I gave them specific instructions and then sent the two vehicles back to base. About thirty minutes later, while we were breaking through some particularly thick jungle, one of the tanks threw a track. When the tank commander and I examined the track we decided it would be best to take the track apart to repair it. I deployed the rest of the platoon around the disabled tank for security and the crew set to work.

About this time I got a call asking when the vehicle with the leaking transmission oil seal would arrive. I was concerned because both vehicles should already have reached their destination. We were only about ten minutes from the base area when they left us. After several attempts on the radio, I finally reached the two vehicles and asked where they work. Neither of the track commanders was sure of their location. Because they thought they knew where they were going, they hadn't used their map or compass. In an effort to determine their location, I had a nearby track fire its .50-caliber machine gun into the ground. I waited a few seconds and then called the lost vehicle commanders and asked if they had heard the firing. Both said no.

While I was sitting there in my sweltering vehicle deciding what to do next, I looked over at the tank with the broken track and saw the tank commander and gunner, both with their shirts off, engaged in a violent fistfight. I jumped off my track and ran over to separate the two combatants. As I stepped between them, the gunner, a very large man, lunged for the tank commander and, in the process, knocked me down. Now, the three of us were tangled up on the ground, their sweat and blood all over me. I drew my .45-caliber pistol and pulled the slide to the rear, cocking it. I pressed the barrel of the pistol hard into the gunner's right cheek between his eye and nose and said, "If you don't stop right now, I'm going to blow your head off!"

The platoon medic, a sensitive young man, jumped up when he saw me put the gun to the soldier's head and ran over, waving his hands above his head and shouting, "No, sir! No! Don't!" Ignoring the medic, I called Sergeant Cowhig over and told him to take charge of the gunner. I told him I was placing the man under arrest and that if the man gave him any trouble at all he should shoot him. Sergeant Cowhig knew I was not serious, but the soldier didn't.

Brushing myself off, I went back to my command vehicle and again tried to locate the lost tracks. With radio reception growing weaker and darkness fast approaching, I instructed the two sergeants to retrace their route. I told them we would move out in their direction until we linked up. With three crews working to repair the broken tank track, we soon had the problem fixed and were able to set out on the trail of the lost vehicles. It was obvious the two vehicle commanders had been inattentive and had wandered around aimlessly before finally heading off in the wrong direction. By the time we linked up with them, we had been forced to turn our headlights on, and the troop commander was calling me on the radio every fifteen minutes demanding a situation report.

There was still much work to be done when we finally returned to base. The troop commander ordered me to send out a six-man ambush patrol, which I had Sergeant Cowhig take charge of organizing. While he was doing that, I turned the unruly soldier over to the first sergeant for reassignment to another platoon and for disciplinary action. Neither the soldier nor his track commander would tell me what the fight was about, so I simply charged the man with striking a noncommissioned officer. As I watched the first sergeant lead the man away, I received a radio call advising me that a resupply request covering our ammunition, repair parts, and C-ration requirements for the next ten days was due at troop headquarters within the hour. While I was figuring that out, the mess hall delivered a hot supper of chili over rice to the platoon area so the ambush patrol could eat before going out.

After chow, I ground-guided the vehicle with the leaking oil seal to the maintenance section, which was located in a tent near the center of the perimeter behind a small clump of trees. The mechanics had planned to work after dark to repair our vehicle but I reminded them of the danger of snipers and said, "Let's leave it until tomorrow."

Private Borgos walked up as I was getting ready to leave and told me I was wanted at the troop commander's vehicle for a platoon leader's meeting. I thanked him and then began picking my way over broken trees and brush to the CO's vehicle. Expecting to get chewed out because of our various problems during the day, I was surprised to find that he wanted to know more about the leprosarium and to compliment me for the way I'd handled the fight earlier in the day. The CO then asked me to make a written statement describing exactly what happened during the fight and to include my recommendations. He said he needed it before we departed in the morning so he could take quick action. He also informed me that two flamethrower tracks were being attached to the troop that night and they were waiting to be picked up at the perimeter barbed wire just off Highway 13.

"Is there anything else, Sir?" I asked.

"Yes, I'm attaching the flamethrowers to your platoon for the rest of the operation," he said. "I want you to personally go and guide them in behind your platoon *right now.*"

Flamethrowers were a novelty, and we had great respect for the courage of their crews. However, no one wanted to be too close to them because of the widely held belief that an RPG or the concussion from an exploding mine would cause the 250 gallons of napalm they carried to explode, taking out the vehicles on either side of them. To me it was just a regular armored personnel carrier with an extra-large gas tank.

I had never been in an ambush with one along or seen them used against enemy troops, but I was aware of the fascination they held for my men. Whenever we saw flamethrowers working my men would stop what they were doing to watch, taking pictures for as long as they were belching fire and flame.

After meeting with the troop commander I picked my way through the darkness from where my platoon was located on the far side of the perimeter. I asked if anyone had seen any flamethrower vehicles around. Nobody had. Finally, a lieutenant whose platoon I'd been harassing told me he knew exactly where they were and led me to their location. Rain began to fall as I approached the two vehicles. I explained to the crews that they had been attached to my platoon, and using a red-filtered flashlight, I quickly guided them back to my platoon area, where I positioned them behind my tracks and used their crews to replace individuals who had gone out on the ambush patrol.

It was after 9 P.M. when I returned to my command vehicle. Private Borgos had already hung a piece of canvas from one side of the vehicle, set up my stretcher out of the rain, and brought the radio extension down beside it. Inside the lean-to, sitting on an ammo box, was a plate of cold chili and rice Borgos had saved for me. He had done all this on his own initiative. I was impressed.

Sergeant Cowhig's driver returned on the resupply helicopter the next evening. He was wearing a clean uniform and boots and looked like a new man, all rested and apparently suffering no ill effects from his near drowning.

After I welcomed him back, he told me that he had begun to regain consciousness as we loaded him on the medevac helicopter. He said he thought that the air stirred up by the chopper's main rotor pressing against his wet fatigues is what revived him. He added that he was feeling fine by the time he reached the evacuation hospital.

I told him it was nice to have him back in one piece and asked him how he had managed to run into the crater. When he told me he couldn't recall anything of the incident, I explained what had happened. I added that Sergeant Cowhig was responsible for saving his life and suggested he hurry on back to his tank, where I was sure Sergeant Cowhig would be very glad to see him.

A Soldier Called "Red"

Within the soul of each Vietnam veteran there is probably something that says, "bad war, good soldier."

—Max Cleland

At the height of the dry season, while we were busy escorting truck convoys from Ben Cat to Dian, I learned that one of my soldiers was not receiving his monthly pay. We had been tasked with providing security for one of the three division truck companies that hauled materials up to a central supply point operated by either division or brigade. Each forward unit then sent its own trucks back to pick up what it needed. The routine sometimes went on for two or three weeks. It was a real vacation compared to our normal mission of beating down the jungle.

This particular day we were lined up along the base-camp road with fifteen to twenty trucks waiting for us to clear the road for them. We began the operation by sweeping the road with two hand-held minesweepers. As we eased out of the compound, I had one tank and two ACAVs in front, followed by five to ten trucks, then three more of my vehicles followed by the remainder of the trucks and, finally, the rest of my platoon bringing up the rear. The truck drivers always felt secure with this arrangement because it allowed for few mishaps.

Although the trucks carried different types of cargo, most were loaded with ammunition for the artillery units, which consumed huge amounts of it with their H and I fires. Several trucks were also filled with supplies for local mess halls.

While we were making the escort run to Dian, one of my vehicle commanders mentioned that a member of his crew, Private First Class Rico, a shy young man with a big, toothy grin whom everyone called "Red," had not been paid for over two months. He wanted to know if I could help. The division finance office was at Dian, so I told the sergeant to remind me when we arrived at Dian and I would go over to finance and see what I could do. Later that day, filthy with road dust, the sergeant and his unpaid soldier reminded me of my offer.

We had about thirty to forty minutes between convoys, so I put the sergeant and Red in my vehicle and drove to division finance. Dian was as far to the rear as you could get and still be in the war— tanks and real fighting soldiers were a rare sight there. We attracted a lot of attention as we drove across the base camp with gunners posted behind our .50-caliber and M60 machine guns.

The division finance office was in a long, low building that resembled a strip shopping center with a parking lot out front. As we wheeled into the parking lot trailing a large cloud of dust, I instructed the driver to pull up to the front door, which was open because of the heat. We stopped with the barrel of the .50-caliber machine gun almost sticking through the front door. I jumped down and entered the building with dust roiling around me. Private Rico and his track commander followed close behind.

The building was empty except for a first lieutenant sitting behind a desk. When I asked where everyone was, he said matter-of-factly, "Everyone's gone to lunch. If you have a pay complaint, you'll have to come back after lunch."

I stood there in disbelief. There we were, dirty, clad in flak jackets and steel helmets and carrying M16s and pistols, and this finance lieutenant in freshly starched fatigues was telling us to come back after lunch! Without mincing words, I explained that we couldn't come back, that we had to rejoin our outfit, which was heading north in just a few minutes, and that my soldier needed his pay straightened out right then. At least that's close to what I told him.

The lieutenant looked at us as if seeing us for the first time, and then said slowly, "In that case, maybe *I* can help you."

It took the lieutenant all of about ten minutes to solve Red's pay problem, give him a partial cash payment, and fill out a money order for his wife. I thanked the finance lieutenant and invited him to ride up to Ben Cat with us someday if he ever wanted some excitement. Leaving the finance office, we climbed up on my track and headed back to the convoy assembly area, where the latest group of trucks was already beginning to assemble.

Red's pay problem was caused by our postal system, which often took two or three weeks to deliver a letter from home. He had a wife and child in Puerto Rico and had taken out an allotment to provide for their support. In the course of transferring to Vietnam he was assigned to a different unit from the one stated on his orders. It took several months for his records to reach our unit because of this. In the meantime, his wife's allotment was canceled. Due to the confusion about which unit he had been assigned to, his mail from home took an additional month to reach him and the cancellation of his wife's allotment became a financial crisis.

Considering the great distances that our mail traveled and the way most units moved around, the army did a pretty good job of delivering the mail. To accomplish this huge task, the army organized its own postal service as part of the Adjutant General Corps. This service was connected at various points with the U.S. Postal Service. Letters and packages bound for Vietnam, many containing homemade cookies and cakes, were mailed from all across America to an army post office in San Francisco. There, the mail was sorted according to zones in Vietnam and then sent on air force supply planes to the appropriate area. When it arrived in country, it was further broken down by postal detachments before being forwarded to individual units, where it was sorted by company mail clerks. These clerks kept track of where each man was assigned, his rotation date, and forwarding addresses. Mail would normally reach a soldier in eight to ten days. If a unit moved around as much as we did, it could take fifteen to twenty days.

As previously mentioned, resupply helicopters made a daily delivery of hot food and also dropped off mail, repair parts, and ammunition. They also brought canned beverages if I sent money back for that purpose. Old-timers left and new men arrived on the resupply choppers, but the most prized item on board was always the mail with news from home.

On a hot day not long after our trip to the division finance office, the first sergeant sent word that we could keep only one pet per platoon. It seemed that with the large number of stray dogs wandering around the country, rabies had become a primary concern to the chain of command.

Rabies infects the central nervous system and can be transmitted to man through the bite of an infected dog or other animal. Its symptoms include choking, convulsions, and an inability to swallow water—hence the name hydrophobia. When left untreated it is always fatal. It is a horrible, Old Testament–type of disease.

What prompted the first sergeant's decree was the fact that almost every vehicle had picked up a mascot in a deserted village or wandering along the road. The list in our platoon included baby ducks on One-Four, a monkey on One-Seven, two small dogs on One-Zero, and a large dog on my vehicle. It was quite a sight to see our column as it rolled by with animals balanced on top of swaying vehicles, heads poking out of hatches, and dogs with their tongues hanging out, panting in the breeze.

The order was specific: only one small animal per platoon. Most of the men understood the rationale behind it, and without complaining, made plans to give away or set loose their pets. The crew of One-Four offered their ducks over the platoon radio net as an early Thanksgiving meal for five dollars each, and then later to anyone who would come and pick them up. When there were no takers, we saw the ducks wandering loose in the jungle.

Red, the young soldier who'd had the pay problem and who looked all of thirteen, was the owner of a large, brown dog. He came to my vehicle the day after the first sergeant's announcement and hung around for the longest time. Finally, I asked him if he had gotten rid of his dog. Tears welled up in his eyes as he told me that he couldn't bring himself to leave the dog he'd had for the last three months. It was smart, and he knew the Vietnamese ate big dogs like his. The poor thing wouldn't have a chance. I told Red we would be rejoining the troop that evening and that if he felt that strongly about his animal he should take it over to the first sergeant and describe how wonderful a dog it was and ask for an exception to the order.

I was well acquainted with Red. He was a good soldier who spoke little English and had served on my vehicle from time to time. Red fit right in and developed a reputation for being fair and considerate of others. He was a good soldier and we all thought a lot of him.

A few months earlier, when Red was riding on my vehicle to round out the crew, I had taken the first watch one night and saw Red up on top of the track rummaging through his waterproof bag looking for a pair of socks. When he couldn't find any, I gave him a pair of mine. The other men had bedded down for the night, so it was just Red and me sitting up on top of the vehicle with the bright stars overhead. As we sat there looking up, the stench that hit me when Red pulled his boots off and began changing his socks would have felled an elephant. I handed him some foot powder and asked him how often he changed his socks. He said he couldn't remember for sure, but he thought it was at least once every two weeks.

Sitting there in the dark, we began to talk about his plans for the future. I asked what sort of work he was going to do when he got out of the army. He told me his stepfather back in Puerto Rico was a barber and made lots of money cutting hair. He said he was planning to attend a barber college, using his GI Bill benefits to pay for it. As soon as he got his license he planned to go into business with his stepfather. It sounded like a good plan, and I told him I thought he'd make a fine barber.

Red told me his stepfather had taught him how to cut hair several years before, and that he'd been cutting his little brother's hair for some time. One of my requirements was that the men shave every day and keep their hair cut short for good personal hygiene, so we were constantly looking for a place to get our hair cut. Occasionally, when we were performing outpost duty on a dusty stretch of road, a Vietnamese barber would come along on a bicycle or motorbike and offer to cut our hair for two hundred piasters or about two dollars. These barbers were good and practiced a little chiropractic therapy by snapping your neck to let you know the haircut was finished. Our soldiers also went into villages and stopped at the local barbershop for a quick cut. I never felt comfortable around those grinning, gold-toothed tradesmen when they were holding a straight-edged razor close to my throat. On one operation in the Iron Triangle, a group of eight Vietcong walked out of the jungle in single file and surrendered to the platoon. Two of those characters had barbering tools and claimed to be simple barbers who had been kidnapped and held against their will by the enemy. It seemed the perfect cover for an enemy agent, particularly one moving up and down the road cutting GIs' hair.

When I asked Red if he could cut his fellow soldiers' hair, he said, "Sure, if I had the equipment I could give them all a first-class haircut."

The next morning I radioed our executive officer and asked if he could locate some hand-operated clippers or an army-issue barber's kit in the inventory. I even offered to pay for it myself if necessary. He added my request to his long list.

About a week later, a large envelope addressed to me arrived on the evening supply helicopter. Inside was a beautiful set of stainless steel hand-operated clippers and a huge comb. Also inside was a note from the XO telling me that he had sent a soldier all the way to Saigon to buy them and that I owed him three cases of Budweiser for his efforts.

On our next road march I dropped Red off with a scout team in a nearby village and he purchased a large paintbrush for brushing off loose hair, as well as a green tablecloth to keep the cut hair off his customers' uniforms.

Red was in business. He charged the princely sum of $1.50 per cut, and from then on, until he rotated back to the States, I don't remember anyone in the platoon getting another Vietnamese haircut. I still remember the first haircut he gave me. I sat perched on a five-gallon oil can with the green tablecloth wrapped around me and watched Red stepping around me with a broad smile as he clipped my hair.

After returning to the troop the evening that Red came to talk to me about his dog, I saw him carrying it under one arm as he headed in the direction of the first sergeant's vehicle to make his case. It wasn't long before the first sergeant called me on the radio and said that Red could keep his dog. Later, I saw Red with a huge smile on his face, still carrying his treasured pet.

The following morning, after a quick departure from base camp, we were lumbering down the road on our way to clear and outpost another road when Red's track commander called me on the radio and reported that Red's dog had disappeared during the night. We never saw the animal again. A few of the men really got some mileage out of the incident by asking each other within earshot of Red, "What do you think that big, brown dog tasted like?"

Tank vs. MP Jeep

Whenever you accept our views, we shall be in full agreement with you.

—Moshe Dayan

Clouds of hungry mosquitoes plagued soldiers in Vietnam, especially during the rainy season. These tiny insects carried malaria, a disabling disease that has a number of strains and varying levels of severity.

To combat the disease, soldiers were issued a large, orange tablet that was about half an inch in diameter and about a quarter of an inch thick. The tablets were only about 80 percent effective and had to be taken on a regular basis if they were to work at all. The major side effect was a very predictable diarrhea and a general feeling of nausea. Most young soldiers didn't take them, preferring to take their chances with the disease.

Despite using repellent sprays and creams, we were constantly being bitten, and a number of men in the platoon developed mild cases of malaria. They exhibited the usual symptoms of low fever, chills, heavy sweating, and mild insomnia, but they were able to function and perform their jobs in a satisfactory manner.

I was lying on the damp, cold ground after a restless night of heavy sweating and chills one morning when Private Borgos came to wake me up for stand-to. My muscles were so cold and stiff I could hardly walk. Our medic, who seemed to have a treatment for everything, looked me over and announced that I had malaria. He told me that I should take a malaria tablet every three days, rather than

191

weekly, in order to get more protection into my body and thus suppress the disease.

I had lost about thirty pounds since arriving in country, with much of the weight loss caused by loss of appetite and diarrhea from the malaria pills. I couldn't imagine doubling my misery. With slightly more than two months remaining on my tour, I decided to wait until my return to the States before seeking treatment.

The troop was once again completing a three-week search-and-destroy mission just south of the Cambodian border where, on three other occasions, we had made heavy contact with the enemy in the vicinity of Loc Ninh and my platoon had suffered twelve casualties. It was an unusual area covered by thick pine forests and was heavily infiltrated by the enemy.

We always felt a certain amount of excitement when coming off an extended operation and heading back into civilization. Once again we could enjoy the simple pleasures of a current movie, mess hall food, hot showers, and a visit to the local PX. These were important things to men who had been eating nothing but C rations, bathing in rivers and streams, and sleeping on the ground for twenty-four days.

As our column headed south on its way to Phu Loi, we passed through a village called Chon Thanh, where forward elements of the division were located. Posted on the road was a sign that read: "Laundry and Bath Platoon—Our Mission Is to Serve and Support." As we lumbered by on the dusty road, the 2d Platoon leader, who was in the rear of the column, radioed the troop commander and asked for permission to stop so his men could bathe and get their uniforms cleaned. The 3d Platoon leader and I echoed the request.

Laundry and bath points had recently arrived in our area and were a great morale booster for the men. These mobile units would set up near a stream that could supply water for their boilers. It was just like a car wash. You entered the first of four tents, removed your uniform, and placed it on stacks of other dirty clothes waiting to be washed. In the second tent you picked up a clean towel and a bar of soap and then walked over a wooden platform to the shower tent, which normally had the sides rolled up and eight or more showerheads spraying warm water. After taking a warm, soapy shower, you moved into the fourth tent, where you were given a clean set of fatigues of the proper size and were then sent on your way. The whole process took no more than fifteen minutes. The only disagreeable part was that if you had a good uniform with your nametag and unit patch on it, you didn't want to exchange it. After listening to our request, which emphasized clean uniforms (we'd been wearing the same ones for over three weeks), the CO said, "Negative. We have a mission to accomplish, so get off the radio with this bullshit."

So much for that idea. We continued south, passing a recently constructed airstrip with a new aviation unit and more new artillery units located along the far side. It seemed that everywhere we went we saw new units and more U.S. soldiers. The countryside was starting to fill up. Thinking back to when I first got my orders in Germany, I recalled asking an old sergeant how many troops were in Vietnam. He said there were fewer than 100,000. Now the number was more than 350,000 and climbing every day. The same sergeant told me that only about one American was killed each day. When I acted surprised, he said, "Look at it this way, lieutenant: If you put all those soldiers in a big football stadium and then had someone come out on the roof each day and shoot one at random, your chances of survival would be pretty good." His example didn't exactly inspire confidence.

About ten miles from Chon Thanh, someone had built a little house or tollbooth in the middle of Highway 13. As we drew closer I could see a Military Police jeep parked along the side of the road. A soldier wearing the hated black MP brassard with block white lettering was walking to the center of the road with his hand up, motioning for the column to stop.

My platoon was leading with two tanks in front and my command vehicle third in line. When the lead tank stopped I immediately radioed the tank commander and asked why. He replied that the MPs wanted to know our convoy clearance number before they would allow us to proceed. I called this information back to the CO, who literally exploded over the radio. A stream of profanity poured into my headset. The gist of his message was that he didn't care what they wanted; I should get the column moving and do it *now!* I toned down the order when I told the lead tank to disregard the MPs and get moving. The column was soon on the move again.

Ever since the division's arrival in Vietnam in the spring of 1965, the cavalry had been regarded as its premier fighting unit. Day or night we were called on to ride to the rescue of units under attack, open roads by clearing mines and barricades, and keep supplies moving by providing heavily armored escorts. Securing the roads was the cavalry's mission and, until recently, the Military Police had stayed within the safety of the compounds. During our long absences out on the border and with the increased buildup of new units, the Military Police were beginning to take over some of our former duties, such as convoy escort and traffic control. The times, it seemed, were changing.

After our encounter with the MPs, the column resumed speed and made good progress. Out of the corner of my eye I saw a jeep with a flashing red light on the hood following in the dust directly behind my track. Completely dumbfounded, I told my driver to pull over and let the MP pass. I figured there must be some sort of emergency up ahead. As the jeep raced past, I got a good look at the two very serious-looking MPs inside. Both of them were wearing pistols, goggles, and MP helmets. They were covered with the thick dust kicked up by our column. Seeing them repeatedly almost drive right into the treads of the lead tanks, I radioed the TCs and told them to move over and allow the MPs to pass. The MPs soon disappeared down the road.

As we drew within sight of Lai Khe, the head of the column rounded a slight bend in the road and there, sitting crossways in a narrow part of the roadway, was the MP jeep. One of the MPs was standing in the road while the other remained behind the wheel.

As we ground to a halt, I again radioed the CO, who was some distance back in the column, and explained the situation. This time he completely lost control of himself, cursing and swearing and demanding that I get the column moving right that minute or he would get someone up there who could. Finally he said, "I don't know what the hell is wrong with you One-Six! I can't believe you'd let one little goddamned jeep stop this column!" I could visualize the foam around his mouth.

Having absolutely no doubt about my instructions, I called the lead tank commander and told him to get moving.

"I can't," he replied. "The MP jeep is directly in front of me."

"Back up and move around the side of the road," I shouted. "Get moving, now!"

A fifty-two-ton tank is not highly maneuverable, and with the driver's visibility severely limited, it's dangerous to be around, particularly at close quarters. As the lead tank backed up and turned to go around the MP jeep, its driver pulled forward in an attempt to further block the tank. From my vantage point in the third vehicle back, I could see the jeep move forward, its red light still flashing, and then the tank's left tread rolled up across its hood, just in front of the windshield. The driver jumped out unhurt and stared with his mouth open as his jeep was mashed into the dusty road. The lead tank continued forward as the second tank rolled over the jeep. I told my driver to go around it and radioed the other vehicles to do the same. The two MPs stood there beside the flattened jeep with blank expressions on their faces as we passed. I radioed the CO that we were moving again, adding that the lead tank had damaged the jeep as it moved out. He did not respond.

A feeling of light-heartedness settled over the column as we passed the crushed jeep. Most of the men had been on the receiving end of heavy-handed treatment at the hands of MPs at one time or another, and they seemed to find joy in seeing their misfortune.

The column moved through Lai Khe past our old compound, where I had reported for duty some ten months before, and continued toward Ben Cat and on to our ultimate destination, Phu Loi, some forty-five miles to the south.

As we approached the small village of Ben Cat I could see a commotion of some kind ahead. The lead tank reported that a Vietnamese logging truck was straddling the road, blocking traffic. Once again, the column ground to a halt. I immediately dispatched the scout teams to find a way around and reported the roadblock to the CO. He let fly another string of profanity before saying, " One-Six, you've got three minutes to get this column moving again. Do you understand?"

I acknowledged and then moved my command vehicle up to the

head of the column to try to move the logging truck out of the way. I dismounted with Private Borgos, and with M16 in hand and the lead tank commander close behind, we marched forward and discovered two MP jeeps on the far side of the truck. As we approached the jeeps, an MP sergeant stepped out from behind one of the mud shacks by the road. He was wearing a .45-caliber pistol in a holster hanging over his right hip and pointing an M16 up in the air.

From twenty feet away I yelled, "Do you know anything about this truck in the road?" "Yes, Sir," he shouted back. "I put it there to stop traffic."

While we were talking, my lead tank commander quietly returned to his tank and within seconds I could hear him charging his .50-caliber machine gun, ready to do battle with the MPs. I didn't know where this thing was going, but I had the feeling it was about to get out of hand.

Facing the MP I said, "You're holding up an armored column and we've got to get moving. I want you to clear that truck out of the way. Do you understand?"

The sergeant responded very politely, "Sir, I can't do that. I've been ordered to block the road."

"Then we're going to move it for you," I said flatly and turned away.

While I was explaining to the lead tank commander how to push the truck out of the way, a runner came forward from my vehicle to report that I had an urgent call from the CO. This time he calmly told me to call in my scouts, mount up all my people, and just sit tight for the time being. I acknowledged his instructions and called in the scouts, and then sat on top of my vehicle, staring now at three more MPs who had come out from behind buildings along the street.

We sat there on the road for what seemed like forever. Finally, a helicopter approached. It landed just south of the village and an MP jeep raced out to meet it. Soon the jeep returned and passed my vehicle headed toward the rear of the column. An MP captain wearing freshly starched fatigues sat in the front passenger seat staring straight to the front.

I climbed to the top of the lead tank and, looking through binoculars, I could see the MP jeep stop at the CO's vehicle. The MP captain got out and handed our CO a piece of paper. The CO glanced at it and then climbed into the back of the jeep, which then turned around and headed back in our direction. I radioed the 2d Platoon leader, who had a better view, and asked if he knew what was going on.

"It looks like the CO has just been arrested," he replied, but he could add nothing more. The CO kept his eyes on the floor and didn't look up as the MP jeep passed my location.

As the ranking lieutenant in the troop, I switched my powerful radios to the squadron frequency and called in for instructions. The radio operator at squadron headquarters could provide me no information on the situation, but he said the squadron commander knew of our CO's arrest. He promised to have the S3 call me back within the hour.

Lacking further guidance, I decided to continue our road march to Phu Loi and remain there overnight.

Dismounting again, I approached the MPs, told them that with darkness coming on fast we needed to get moving, and asked if they would move the logging truck.

"Yes, Sir, just give us a couple of minutes," said the sergeant in charge, and they immediately began moving the truck. When I returned to my vehicle, the squadron S3 was on the radio. After I told him what had happened and about my assuming command, he ordered me not to do anything. He said our executive officer was on his way out to take command and that he would be there within a few minutes.

It was now after 5 P.M., and several of the men asked if they could break out the cold beer. Unable to think of a good reason not to, I gave the OK.

After arranging something down inside my vehicle, I stood up and saw two MPs standing beside my vehicle. Thinking they were going to arrest me, I said, "What do you gentlemen want?"

The MP sergeant explained that his headquarters had called and directed them to bring in the commander of the tank that had run over their jeep.

"Why do you want him?" I asked. "He was only following my orders."

They said he was being charged with leaving the scene of an accident and failing to render assistance.

Despite my low opinion of the CO, who had been with the troop only a few weeks, I had begun to feel badly that I hadn't blocked the road with my vehicles and demanded that the MPs explain why they were carting him off. I wished that I had confirmed that the CO did not want me to intervene and get him out of the jeep.

Those were some of my thoughts as I told the MPs they were not taking my tank commander anywhere. I explained that I needed him to fight his tank, and told them they were interfering with our combat mission. As they continued to talk, I radioed the lead tank commander and told him he was not to go with the MPs under any circumstances.

The MPs left and soon our executive officer arrived in a jeep coming from the direction of Lai Khe. He drove up beside my command vehicle and, after a brief greeting, took me aside and quietly said, "Paul, I have no choice. I've been ordered to turn your tank commander over to the MPs. This is way over my head. Apparently someone's having a pissing contest and we're caught in the middle." As I stood there in disbelief, he said, "I'm sorry, but I'm ordering you to turn him over to the MPs."

I immediately called the lead tank commander and told him to go with the MPs and try to rejoin the platoon at Phu Loi later that evening. Then I watched as the tank commander slowly climbed down off his tank, sadly got in the MP jeep, and disappeared down the dusty road. The gunner became the new tank commander of the lead tank and a man from my vehicle filled out the crew.

The executive officer came on the radio after the MPs carted off my sergeant. He said he didn't know all the details about what had happened or why, but he assured me answers would be provided later. Our immediate concern was to get the troop down to Phu Loi before nightfall and get ready for the next day's mission.

We continued on to Phu Loi without further incident, parked our vehicles, and prepared to spend the night in an open field inside the security perimeter.

After dinner in a nearby mess hall, the XO took us officers over to a small artillery officer's club. There, in a quiet corner of the club, we discussed what had transpired earlier in the day. The consensus was that the squadron commander and the division provost marshal were involved in a disagreement over who would control the roads in our sector, and that the division commander had sided with the provost marshal. We agreed that a showdown between the MPs and the cavalry was inevitable after that. We just happened to be the ones who were in the wrong place at the wrong time.

The XO said no one at squadron headquarters knew anything about convoy clearance numbers or even how to get one. That was a new wrinkle that was totally uncoordinated by the MPs. We also discussed the heavy-handed manner in which the column had been stopped, and the arrogant and brazen way the CO and my tank commander had been arrested in front of the entire troop. In a unit with a few more hotheads it could easily have turned into a situation in which shots were fired and people hurt. Why, we wondered, hadn't the MPs waited until we reached our destination and then quietly arrested the CO and my NCO? Why the big grandstand show? Except for the mashed jeep, we finally decided the incident was a setup for a showdown aimed at bringing the cavalry down a notch or two.

I always thought the way we lived and acted in the cavalry was very humble, certainly never arrogant. The only time I was ever accused of being anything other than humble was during the previous month, after my platoon had finished clearing a five-mile section of road that was to be outposted by ARVN troops assisted by our MPs, who would provide convoy escorts in jeeps outfitted with pedestal-mounted M60 machine guns.

As we finished clearing the road, the convoy commander called on the radio and ordered me to remain in place until the two-hundred-vehicle convoy had cleared my position. At the time he called, we were in the process of crossing over Highway 13 and heading cross-country back to our troop's night defensive position. Earlier, troop headquarters had called and informed me that the mess sergeant was holding some hot pastries for us, and my thinking may have been momentarily clouded by visions of hot cinnamon rolls.

I understood what the convoy commander was trying to do, but since my vehicles were not on the road, I didn't think there would be any harm in continuing to move cross-country to our troop area.

Shortly after the convoy commander's call, a Huey helicopter flew over us, circled, and then set down in front of my lead tank, almost cutting off his antenna. An older lieutenant colonel with a red face and bulging eyes got out and yelled at the lead tank crew to "get your commander up here on the double!"

I was in my usual spot three vehicles back in the column when I received the message. I slowly dismounted and moved forward. Dirty and unshaven, I knew there was going to be trouble.

Approaching the colonel, who was standing under the whirling blade of his helicopter, I saluted. Glowering at me with a look on his face that would have stopped a bull in its tracks, he ignored my salute and jerked his thumb over to the side, motioning for me to follow.

As soon as we were out of earshot, he snapped, "What the hell do you think it means, Lieutenant, when I say remain in place?" I started to answer but he cut me off by getting right up in my face and saying, "Do you want to be a lieutenant the rest of your life, or are you going to get some smarts and leave these tin cans parked until I tell you to move them?"

He stepped back, folded his arms across his chest, and glared at me. Figuring he was ready for my answer, I replied, "Sir, I'm going to leave these vehicles right where they are until you tell me to move them."

"Make sure you do, Lieutenant," he said in true Major General Depuy style. "If I have to land again, I'm gonna take you back in with me."

I stood there at attention, with my platoon looking on, as the lieutenant colonel, cussing under his breath, turned and walked back to his helicopter.

I stood there for a minute and watched the chopper depart. I could just barely see our mess tent off in the distance. When the helicopter was out of sight I slowly walked back to my vehicle. My men cheered and hollered as I walked by, saying things like, "Give 'em hell, Lieutenant," or "Knock him on his ass next time, Sir." Their response took some of the sting out of my public humiliation.

I radioed troop headquarters and explained to the CO that we had been ordered to remain in place by an MP lieutenant colonel from division headquarters. I then asked if we could have a truck bring the pastries and coffee out to the platoon, as we were only about three hundred yards away.

The CO told me to wait a minute. I saw him off in the distance climbing onto the hood of his jeep and looking over the entire area. Returning to the radio, he said, "I don't know why the colonel ordered you to stop there. You're not blocking a thing." Then he added, "Go ahead and move your platoon over here to my location and feed your troops."

"Should I call the colonel and tell him I've received a new mission?" I asked.

"You were only tasked to clear the road. It's been cleared. Now you're back under my command. It's as simple as that."

"Yes, Sir," I replied. Despite his calm assurance, I scanned the horizon for the convoy commander's helicopter before giving the order to move.

As soon as we were inside the perimeter we pulled into our night defensive positions and I released the men to go to the mess hall for sweet rolls and coffee. A few minutes later, the CO joined me in the mess tent. Shortly afterward we heard a helicopter hovering overhead. Staying out of sight, we slowly pulled the tent flap back. The red-faced lieutenant colonel's helicopter was hovering about fifty feet above our vehicles, looking for me. The men, enjoying the moment, began whistling and making whoops and catcalls until the CO and I motioned for them to be quiet as we peered out of the mess tent door at the departing helicopter.

I never heard from the red-faced lieutenant colonel again, but at the time I was certain my career hung in the balance. I even imagined how court-martial charges might read: "Willful disobedience of a direct order from a superior officer," et cetera, et cetera, et cetera.

It was easy to understand why that misguided lieutenant colonel might have thought the cavalry was arrogant and needed to be brought down a notch or two.

• • •

The troop executive officer, a by-the-book cavalryman, was highly thought of by all. He kept food and supplies coming from the rear and often visited our platoons in the field to make sure we were getting everything we needed. As he dropped us off in the darkened field where our men and vehicles were already bedded down for the night, he said, "Get a good night's sleep and let's try to put this thing behind us."

Before moving out the next morning, the XO held a quick meeting and he handed out copies of an appointment order signed by the squadron commander designating him troop commander. He explained that the CO had been relieved of his command and reassigned.

No one was sorry to see him go. A short man who always made sure you knew he was in charge, he would go into fits of towering rage at the slightest hint that someone hadn't done his job. He seemed to enjoy insulting officers and NCOs in front of their men.

I recall his track driver asking me one day if my platoon had any openings for a good driver. "Sure," I said, "but why would you want to leave the CO's vehicle, that's a good job."

His response was very enlightening. He said the CO had a lot of enemies and a couple of them had said to him, "when we hit the next ambush, the CO's going to get an M16 bullet right through the head." He said he was afraid that if he stayed he might get caught in the crossfire.

Life soon returned to normal. However, about a week later, while we were out on the Cambodian border conducting search-and-destroy operations, the evening supply helicopter landed and a CID warrant officer got off. He said he was supposed to get sworn statements from me and the crew of my now infamous lead tank.

In my statement, I strongly emphasized that the lead tank commander had been acting under my direct orders. When the CID man asked why we continued on after the accident, I explained that it was no accident, that the MP deliberately drove his jeep in front of a moving tank. What did he expect? As for not stopping to render assistance, I explained that I could plainly see as we passed that no one had been injured. Finally, I told him we were the division's ready-reaction force and that when we were moving as we had been that day it was normally to rescue a unit or patrol that was under attack and to save American lives. People depended on us. Like a fire truck, we couldn't be delayed.

The final chapter of this sad story came about a month later when our troop was pulling outpost duty on an abandoned jungle road about as far north as we'd ever operated. It was afternoon and, with my vehicles positioned about fifty yards apart and with heavy brush right up against the old asphalt, we were taking almost constant enemy sniper fire from one particular area along the road. My vehicle had been hit there by enemy small-arms fire earlier in the day. Troop headquarters called telling me that the troop commander was en route to my location and that he had the squadron commander with him. I was to meet them at the north end of my sector.

Within five minutes I was at the appointed place. I had just brushed the dust off and straightened my uniform when two armored vehicles roared up and ground to a halt. The squadron commander jumped down, shook my hand, and said, "Let's go for a walk, Paul." We walked in the center of the road with the two armored vehicles following about thirty yards behind us. As we walked he asked me about my personnel strength, how the operation was going, and if we were getting regular supply deliveries—all small talk.

We continued walking in silence for a moment and then he said, "Last month we made some bad decisions with regard to the MPs. You know, they're personal representatives of the commanding general, and when they speak it's as if he's speaking. We've got to start obeying their directions." Then he opened a manila folder and took out a typed letter and handed it to me. "I had no choice in this matter, Paul. This is an official reprimand for your actions on 16 June 1967." As I looked over the document he added, "A copy of this letter will be placed in your field personnel file and removed when you depart." After a brief pause he handed me two more letters and said, "I want you to give these to the tank commander and driver of the tank that ran over the MP jeep." They were similar in wording to mine. He motioned for the two vehicles to come forward. Then, patting me on the shoulder, he said, "Don't worry too much about this, Paul. In a couple of years we'll all have forgotten about it."

We exchanged salutes and the squadron commander climbed back on his track. He waved as they turned around and disappeared down the road in a cloud of dust.

I stood there in the road for a few minutes reading the ridiculous letters and shook my head. It was like the old sheriff who tamed the lawless frontier town when no one else could. With the bad guys gone and prosperity at hand, he was no longer needed and his rough and violent ways were an embarrassment to the good and decent townsfolk. He had served his purpose and now they wanted to get rid of him.

As a final note, about a week after I received the letter of reprimand my track struck a mine and was destroyed by fire. My copy of the letter burned up with it. It was never mentioned again during my long career in the army.

The Battle of Bau Bang

They've got us surrounded again, the poor bastards.
—Gen. Creighton W. Abrams

As the scout teams swept through the outskirts of an abandoned village on the Cambodian border near Loc Ninh, Team Bravo called to report the discovery of banana and mango trees loaded with ripe fruit. The team commander said they were preparing to pick some for the platoon.

Private Borgos was my fruit tree expert. A native of Puerto Rico, he was knowledgeable about most tropical fruits and would climb the highest trees in his quest for them. Since I was nearby I told the team to hold up on trying to reach the fruit until I got there with our expert to help them look for booby traps and ensure that the fruit was edible.

We'd been warned about eating food prepared in Vietnamese restaurants or buying any fruit from village markets because of the danger of hepatitis or intestinal parasites. Bananas, because of their protective peel, were an exception, and our soldiers were always being encouraged to eat them.

When we were pulling outpost duty on a road and a truck carrying bananas entered the sector, a radio call would go out to the last vehicle in the platoon to get someone up on the road to stop the truck. Then one of the men would buy a large stalk of bananas for about a hundred piastres.

When we arrived I found six men standing on the ground inspecting the trees and discussing how best to get the ripe fruit down.

This scout team carried most of the platoon's explosives, normally consisting of two cases of TNT, a case of C-4, and four rolls of detonating cord. A soldier who claimed to have worked with explosives in his father's construction business was our unofficial demolition man.

The men enjoyed blowing things up, and they were proud of the fact that they'd destroyed just about every type of bunker or building that might have been of use to the enemy. I was not surprised when the section leader suggested putting blocks of TNT around the base of each banana tree. "With all those palm fronds, the bananas will just float down to the ground," he added.

Thinking that the displaced villagers might someday want to take up residence in the area again, I told him, "No, let's try something else."

Private Borgos quickly sized up the situation and had our driver pull over to within six inches of a nearby banana tree. Before I could tell him to slow down and watch for trip wires, he jumped onto the tree and shimmied his way up to a large clump of bananas.

Obviously, he had done this many times before. Then, with me yelling at him to look for wires and watch out for grenades hanging in the tree, Borgos took out his pocketknife, cut off the stalk, threw it down to the men on the ground, and slid down the tree.

There were about fifty bananas on the stalk, each about half the size of the Central American bananas we were familiar with, but they tasted just the same.

Satisfied with their quality, Borgos climbed back up the tree and cut enough stalks so that there was one for each vehicle. That done, we moved on to the mango trees. However, that fruit was too green to pick. Borgos told us it needed to ripen for at least another two weeks.

While we were delivering stalks of bananas to the various vehicles, I received a call to move my platoon and attached vehicles out onto Highway 13 for refueling and ammunition resupply. This procedure occurred about every two to three days, depending upon how far we'd traveled or whether we'd fired our weapons recently.

We reached the highway just as 2d Platoon was finishing up. The resupply trucks were positioned one behind the other in an open area fifty yards from the road. I formed the platoon into two lines on either side of the trucks so two vehicles could be serviced at the same time. We pulled our tracks up to within a few inches of the trucks and our supply people set the ammo right on the back of each vehicle without any awkward lifting.

We were next in line for refueling when Private Borgos yelled, "The hose broke!" Gasoline was spraying twenty feet in the air from the back of the fuel truck. I immediately jumped down and ran over to the five-thousand-gallon tanker to try and find a shut-off switch for the motorized fuel pump. The pump was being saturated by the fuel spewing from the broken hose and had begun to smoke. I feared it might burst into flames at any moment.

I finally found the switch and shut off the pump. Then, wading through the gasoline, I moved to the rear of the fuel truck, where I found the injured operator clutching his eyes and screaming for help. Grabbing the soldier and telling him to calm down, I led him out of the standing gasoline and shouted for the crew of the nearest vehicle to bring me all of their drinking water. After helping the soldier lay down, I began pouring water from three five-gallon cans over his face and eyes. This helped, but it failed to remove all of the gasoline from his eyes. Leaving the soldier with our medic, I ran to the closest vehicle and called for a medevac helicopter to take him to a nearby hospital that could deal with this potentially serious problem. Soon a helicopter arrived and, since the injured soldier could not see, I sent one of my men with him, telling the trooper to come back out on the evening resupply chopper.

We attached a nylon rope to the fuel truck, pulled it out of the pool of gasoline, repaired the hose, and resumed our refueling operation. About two weeks later, I saw the injured soldier back on the job, pumping fuel. His eyes were still red, but he said the doctor had assured him he would recover completely.

Our next day's mission was to escort a large convoy from Phu Loi to Loc Ninh, a distance of nearly a hundred miles. In preparation for the mission, we would move south and spend the night in the vicinity of Lai Khe, clear the road down to Phu Loi the next morning, and then pick up our designated convoy for the move back up north.

Since the division commander's policy prevented us from staying in a base camp, we frequently set up in Bau Bang, an abandoned village located a short distance north of our old base at Lai Khe. It had been a large village for the area, with approximately six hundred inhabitants, most of whom were employed as workers on the Michelin rubber plantation that surrounded it. Because of its key location on Highway 13 with good access to the Cambodian border, it was a popular base for the Vietcong. It was this popularity with the Vietcong that caused the army to relocate the villagers to an area near Saigon early in 1965 and then completely demolish every structure and well, leaving only an open field covered by dry, hard-packed mud.

The enemy high command had subdivided South Vietnam into sectors and zones, assigning areas of responsibility from corps down to company-sized units. The area around Lai Khe belonged to the 272d Main Force Vietcong Regiment, a unit whose strength varied from eighteen hundred to twenty-two hundred men. Our troop had often been engaged in battle with this unit and on two occasions had mauled it rather badly.

Several captured documents belonging to the 272d VC Regiment explained in great detail how to bury and aim command-detonated mines using a stick or bush as an aiming point. The pictures accompanying the documents were of crudely drawn armored personnel carriers with the mine's blast shown directly under the driver.

Late in the evening, as we approached Bau Bang, our lead platoon notified the troop commander that another unit from the 3d Squadron, 5th Cavalry was already occupying the area. The CO directed the lead platoon to continue on south through Lai Khe and set up near the village of Ben Cat.

As we passed through Bau Bang, we noticed that the 3d Squadron, 5th Cavalry unit had set up in a circular formation to the west of the road and was already putting up barbed wire.

The unit had been in country about eight weeks and, before their vehicles arrived, had sent their officers and senior sergeants to spend three days with us learning how we operated as an orientation to the new environment in Vietnam. But this was not their area of operation, they were normally based closer to Saigon.

One of the lieutenants who came over for the orientation had been a classmate of mine at the Jungle Warfare School. His name was Frank Livolse, and he had a peculiar habit of greeting everyone with a thumbs-up sign and saying, "Hubba, hubba."

I recall being in class with Frank when an instructor called him down for talking. Frank leaned over to me and jokingly whispered, "When we get to 'Nam, he's gonna be the first one to get it." Frank was seriously wounded in the battle of Bau Bang and evacuated back to the States.

Our troop continued on to the outskirts of Ben Cat, set up a normal defensive perimeter, and spent a very routine and uneventful night there. The only unusual thing was an announcement by the CO that we couldn't set up south of Ben Cat because of a Boy Scout encampment there. This brought an immediate "Say again?" from one of the platoon leaders.

"You know, Boy Scouts, like in the States," the CO replied. "They have 'em here and this is some sort of jamboree."

That evening, just before dark, I got permission to take two vehicles south of Ben Cat to see what a Vietnamese Boy Scout jamboree looked like. The CO cautioned me to keep my distance and not interfere in any way.

As my two vehicles passed south of the village, off to the west of Highway 13 about a hundred yards we saw three hundred or so youngsters. They were going in all directions, busy cooking over open fires or chasing each other around U.S. Army–style pup tents. They looked like typical children playing. Most wore the old-style drill sergeant campaign hats and brown shirts with yellow scarves and brown shorts.

There were no soldiers to be seen, American or Vietnamese. Arrangements for their jamboree must have been worked out through an agreement with the Vietcong, who otherwise would surely have tried to disrupt it to show that the government couldn't protect the people. It was pleasant to see the young boys having such a great time, but strange to see it here in the midst of the war and so far from the protection of Saigon.

As they would soon discover, the men of the 3d Squadron, 5th Cavalry were in the wrong place at the wrong time. Our old nemesis, the 272d VC Regiment, had plotted one of the largest ground attacks ever to be conducted in our area. Bau Bang was the site and our troop was the intended target, but the 3d Squadron, 5th Cavalry entered the picture and would suffer in our place. Several days after the battle, I spoke with one of the officers from their B Troop and heard a complete description of this classic battle at Bau Bang.

He told me his troop was deployed to the west, about twenty yards off Highway 13. They followed the usual SOP of setting out barbed wire and trip flares. However, since they were so close to Lai Khe, they didn't bother to send out any listening posts or ambush patrols. First Platoon was positioned from ten to two o'clock in the perimeter, 2d Platoon had from two to six, and 3d Platoon was assigned six to ten, with the troop's three headquarters vehicles in the center. The distance from the vehicles to the thick brush surrounding the clearing was about thirty yards.

The area was covered by old-growth rubber trees about fifteen to twenty feet apart and maybe thirty-five to forty feet tall. Since the plantation had not been worked for some time, thick, waist-high brush covered the base of each tree. On the east side of the road, opposite the encampment and running parallel to the road, was an old railroad bed, minus the rails, which was about five feet higher than the surrounding ground.

At about 11 P.M., with the unit settling down for the night, the 1st Platoon leader started receiving reports from nervous vehicle commanders of mysterious noises to their front. After listening carefully, the troop commander determined that they came from a loudspeaker amplifying sounds similar to those made by a Vietnamese stringed instrument. He called for artillery fire on the loudspeaker's suspected location and the noises ceased.

Later, around 2 A.M., the perimeter guards were startled to see five water buffalo running down the road from north to south setting off trip flares and knocking over barbed wire as they went.

About a half an hour later, after the commotion died down, two enemy machine guns opened up on the perimeter from behind the railroad berm. Simultaneously, several hundred enemy soldiers stood up in the streambed that ran from east to west just south of the village and started running toward the cavalrymen's positions, yelling and firing their weapons as they came.

Because of the earlier activity around the perimeter—noises, water buffalo, and machine guns—the troop was at 100 percent alert. The crews immediately returned fire with everything from M16s to 90mm tank main guns, and the battle was on.

At least twenty enemy rocket-propelled grenade launchers began to take their toll of vehicles on the south side of the perimeter. Soon, the enemy was inside the perimeter and anyone not on a vehicle was an easy target.

The troop commander called for artillery support, which, because of the close quarters, was largely ineffective. He also called for illumination and soon artillery and 4.2-inch mortar flares began bursting overhead, starkly dividing the battlefield into areas of light and darkness.

Three minutes into the battle, four armored vehicles were on fire and at least a dozen men had been killed. The waves of enemy soldiers continued to move forward as the remaining armored vehicles, their machine guns blazing, poured fire into them.

Flares illuminated moving figures in the trees on the west side of the perimeter, and the 3d Platoon took them under fire.

The troop commander at that point determined that the main attack was coming from the south and moved four vehicles from the 1st Platoon's sector to the south side of the perimeter to replace the three that had been destroyed.

The troop had been keeping up a heavy volume of fire for about twenty minutes and some of the vehicles were running low on ammunition. The CO tried to redistribute what little remained.

The enemy continued the attack, firing RPGs when the flares were bright and attacking with his infantry when the light faded.

Realizing they were in danger of running out of ammunition, the CO placed an urgent call to Lai Khe requesting tank main gun and .50-caliber ammunition. Explaining the seriousness of their situation, he asked that it be delivered with all possible speed. Officials at Lai Khe had a tank platoon alerted just for that purpose, and it quickly assembled with additional ammunition strapped to the tanks' back decks. Then, with headlights on, they started it in the direction of Bau Bang.

The five tanks were approaching a slight turn in the road about a mile from the village when several RPGs hit the lead tank, which was carrying the platoon leader, in the turret. They had been ambushed by a group of Vietcong whose mission was to keep the road closed and isolate the battlefield.

The explosions set off the ammunition piled on the vehicle's back deck, destroying it. The lieutenant, his loader, and the driver were all severely wounded, suffering horrible burns over much of their bodies caused by exploding white phosphorous rounds.

The tank platoon leader, 1st Lt. Burt Lewis, had worked with our troop on several occasions. He had never had his entire platoon of five tanks when he was attached to us. He'd always come with just three. The others were inoperative because of maintenance problems.

Burt was a very quiet and studious officer. He was always carrying a book in his hand. Twice before, when his platoon was attached to me for a few days, I put him in charge of all six of the tanks. That allowed me to work with the scouts and, if needed, he would bring up the tanks with their heavy firepower.

He was great company at night as we checked the perimeter and planned the next day's mission together. He spoke of his plans to teach school after the war. Unfortunately, he died from the wounds he suffered during that daring night resupply mission.

The second tank was also badly damaged and, although the platoon put up a valiant effort with all remaining guns blazing, the decision was made to abandon the resupply attempt. The crews loaded the wounded onto the three remaining tanks and then withdrew back to Lai Khe, leaving behind the two burning vehicles.

With daylight still an hour off, the B Troop commander carefully redistributed ammunition from those vehicles not fully engaged and set up an aid station behind his three headquarters vehicles for the forty to fifty wounded.

About six weeks before, the troop had been issued experimental antipersonnel tank ammunition that had never been tested in combat. It was acknowledged that the old 90mm canister rounds were only effective out to about fifty yards. If any type of vegetation was present, their effectiveness was even further reduced, so in a jungle ambush, they were of limited value.

The old rounds were packed with several hundred steel pellets, each of them a quarter of an inch in diameter and about half an inch long. The new "beehive" rounds, as they were known, were packed with thousands of tiny arrow-like darts, each a little over an inch long. These would penetrate dense foliage and were effective out to a range of a hundred yards and beyond. They also had a larger dispersion pattern than the canister rounds. Only three of the new beehive rounds had been issued per tank, and the CO directed that all of them be loaded into the tanks on the south side of the perimeter.

The last ground attack occurred around 4 A.M. When the enemy stood up and ran forward, supported by machine guns and RPGs, five tanks positioned not more than three feet apart and directly facing the streambed opened up with 90mm canister and beehive rounds, ripping the enemy formations to pieces. The attack lasted about five minutes. Then there was silence as the troop, its ammunition nearly gone, braced for the next wave, which never came.

When daylight arrived, helicopter gunships hammered the area in and around the streambed. A little later in the morning, an infantry battalion was airlifted into an area two miles to the west in an effort to block the retreating enemy.

With the battle over and the smoke beginning to clear, the troop commander began to take stock of what remained of his two hundred–man troop: eighteen men were dead and sixty-three more were wounded; five ACAVs had been destroyed and one tank was badly damaged. Supporting 105mm and 155mm artillery batteries provided effective fire support during the night, and the air force flew twenty-six sorties, losing one F-101 jet fighter-bomber. The pilot's body was recovered later in the day.

There were 227 enemy dead. About a third of the bodies were found within the perimeter wire. Three enemy wounded and forty-eight weapons of all descriptions were captured. Given the enemy's practice of carrying away their dead and wounded, the actual figures were probably much higher.

Later in the day, a bulldozer brought out from Lai Khe dug a mass grave for the enemy dead. The five destroyed vehicles were also buried in the place where they'd burned.

The officer relating the events of that night also explained that one of the eighteen Americans killed was the unit's 1st Platoon leader. Since his platoon was on the side away from the main attack, he had organized ten men armed with M60 machine guns and M16s to fight on the ground and cover the areas between vehicles to ensure that no enemy got inside the circle of vehicles. Several enemy rounds hit the lieutenant in the chest, penetrating his flak jacket and killing him instantly.

He said their examination of the battlefield the next day revealed that the enemy had hung 105mm ammunition boxes in the trees to the west to make it appear that the unit was also being attacked from that side. This apparently worked, because when artillery flares illuminated the boxes, the defenders expended much ammunition shooting at them.

Finally, he told me it was difficult for him to comprehend how a lightly armed enemy force like the one that had hit them could attack with such ferocity a heavily armed American unit. "One has to ask why," he said, shaking his head. The only reasonable answer I could offer was for political effect—to wear the Americans down, impress the South Vietnamese with their strength, and make the American people think the war was unwinnable.

My friend had a simpler explanation for the almost willing manner in which those fearless Vietcong allowed themselves to be slaughtered. On each enemy body they recovered there was a small plastic bag of red betel nut, a strong local narcotic. His theory was that the enemy was hopped up on betel nut and had blindly charged into the American positions feeling no pain.

One final note on the battle. About two months later our troop moved into Bau Bang and set up for the night. The battle damage had been washed away by recent rains or covered by the growth of new underbrush. We set up a solid defense and even placed an ambush patrol in the streambed approximately 150 yards out. It was the dry season and very warm, so most of the soldiers set up cots or stretchers on the ground near their vehicles. As usual, I had stretched a canvas from the side of my track to form a lean-to and set up the radio extension next to my stretcher. Around midnight, I settled down on my stretcher and was soon asleep. About two hours later something bumped my back. I lay there for a few minutes trying to figure out what it was, then turned on my flashlight just in time to see two large, black, hairy rats disappear under my stretcher. All I could think about was rabies as I leaped off the stretcher and scrambled on top of my vehicle. I radioed the rest of my platoon and ordered everyone sleeping on the ground to get back on top of their vehicles. No one questioned my order after I explained the rat situation to them.

The next morning as we were preparing to move out, I discovered about a thousand other rat holes. The area looked like a prairie dog village, with the heaviest concentration of holes over the mass gravesite. The rats were apparently living off the remains of the dead Vietcong soldiers, a really grotesque conclusion.

I am convinced that the 272d Vietcong Regiment had planned the battle of Bau Bang for our unit in retaliation for the many casualties we had inflicted on them. As with so many things in this war, it was a quirk of fate that 3d Squadron, 5th Cavalry arrived there first.

Tour's End

You will kill ten of our men and we will kill one of yours, and in the end it will be you who will tire of it.

—Ho Chi Minh

At one-thirty one afternoon, while we were pulling outpost duty along a dusty section of Highway 13 north of An Loc, I received a radio message from troop headquarters advising me that I had been selected to attend an awards ceremony. The caller instructed me to report to squadron headquarters early the next morning. Furthermore, he said, upon completion of the awards ceremony I would begin outprocessing and preparation for my return to the United States.

The message finally sunk in: I was going home! This was to be my last day as platoon leader!

During the past eleven months there had been a complete turnover of the men in my platoon. Of the original sixty-three, all were either dead, wounded, or had completed their tours and returned home. Even Private Borgos was gone. As the platoon filled up with newer and, it seemed, younger and more inexperienced men, I had taken on more and more responsibility and become less tolerant of careless mistakes.

During the last few months my physical condition had gotten worse. I'd lost more than thirty pounds, my hands trembled, and I was sick with malaria and couldn't sleep at night. Standing there in my faded, threadbare jungle fatigues, which were by then a whitish-green and had penciled-on rank instead of sew-on insignia, I felt very old and tired. I was definitely ready to go home.

216

There was little fanfare as I shook hands with my crew and then called my platoon sergeant to wish him luck. After telling him he was in charge, I grabbed my waterproof bag and two cans of C rations and flagged down one of the empty five-ton artillery trucks streaming down the dusty road behind us headed for Saigon. I rode up front with the young driver. He had the cab top and windshield down and was wearing goggles. Although he maintained an interval of about fifty yards between us and the truck to our front, we were in a thick dust fog the entire way.

As we began moving south along Highway 13, I waved good-bye to my platoon. Later, as we passed familiar points along the way, I was reminded of mining incidents, ambushes, and the arrest of our CO, all of which had occurred on that road over the past eleven months.

After three hours in the truck we finally reached the little village where the road forked to Phu Loi. As the driver slowed to let me out I jumped down. He waved and then shouted, "Are you sure you want out here?" When I nodded, he tromped on the accelerator and then disappeared down the road.

It was about three miles to Phu Loi. Wearing my flak jacket and helmet, and armed only with my .45-caliber pistol, I slung the waterproof bag over my shoulder and started walking. As I passed villagers herding their water buffalo beside the road and families working in the lush rice paddies, I drank in the quiet beauty of the day. An army three-quarter-ton truck soon stopped and the driver offered me a ride to the military compound at Phu Loi.

It was dark when I finally reached squadron headquarters. All the offices were closed, so I walked over to the tiny officer's club near the airstrip. A small group of warrant officers from the air cavalry troop were the only ones present as I settled in at a small table and ordered a drink with quinine water to help suppress my malaria. Later, I ate the crackers and cheese from one of my C-ration meals. When I finished eating I set out to find a shower. After cleaning up, I was able to locate an unused bunk and settle down for the night. It was the first time in a long while that I had no responsibilities at all.

I got up at my regular time the next morning, quietly left the tent, and went over to the mess hall for an early breakfast with the cooks. At seven-thirty I was standing at the door of the personnel of-

fice when the adjutant arrived for work. After exchanging greetings
and making a comment about the early hour, he told me I was being assigned to the headquarters troop as executive officer, but that
I would be the acting commander while the commander went on
leave. Next, he said I would receive an award at a ceremony at division headquarters in two days. He paused and looked me over, then
said, "General Westmoreland will be there, so get rid of that ratty
uniform and draw a new one from supply."

My feelings were hurt by his comment. A sergeant had given me
the uniform when my vehicle was blown up and burned. It still had
faded sergeant stripes that had been drawn on the sleeves with a
permanent marker. It was the same uniform my men had fished out
of a trashcan at the evacuation hospital. I had no intention of parting with it. However, I did decide to send it to the laundry and have
the rips and tears sewn up and real rank and unit patches sewn on.
In the meantime, I went ahead and drew two new uniforms from
supply so that I'd fit in around headquarters.

On the day of the awards ceremony I boarded a C-123 and,
along with ten other men, flew to Dian. My old jungle fatigues had
come back from the laundry looking so nice with the new insignia
sewn on them that I decided to wear them in spite of the adjutant's
admonition. No soldier from my platoon had ever had the opportunity to participate in an awards ceremony. Normally, one or two
replacements wearing new uniforms and eager smiles arrived on
the resupply helicopter each week. The same number of old-timers
would depart with their threadbare uniforms and haggard faces. I
often wished we could have thrown a party for those loyal and
courageous young men as they left. However, living constantly in
the field as we did, it just wasn't possible. Most had been recommended for an award during their tours and they were simply
handed the medals as they cleared the squadron personnel office.
Sometimes, a departing sergeant on his last night in the squadron
would celebrate a little too much at the NCO club. Fortified with
liquid courage, he would then stumble over to the operations center and call up on the platoon radio frequency to bid a final tear-
ful good-bye to his crew and express a wish for us all to get back
home safely. The ceremony I was about to attend would be the

recognition for all those who had served in my platoon during the past year.

When we arrived at Dian we were greeted by the division G1 and taken to the far end of the local airstrip, where a reviewing stand had been set up and the division band was busy rehearsing.

After a stand-up lunch of cold cuts and potato salad, the rehearsal began with the troops assigned at Dian assembled in formation and the twenty honorees lined up in front of them. As we waited for the band to play its sequence of bugle calls and musical numbers, several captains and majors who were also getting awards came down the line shaking hands and visiting with us about recent operations on which we'd served together.

One of the captains who came down the line stopped in front of me and said, "Lieutenant, you sure look familiar."

"I'm the one who brought in the bodies of your Slingshot Platoon, Sir," I replied.

"Oh, yes, I remember you," he said. "A day doesn't go by that I don't think of those poor men." He patted me on the shoulder as he moved on to talk to the next man and said, "I'm glad to see you're going home in one piece."

Those informal conversations were the highlight of the awards ceremony.

We took a break in place for about thirty minutes and then a shiny new helicopter settled onto the helipad at the end of the field, and General Westmoreland, the commander of all U.S. forces in Vietnam, emerged.

His arrival started the ceremony. The band played "Ruffles and Flourishes" and "The Star-Spangled Banner." The division commander followed with a short speech about courage and heroism and then introduced General Westmoreland.

The general gave a far-ranging speech about the Civil War, World War I, and World War II, but said little about Vietnam. When he finished, the honorees were called to attention and marched to the center of the field. As the general moved in front of each of us, a citation was read over the loudspeaker describing the act of heroism for which the medal was being awarded. Then the general pinned on the medal and shook each hand. My award was for rescuing a soldier from a burning vehicle. The citation made my actions sound very impressive. I'm sure my mother would have been very proud.

We stood there at attention or parade rest under a blazing sun for the forty-five-minute ceremony. Afterward, we congratulated each other, had cold punch and cookies in the shade of the reception tent, and then boarded trucks that took us to the other end of the runway where we boarded a large helicopter waiting to take us back to Phu Loi. The ride back was uneventful, and my company clerk was there with a jeep to greet me.

The next day, after rising early for breakfast, I visited with some young medics who were gathering up leftovers and scraps from previous meals. In answer to my inquiries I found out they were supporting an orphanage located in the nearby village with food and medicine. Curious, I asked if I could visit their orphanage sometime. They quickly agreed and arranged for me to accompany them later that afternoon.

The orphanage was located on the side of a small hill near the entrance to Phu Loi. The three buildings were of masonry construction and appeared to date from the French colonial period. A very leathery-looking Caucasian woman in her fifties greeted us with a pleasant smile and, in a Scandinavian accent, explained how helpful the two medics had been in keeping the orphanage going. She belonged to a church group in Sweden and was only funded to support about thirty children. With the medics' help and the aid of five Vietnamese assistants, she was able to care for more than a hundred.

The children ranged in age from several months to ten years. They had either been brought in by relatives or found wandering the streets. Most of them were dressed in typical Vietnamese clothing, but here and there I saw Disney characters and baseball-team logos on clothing sent from the United States. The children were cared for, taught in the little classroom, and then, at age ten, placed with local families that were happy to take them since they could then work in the fields to pay for their keep.

The woman was very gentle and soft-spoken and obviously enjoyed caring for the children. She had been there for thirteen years and had made it her life's work. It was a noble effort there in the midst of this ugly war.

My new job, which would last for about three weeks, looked like a good one. I had very few subordinates because soldiers assigned to the troop actually worked for someone else: supply, maintenance, the mess hall, and the medical and staff sections. The only person who worked directly for me was the company clerk. Squadron headquarters was arranged around a fifty-yard square that was lined with empty 90mm shell casings hammered into the ground every three feet. I had my own jeep and used it to explore the compound and local area. Compared to my platoon with its sixty-plus men and ten combat vehicles, my new responsibilities were insignificant.

The day's work was over every evening at five. Then it was dinner at the mess hall, off to the club or to a movie, and then to bed on a bunk with a real mattress and clean sheets. After a few days of this quiet routine, I began to miss the excitement of life in the field with my platoon.

Just about the time I was getting comfortable with this peaceful job, it was time to go home. On my last night in the squadron, the maintenance section threw a party for me. It was just Chief Warrant Officer 4 Lew Hudson, myself, and his clerks and mechanics— about fifteen people. Someone had acquired a case of T-bone steaks, two one-gallon cans of pork and beans, and two cases of beer—a real feast!

While the steaks were cooking over a fifty-five-gallon drum we used for a barbeque, we had a shirts-off volleyball game pitting the clerks against the mechanics, with me playing for the clerks. The steaks were delicious and, as I found out later, had been obtained from another unit in exchange for some excess repair parts.

After dinner one of the mechanics played a guitar and we all joined in singing some of our favorite songs. Finally, Chief Hudson called me up front and said some very nice things about my old platoon having been their best customer. He said we held the record for the most blown-up vehicles in the squadron. Then he took an engraved cigarette lighter out of his pocket and presented it to me. Moved by this gesture, I stood silently for a few seconds and then made a little speech about how important they were to the squadron. I appreciated the fact that they were always picking up

the pieces of my tracks and keeping us at full strength in fighting vehicles. These were the dedicated men behind the scenes, the real
strength of the squadron, and I truly appreciated their honoring
me on my last night at Phu Loi.

Our flight section had arranged for me to fly to Saigon on one of
their fixed-wing aircraft, a single-engine Beaver that looked like
something Charles Lindbergh might have flown. I was the only passenger as we lifted off the runway and headed south. The Beaver
was used primarily for hauling repair parts and personnel on long
flights. We flew at about three thousand feet and at approximately
one hundred miles per hour, which allowed for a good view of the
ground below. As we neared Saigon, it began to rain and visibility
dropped to zero. Suddenly, there were several loud explosions directly under us. As the pilots put the old plane into a steep dive, I
asked myself why I hadn't taken a truck to Saigon. Briefcases, bags,
and boxes bounced off the back of my head as I braced myself for
the impact.

The pilots leveled off just above the treetops, and we soon landed
at Tan Son Nhut Air Base in Saigon. We'd flown directly over an artillery battery that had just begun firing as we passed overhead.

The warrant officer pilots apologized for their daredevil flying as
I said my good-byes. Leaving them, I headed over to the personnel
office to begin my outprocessing. Everything was in order except
that two of my shots needed updating and I needed to attend an
outprocessing briefing. The clerk told me I was to report to the passenger terminal at 8 A.M. the day after tomorrow. Armed with this information, I put my bags in the supply room, walked outside the
compound, and caught an old blue and beige taxi, a leftover from
the French colonial period, into the city.

The French had built Saigon on the order of Paris, with wide,
tree-lined streets and wide sidewalks for shops and restaurants. It
was an impressive city and—with all the trucks, taxis, motorcycles,
shops, and restaurants—appeared to be very prosperous.

My destination was the Rex, a hotel leased by the U.S. government. It was a twelve-story building with a garden restaurant and observation deck on the top floor. Arriving at the hotel, I entered a
lobby crowded with Vietnamese women, Americans in civilian

clothes, and senior army officers in uniform. I found the elevator and, jammed inside with twelve other people, began the creeping ascent to the top floor.

A beautiful sight greeted me as I stepped out of the elevator— there were plants and flowers hanging everywhere. It was a lush garden. American music was playing and, when I sat down at a table, the waiter placed an American menu in front of me. Scanning the menu, my eyes settled on an American-style hamburger and french fries. I ordered that and a large strawberry milkshake. It took me an hour to finish this delicious meal as I savored every bite while looking out over the beautiful Saigon landscape.

After spending a couple of hours in the rooftop garden, I went down to the front desk and asked for a room. An older Vietnamese man politely told me they had none, but that I could find one at the nearby President Hotel.

I walked the three blocks to the President Hotel. Along the way, beggars, street vendors, and merchants of every description tried to sell me something. By the time I reached the hotel, a small army of kids and beggars trailed behind me, all of them chanting for a handout.

I spent the remainder of the evening watching a couple of episodes of *Bonanza* on Armed Forces Television, and then went to bed at ten. I slept soundly throughout the night.

The next morning, after a breakfast of coffee, French bread, and jam, I caught another little blue and beige taxi and began a sightseeing trip around the city. Our first stop was at the docks along the Saigon River, where most of our war supplies were off-loaded. Although the area was restricted, I was able to get an MP to allow my taxi to enter. We drove along beside twelve ships in various stages of unloading. Most of the ships were unloading grain or rice packed in large, brown burlap bags imprinted with the symbol of two hands shaking and the inscription "Hands Across the Sea." The cargo was part of our foreign aid from the Agency for International Development to the government of Vietnam. The bags of grain and other goods were placed in American-made trucks with Vietnamese drivers and delivered to warehouses scattered around the country. Occasionally a truckload of goods disappeared into the black market.

Sometimes both the truck and cargo disappeared. Once in a while, an American truck sporting a blue paint job and minus its serial number would reappear hauling logs or rubber for a Vietnamese company. It was often said that the Vietnamese black market could get anything you wanted for a price—trucks, tanks, airplanes—anything.

I had been told to avoid the food sold by street vendors and Vietnamese restaurants because of poor sanitation practices. Not wanting to get dysentery on the eve of my departure, I stopped at a small American compound for lunch. Later, I was out on the street trying to hail a taxi, when a motorcycle cab stopped in front of me and the toothless driver motioned for me to get in. The contraption consisted of a motorcycle with its front wheel removed and the front fork attached to the rear of a rickshaw. I climbed in, and we rode along breathing in the thick, choking fumes rising from every sputtering, poorly tuned vehicle on the road. To add to my discomfort, the driver was constantly darting in and out of the oncoming lane of traffic. He seemed to be at war with everyone as he yelled and gestured at passing vehicles.

I was somehow able to make the driver, who spoke almost no English, understand that I wanted to go sightseeing. We spent the next couple of hours visiting the parliament building, the military statue, the U.S. embassy, and the Cholon PX, which was much like an American supermarket in the heart of Saigon. At each stop I tried to pay the driver and get another taxi, but he stuck to me like glue and chased other drivers away. Finally, I was able to get across to him that I wanted to play golf, so he took me to the Saigon golf course. After convincing him that this was my last stop, I paid the driver and, after much grinning and bowing, he left in a thick cloud of exhaust.

The clubhouse, which was in a former French château surrounded by large trees with what appeared to be Spanish moss hanging from their limbs, had cathedral-like ceilings and polished wood floors. Apparently the golf course's owners paid the Vietcong to allow them to operate, because there were no guards anywhere. It was a beautiful setting. There were about forty people in the clubhouse. They appeared to be State Department personnel, with a few senior military officers mixed in. Feeling out of place, I asked the Vietnamese clerk for a putter and some balls and went outside to practice on a very rough putting green. As I was enjoying the peace and quiet and beautiful scenery, a large Vietnamese dressed in civilian clothes walked up to me and asked in clear English if I was a member or a guest of a member. When I said neither, he said, "Then, Sir, you'll have to leave." I'd been there for about thirty minutes and was about ready to leave anyway, so I handed him the putter without argument and left.

I walked around the adjoining barbed-wire fence until I came to a gate guarded by American MPs. I asked for directions to the Tan Son Nhut Air Base departure terminal and found out that it was nearby.

On my last night in country I saw a Western starring Kirk Douglas in an outdoor theater near my barracks in the air base compound. It began to rain about halfway through the movie. The audience dwindled as the rain's intensity increased until only five of us remained seated on the wooden benches. Finally, the screen went dark and a voice announced from the rear, "The projector's getting wet. We'll show it again tomorrow night."

The next morning I got up early, put on my khaki uniform, and ate my last meal in Vietnam at the nearby mess hall, one of the army's finest. We had been told to report to the terminal three hours before flight time, so after breakfast I gathered up my suitcase and duffel bag and walked the short distance to the terminal.

The waiting area was already crowded when I arrived. Although getting soldiers to report on time has always been a problem, I've never heard of a soldier who missed his flight home. The staff seemed confident enough that we were all there that they waited until thirty minutes before departure before conducting a roll call.

As I sat at a table on the second floor of the former French terminal building, several other lieutenants joined me. Soon, eight of us were seated there. While exchanging war stories with the lieutenants, I got up and looked out the large picture window in front of us to see how the refueling of our plane, a civilian Boeing 707, was coming along. Not far from our aircraft, I spotted a row of Vietnamese World War II–vintage propeller-driven fighter-bombers.

Curious, several of us walked out the main terminal gate and headed over to the planes. They were working planes, not museum pieces, and some were already armed with 250-pound bombs and fresh belts of ammunition, ready for their next mission. As we stood there admiring the planes and commenting on how well maintained they were, a Vietnamese sergeant came over. We told him the planes looked like they'd be fun to fly and asked if he'd ever been up in one. After joking with us briefly, he said if any of us were interested he would see if his captain would take one of us up.

What an offer! We all looked at each other for a few moments. I'm sure each of us was thinking what it would be like to fly at three hundred miles an hour over the countryside, bombing and strafing the Vietcong and then returning to base. I finally told the sergeant that we were headed home and that our flight was departing within the hour. I thanked him for the offer and then we walked back to the terminal, arriving just in time to hear the final boarding call being made over the loudspeaker.

Outside, an air force sergeant was busy herding 130 soldiers up the steps and through the single door of the plane. We attached ourselves to the end of the line and followed them into the aircraft. As the engines started to whine, the GIs began to cheer. Then, as the plane moved down the runway and lifted off, there was another wild cheer.

The flight back to the United States seemed to be one continuous night. I sat next to a window and could see thousands of stars and moonlight on the ocean below. Occasionally I spotted another plane passing at a lower altitude in the lonely sky. As I sat there in the dark, my thoughts drifted back to the many other moonlit nights I spent sitting on my command vehicle wondering what the next day would bring.

It was daylight when the pilot came on the intercom and announced that we would be landing in thirty minutes. Then, as the plane's wheels touched down at Travis Air Force Base, California, a final cheer went up from the tired soldiers. Our long journey was over at last.

Epilogue: The Dream

The dream in question is always the same: My armored cavalry platoon has just pulled into its night defensive position and, as always, the crews immediately begin cleaning their weapons, breaking them down and soaking them in .50-caliber ammo cans filled with a mixture of gasoline and motor oil.

Then, without warning, while all the crew-served weapons are disassembled, the enemy launches a powerful attack. Waves of North Vietnamese soldiers sweep over my unsuspecting platoon as the men frantically try to assemble their weapons. I'm desperately fishing parts of a .50-caliber and an M60 machine gun out of the cleaning solution, trying to put together a working weapon.

That is the point at which I usually wake up: with the enemy horde slaughtering my men and me fumbling with parts of two machine guns as bullets fly everywhere.

I'm not sure what causes this dream, but I do recall that everyone cleaning weapons at the same time was a concern of mine—along with a hundred other things. Apparently this one stuck.

The dream is now like an old friend, making an appearance once or twice a year. I greet it more as a harmless visitor from the past, with little left of the stark terror it once produced.

Glossary

ACAV Armored Cavalry Assault Vehicle
AG Adjutant General
ARVN Army of the Republic of Vietnam
ASAP As Soon As Possible
BOQ Bachelor Officers' Quarters
C rations The army's standard field rations
CG Commanding General
Chicom Chinese Communist
Chinook Nickname for the CH-47 series cargo helicopters
CID Criminal Investigation Division
CO Commanding Officer
CQ Charge of Quarters
CS A potent form of tear gas that often produces nausea
deadlined A vehicle that is not operationally ready and cannot be operated
Duster Nickname for the M-42 antiaircraft weapon, which consisted of twin-40mm cannon mounted on a tank chassis. It was used in Vietnam primarily for base defense and convoy escort
FDC Fire Direction Center
Flak jacket A sleeveless armored vest designed to protect the wearer from shell fragments
G1/S1 Personnel
G2/S2 Intelligence
G3/S3 Operations and Training
G4/S4 Supply
Grunt Slang for infantrymen
Huey Nickname for the UH-1 series utility helicopters
KP Kitchen Police
MACV Military Assistance Command Vietnam
MI Military Intelligence

MP Military Police
NATO North Atlantic Treaty Organization
net call A radio call made to all stations operating on a single net
NVA North Vietnamese Army
PIO Public Information Office
PSP Pierced-Steel Planking
PX Post Exchange
R and R Rest and Recuperation. Each soldier was granted a seven-day break from the war in an exotic Far East locale not chargeable as leave. Most married soldiers opted to meet with their wives in Hawaii
ROTC Reserve Officers' Training Corps
RPG Rocket-Propelled Grenade. The enemy employed several different models. However, all were shoulder-fired rocket-launchers similar to the U.S. bazooka of World War II fame and were effective antitank weapons, especially the Soviet-made RPG-7
RTO Radio-Telephone Operator
SITREP Situation Report
SOP Standard Operating Procedure
TC Track or Tank Commander
TO&E Table of Organization and Equipment
Track Slang for armored vehicles
VC Vietcong
XO Executive Officer